AF395131

# BERMONDSEY & ROTHERHITHE

## THROUGH TIME

Debra Gosling

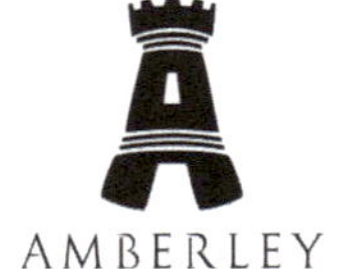

AMBERLEY

# Acknowledgements

I am indebted to David Toogood, not only for his brilliant photography, but also for enduring my endless wittering on. What a hero! Thank you.

Also thanks to Michael Holland, my mum Mary Gosling, Fred & Christine Low, Chris Lordan, Boyd Sofield, Metropolitan Police, Peter Voss, Millie Padbury, Fr Andrew Doyle, Tony Young, Dawn Irvine (Guinness Trust), Kathryn Parish, Freddie Roll, Shirley Chapple, Charlie (Southern Railway stables), Robert Hulse (Brunel Museum), John Beasley and Ingrid Uhlén Gray for sharing their family photographs, postcard collections and stories. All new photographs are © David Toogood, 2011 unless stated.

Debra Gosling
2012

**Front Cover: Dock Offices, Surrey Docks, 1910**
These offices have been very sympathetically restored and serve as a reminder that this area was a busy commercial hub, teeming with dock workers, cranes and tall masted ships. The masts have disappeared, to be replaced by water sports and leisure boats. The gateway has also disappeared and where the view in the background showed timber sheds the new library now stands.

First published 2012

Amberley Publishing
The Hill, Stroud
Gloucestershire, GL5 4EP

www.amberley-books.com

Copyright © Debra Gosling , 2012

The right of Debra Gosling to be identified as the Author of this work has been asserted in accordance with the Copyrights, Designs and Patents Act 1988.

ISBN 978 1 4456 0644 6

All rights reserved. No part of this book may be reprinted or reproduced or utilised in any form or by any electronic, mechanical or other means, now known or hereafter invented, including photocopying and recording, or in any information storage or retrieval system, without the permission in writing from the Publishers.

British Library Cataloguing in Publication Data.
A catalogue record for this book is available from the British Library.

Typeset in 9.5pt on 12pt Celeste.
Typesetting by Amberley Publishing.
Printed in the UK.

Appointed GPSR EU Representative: Easy Access System Europe Oü, 16879218
Address: Mustamäe tee 50, 10621, Tallinn, Estonia
Contact Details: gpsr.requests@easproject.com, +358 40 500 3575

# Introduction

Bermondsey and Rotherhithe are a contradiction in terms; linked but quite separate, united but individual. You cannot have one without the other! People from these areas are very passionate about the neighbourhood they grew up in. They have a strong identity, with a history and legacy to be proud of.

Rotherhithe was dominated by the docks before they were closed in the 1970s, while Bermondsey saw its leather industry and factories disappear around the same time. Happily, numerous buildings associated with these occupations have survived, albeit with different uses. Some parts cannot be changed; the railway dominates much of the area and the river just keeps rolling on through time. There are wonderful chapels and churches, but there was a time when the public houses outnumbered them. Particularly noticeable now is how many pubs have been demolished or converted into flats. Rotherhithe Street had pubs on just about every corner, serving the busy maritime community. It is a long street, which has lost its character following the disappearance of so many inns.

The dust of many centuries still blows across Bermondsey and Rotherhithe. The monks of medieval Bermondsey Abbey, tanneries, glue works, biscuit works, chimneys and old sea captains are the ghosts in the shadows.

For aeons the lie of the land remained the same, until the Second World War caused so much damage, both physically and emotionally. Despite it happening over seventy years ago, the annihilation of so much of both areas still resounds.

Redevelopment can be controversial, but in most instances it is positively flourishing. Areas that were dark, claustrophobic and somewhat threatening are now light, with open spaces and trees. Bermondsey used to boast the highest tree count in London. In the 1920s, Mayor Ada Salter worked tirelessly on her beautification scheme to put a bit of greenery into the industrialised, murky little byways. It has certainly paid off now, along with a little input by developers, to make the area a very pleasant location in which to live.

The new Shard of Glass dominates the skyline; it is a beautiful and graceful structure that reflects the sky, sometimes making it almost invisible. It stands adjacent to Stainer Street Arch, where so many lives were lost in the Second World War and seems to act as an informal marking-place for all those souls, reaching up into the sky.

Some places have simply barged their way into this book, due to the sheer reverence in which they are held. Tower Bridge and Southwark Park are jewels in this area's crown, both beautiful and a pleasure to visit. Others, such as the Blue Anchor Fish Bar and the Brunel Engine House, have made it because of their age and endurance. Some are here purely for the quirkiness factor!

Bermondsey and Rotherhithe are survivors. Both are now very different from even ten years ago but the atmosphere remains the same. The characters are still larger than life and there is a heritage that is positively uplifting.

'Where your treasure is, there will your heart be also.'

Matthew 6:21

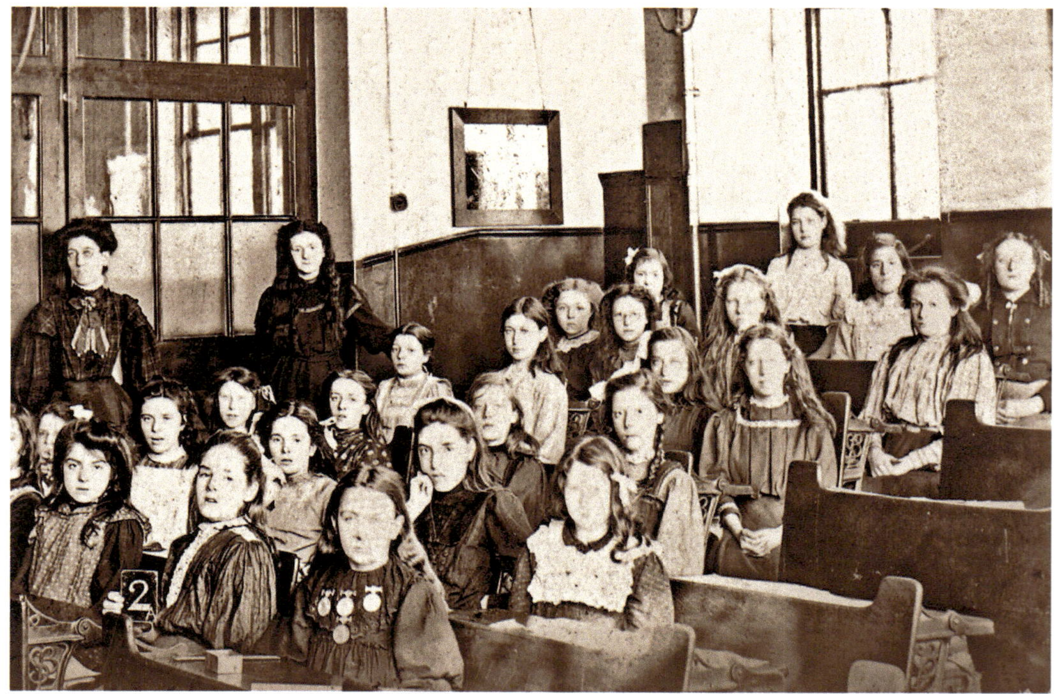

**Rotherhithe School, 1910**
Ethel Marshall is one of the girls in the front row, but it has not been established which one she is! She sent this photograph to her brother, Willie, at midday and then went skating in the afternoon. It would be nice to think she is the one with all the medals – possibly one for skating? This was a board school, as can be seen by the monograms on the desk sides. (1910 Photograph © Debra Gosling)

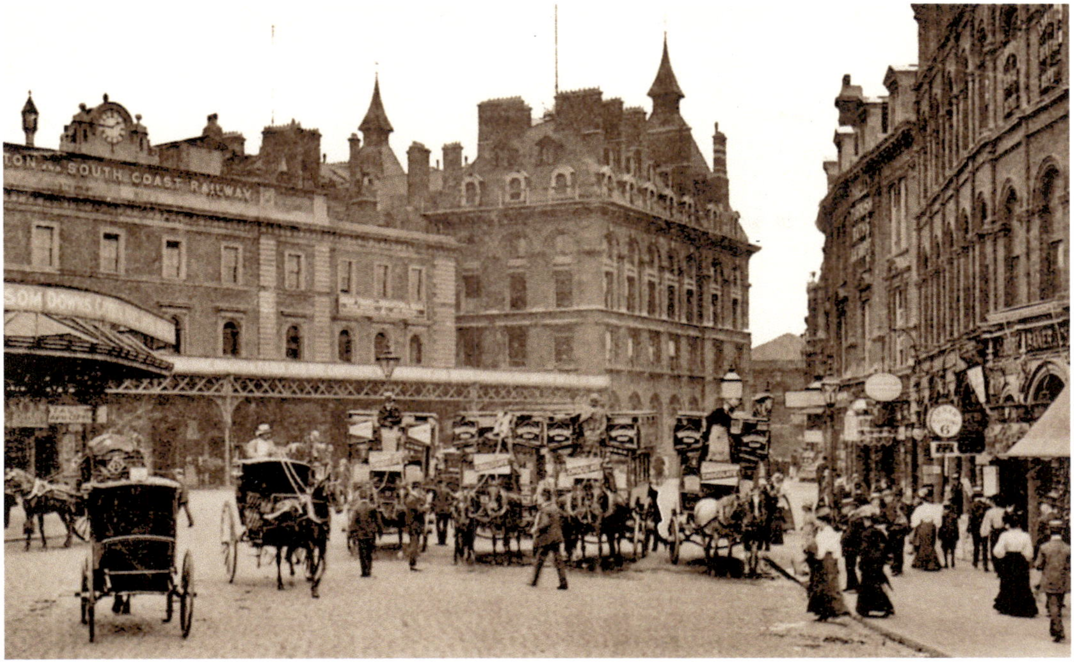

**London Bridge Station, 1900**

The London & Greenwich Railway opened up the world to local people. Trips to the coast, shopping and even the chance to travel abroad all beckoned for those who could afford the fare. The large Gothic building in the centre was a hotel, later demolished to make way for a very ugly 1970s lump of concrete. Happily, that has been replaced by the sparkling Shard of Glass.

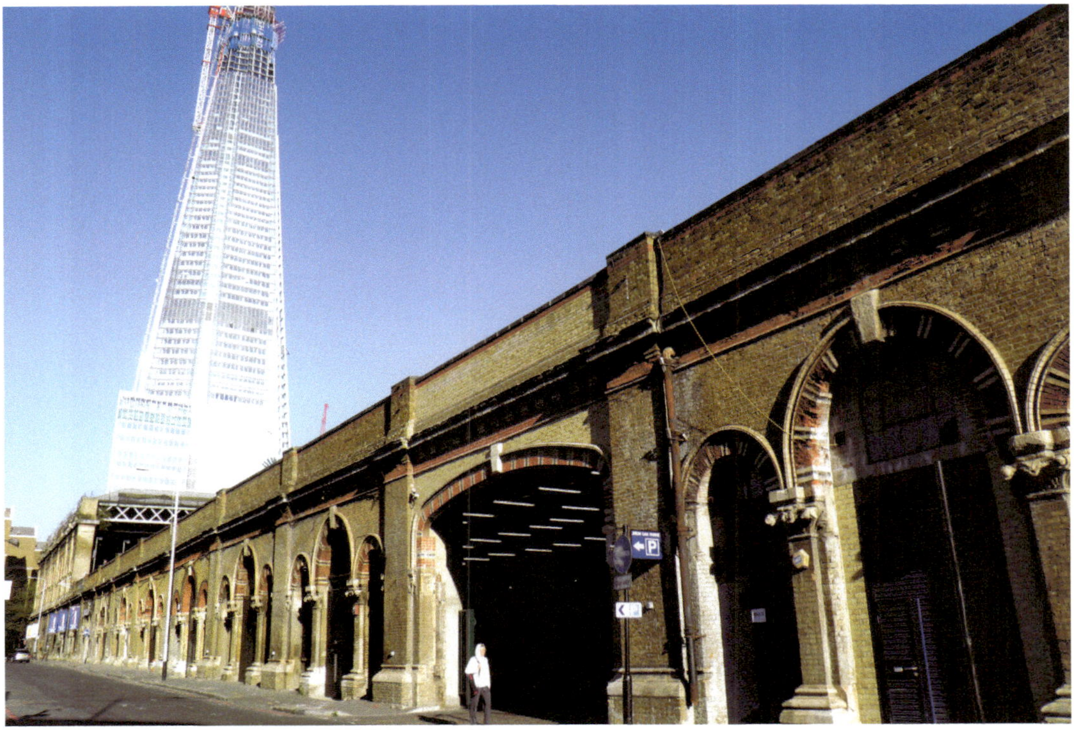

### Hays Lane, 1920

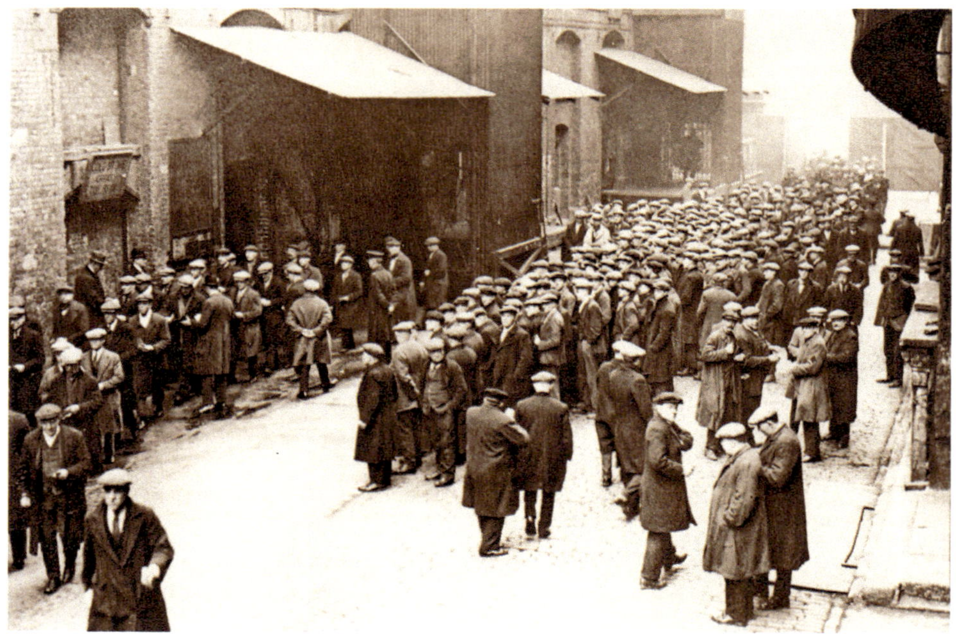

This was London's larder, where everything from tea and coffee to ham, cheese and bacon was stored. Labourers were paid on a daily rate and here they queue up to be called on to unload cargo. Re-branded Hay's Galleria, it has to be said that this conversion is a big improvement from the days when Tooley Street was a dark, rather sinister place in which to find yourself.

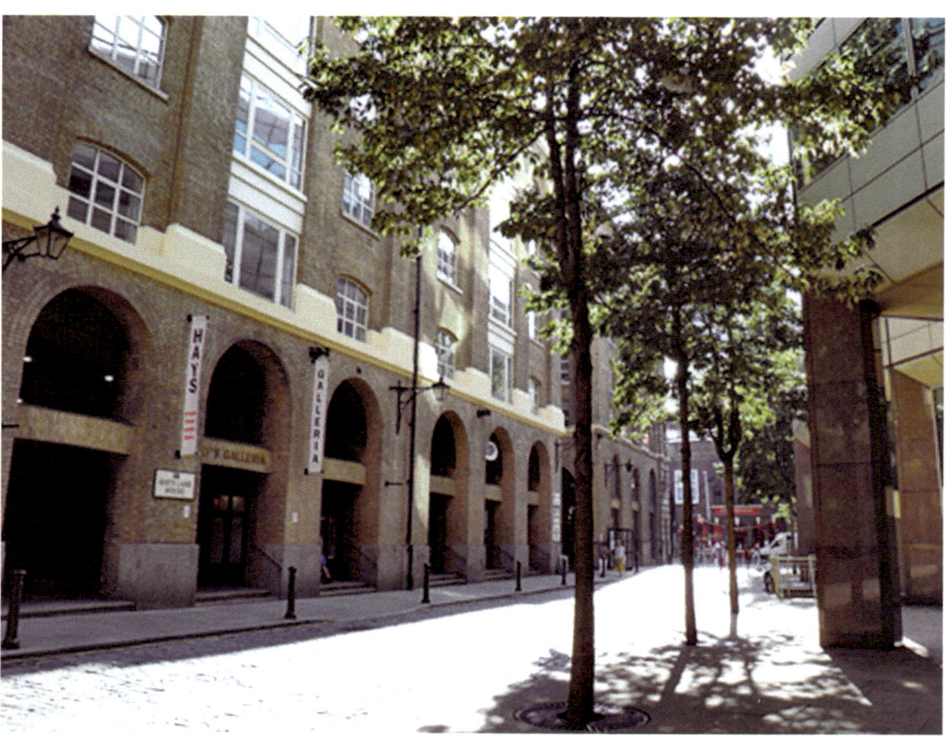

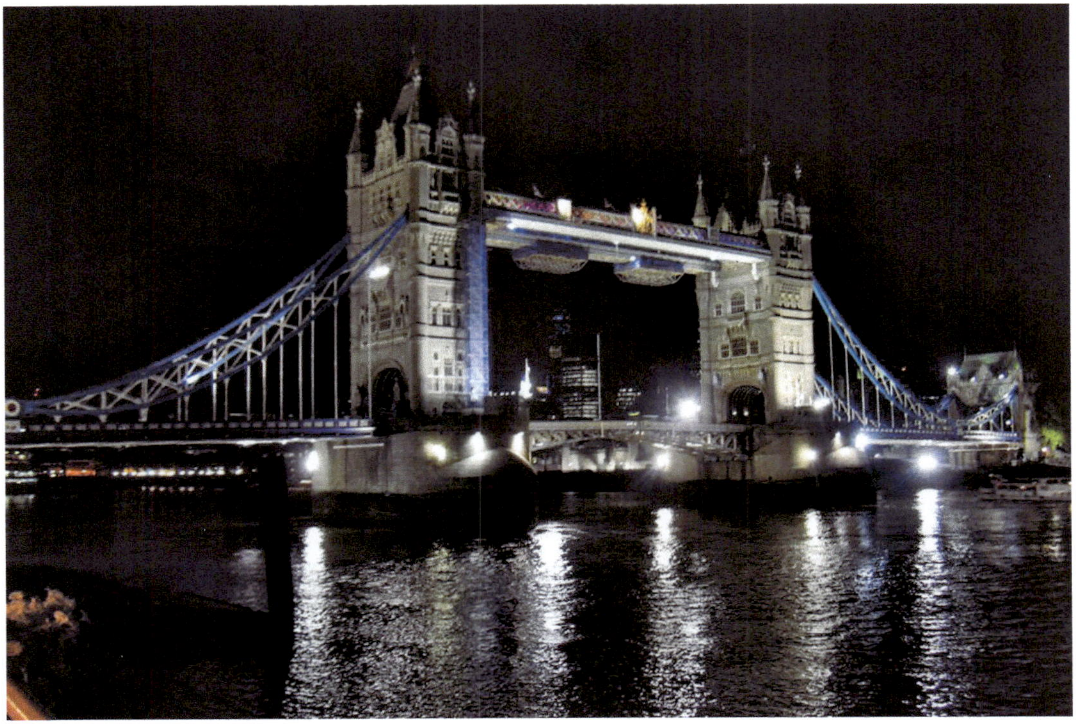

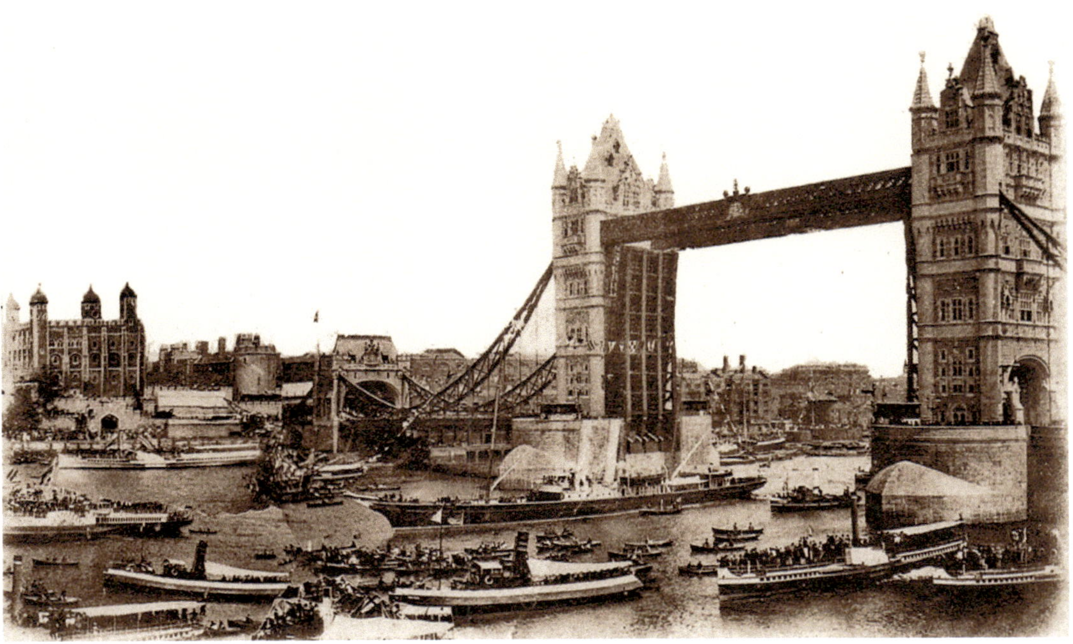

### Opening of Tower Bridge, 1894

Like a fairytale castle it rises up before the eyes! Created by Sir Horace Jones and John Wolfe-Barry, the bridge was officially opened by the Price of Wales on a sunny June afternoon. The Pool was awash with spectators when the Prince declared the bridge open and set the bascules in motion. The cheers, whistles and ships' horns were deafening, along with the Tower's cannon firing. HMS *Landrail* was the first ship to pass through. (Top photograph © F. Low)

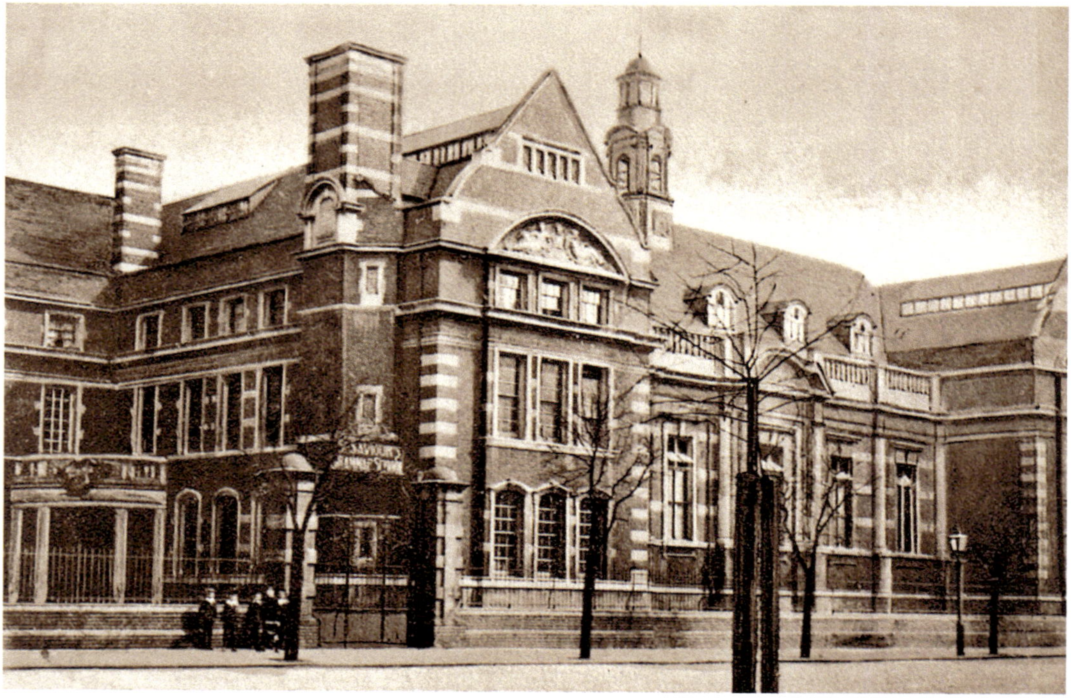

St Saviour's & St Olave's Grammar School, Tooley Street, 1905

Founded in Elizabethan times, the school moved to various spots around the parish before settling in its final resting place in the shadow of Tower Bridge. After much local opposition, the school has now been saved from the bulldozers and awaits a new life as a housing complex.

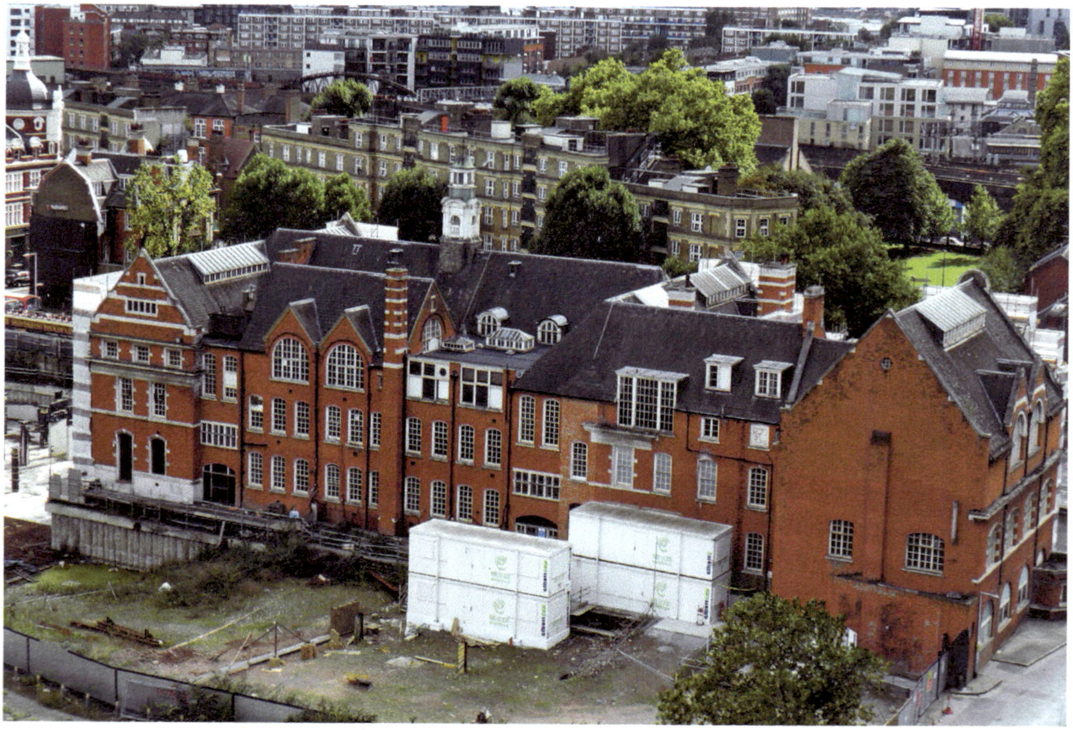

### Hunts House, Guy's Hospital, 1903

It is believed this steeple-like tower burnt the hospital's hazardous waste – mucky, but they did it with style! Hunts House suffered badly in the war, with whole sections demolished, but it recovered sufficiently to carry on until the late 1990s, when it was replaced by the new medical school. This fragment of the old building, bearing the Guys' motto, which translates as 'it is better to give than receive', seems to serve as a monument, but has no plaque to satisfy the curious!

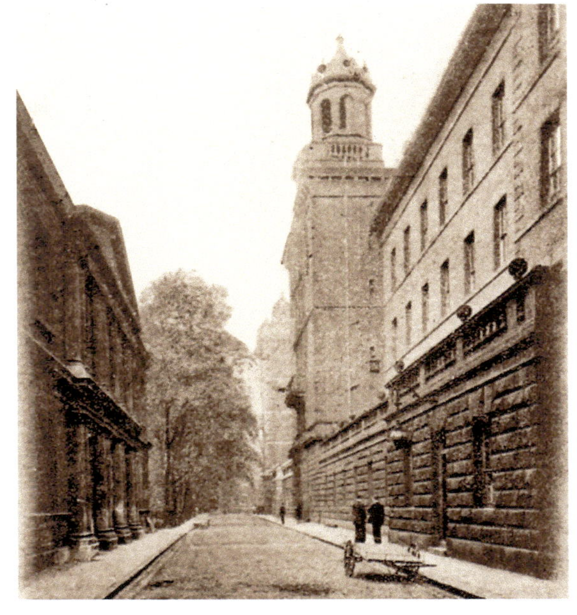

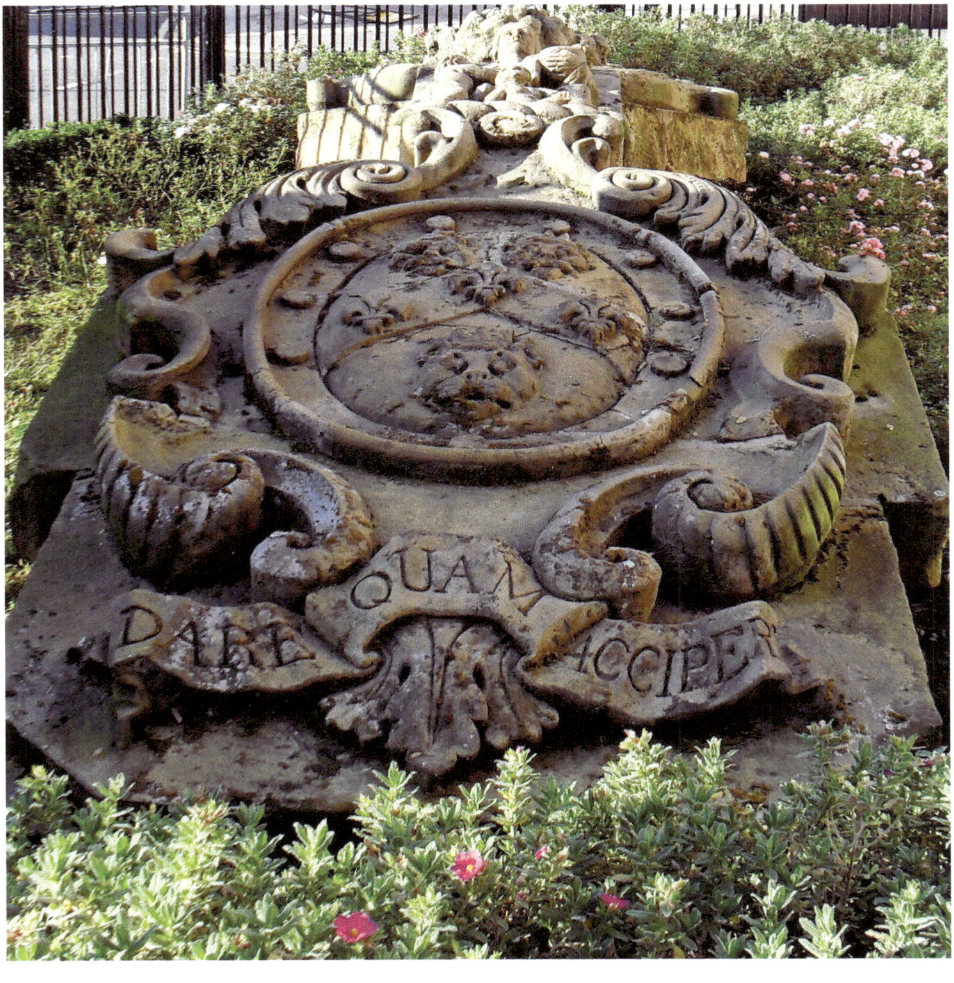

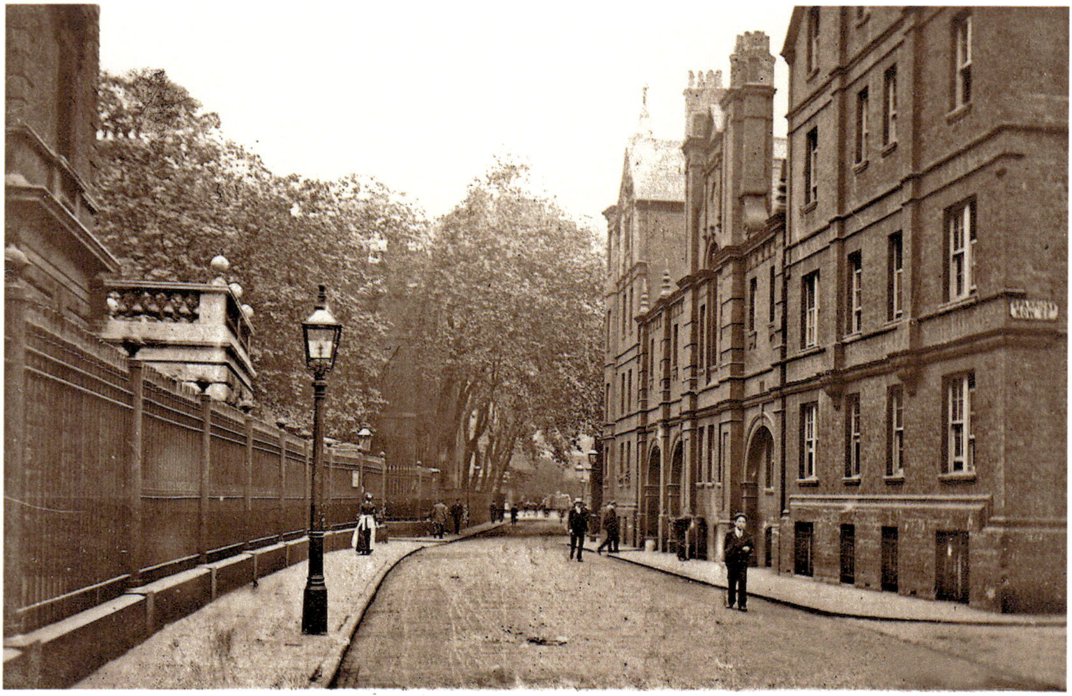

### Guy's Hospital & Sparrick's Row, 1920

Bookseller Thomas Guy was born in 1645 upon Horselydown. He invested wisely and made a fortune from the South Sea Company just before it crashed, donating much of his wealth to the building of Guy's Hospital. It holds a special place in the hearts of Bermondsey people, as so many were born here, treated here and maybe even died here in their later years. Only the railings remain of this building, amid the futuristic, shiny structures that dominate the skyline today. (1920 © Debra Gosling)

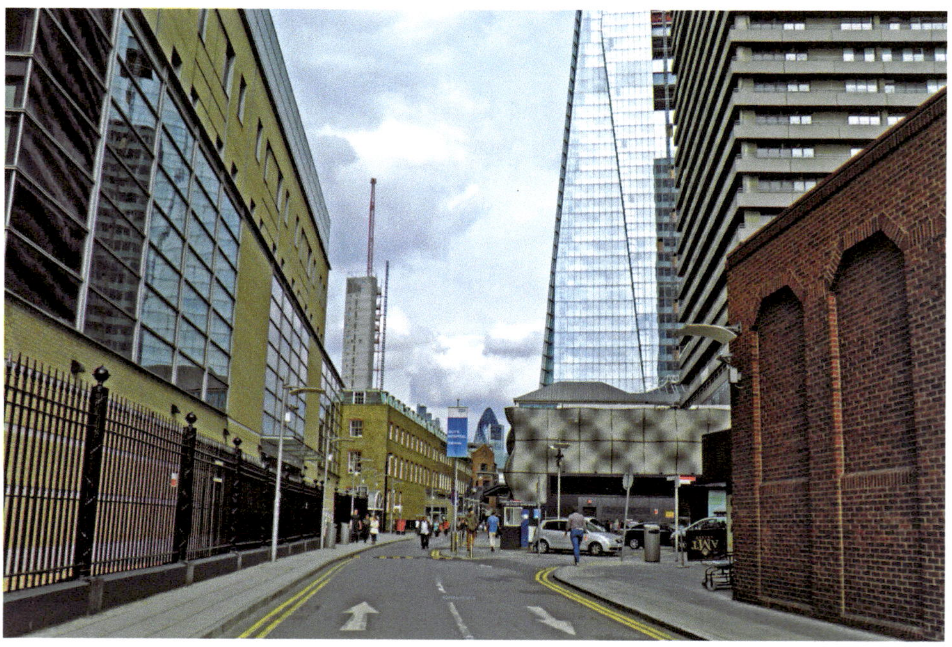

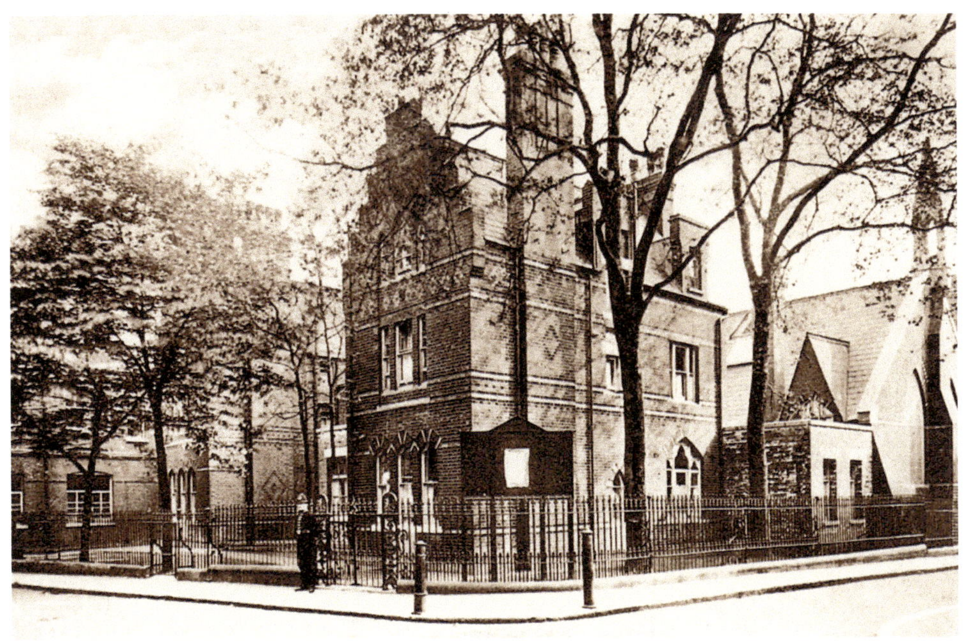



**Newcomen School, 1920**

Elizabeth Newcomen was the widow of a wealthy city merchant. She died in 1674 and left a legacy to provide clothing and education for poor children. The school was remodelled in 1913 and then unsympathetically rebuilt in the 1980s, and now belongs to Guy's Hospital across the road.

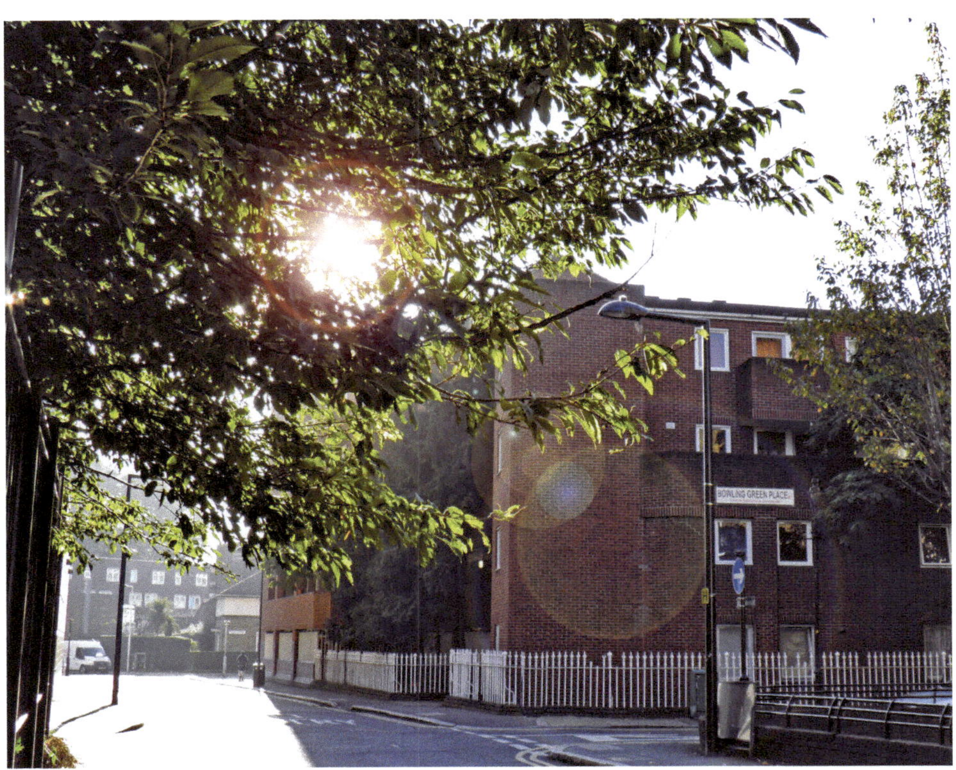

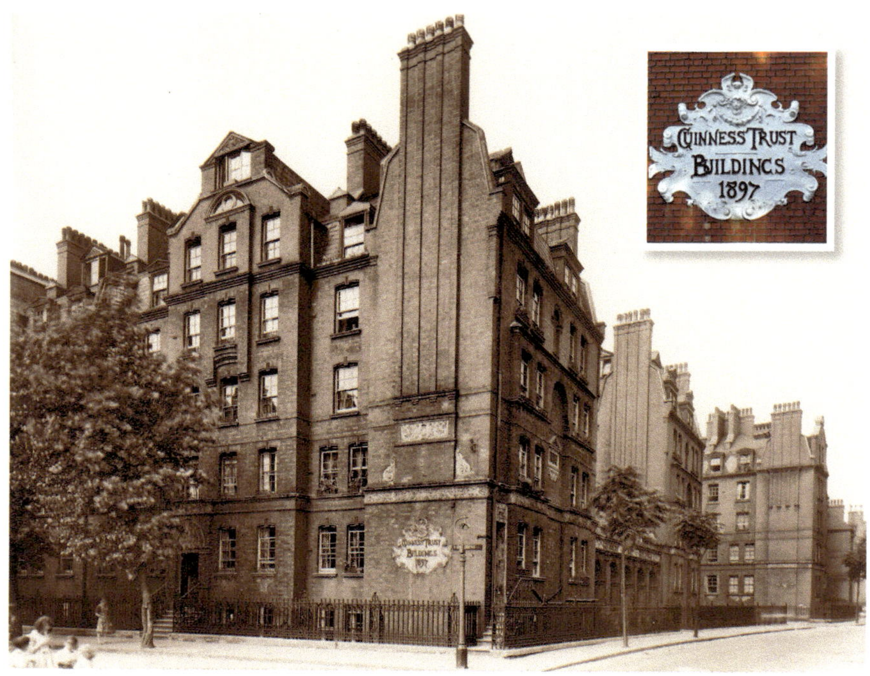



## Guinness Buildings, Snowsfields, 1939

These attractive, rather art nouveau dwellings were built by the Guinness family, of the famous brew. Victorian Snowsfields was an impoverished area with a need for decent housing, so these flats, built in 1897, were welcomed with open arms. Being so close to the railway, they were vulnerable to Luftwaffe attacks. Time after time they were hit, causing extensive damage with many fatalities. In one raid, a whole family was tragically wiped out in one fell swoop. (1939 photograph © Guinness Trust)

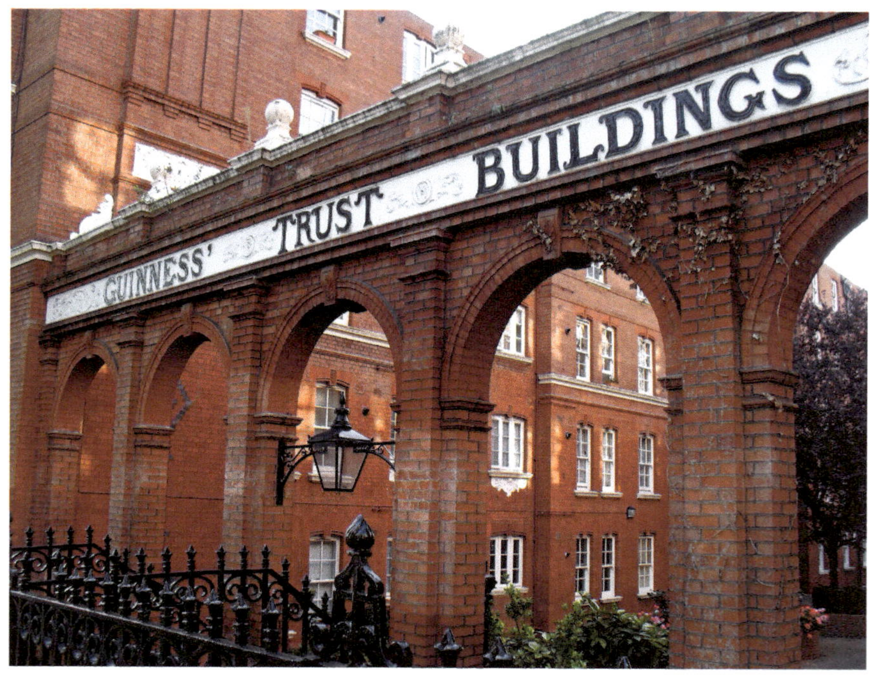

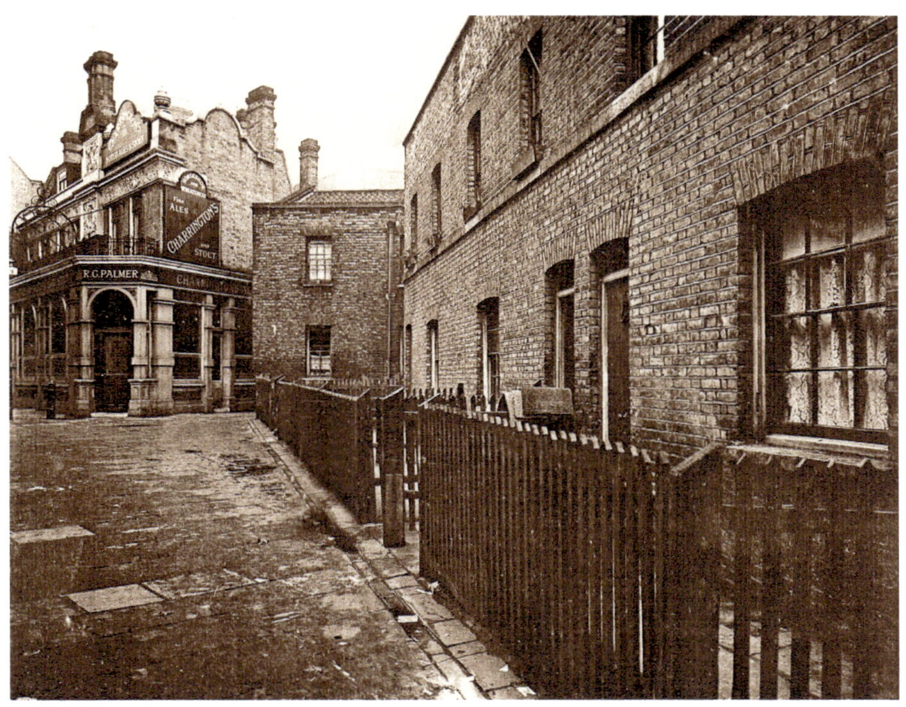

## The Horseshoe, Melior Street, 1935

While so many public houses are closing down, the Horseshoe is flourishing and enjoying something of a renaissance. Originally called the Horseshoe and Wheatsheaf, it nestles in this quiet cul-de-sac, in an area now eccentrically renamed Bermondsey Village. This turning was called Melior Place and, despite the disappearance of the cottages, it still retains its air of serenity.

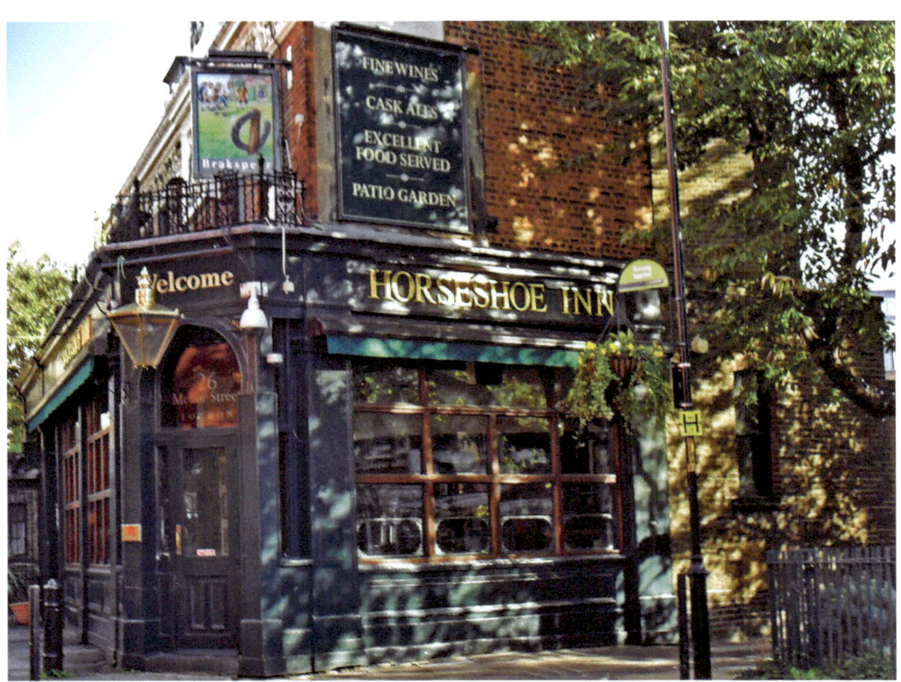

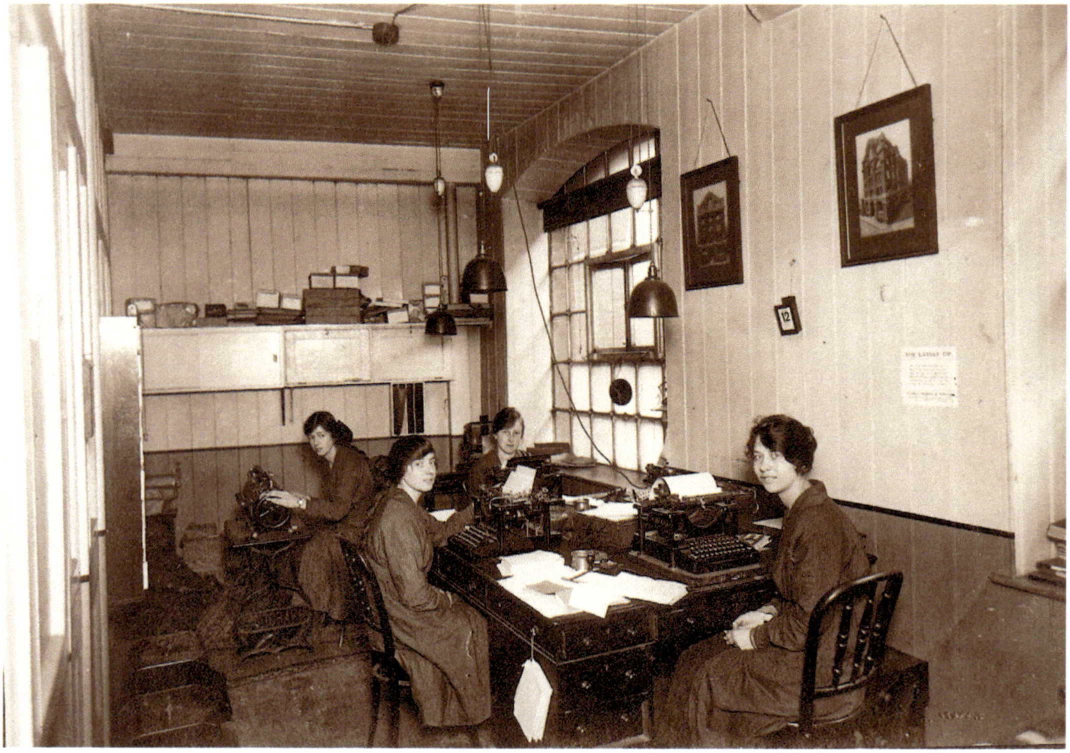

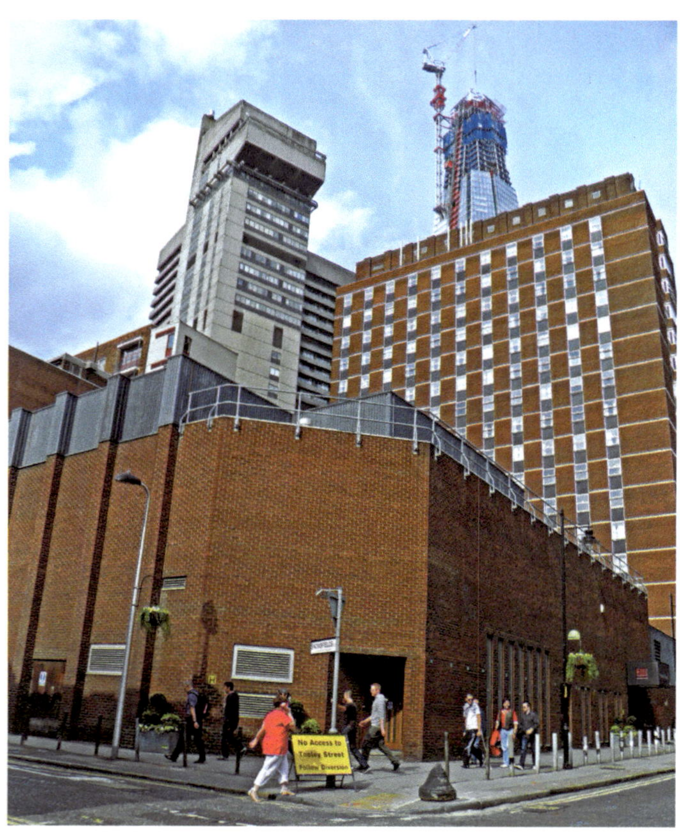



### George Morris & Son, Weston Street, 1918

The photograph on the wall of this early typing pool shows the building in which these girls are working. They were probably the first female administrative staff Morris & Co. had employed, as by this date so many men had been lost in the fields of Flanders. The Greenwood Theatre, where *Jackanory* and *Question Time* were televised, was built over the site, but those days have also gone and the theatre is now owned by King's College London. (1918 photograph © Debra Gosling)

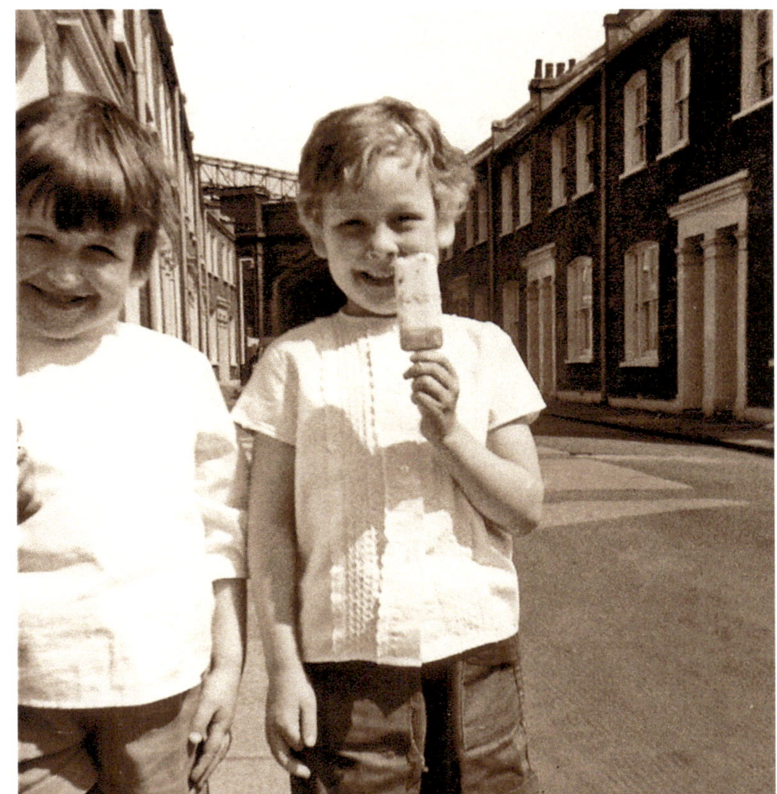

Summer in the
1960s meant a
Fab ice lolly! The
houses where
these two girls are
standing were built
on what had once
been Bermondsey
Abbey's vineyards
and fishponds.
Erected in the 1790s,
the houses stood
the test of time, but
by the 1970s they
had serious damp
and subsidence
problems. The new
developments to the
right of the current
view are faux
warehouses with
ineffectual cranes,
all built to satisfy
the loft experience
that today's buyers
seem to crave. (1968
photograph © Debra
Gosling)

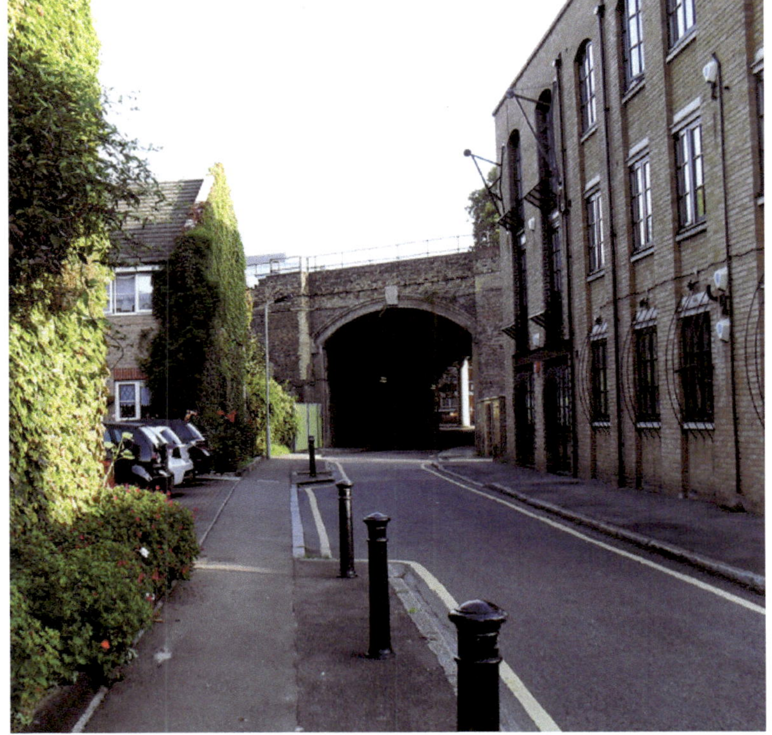

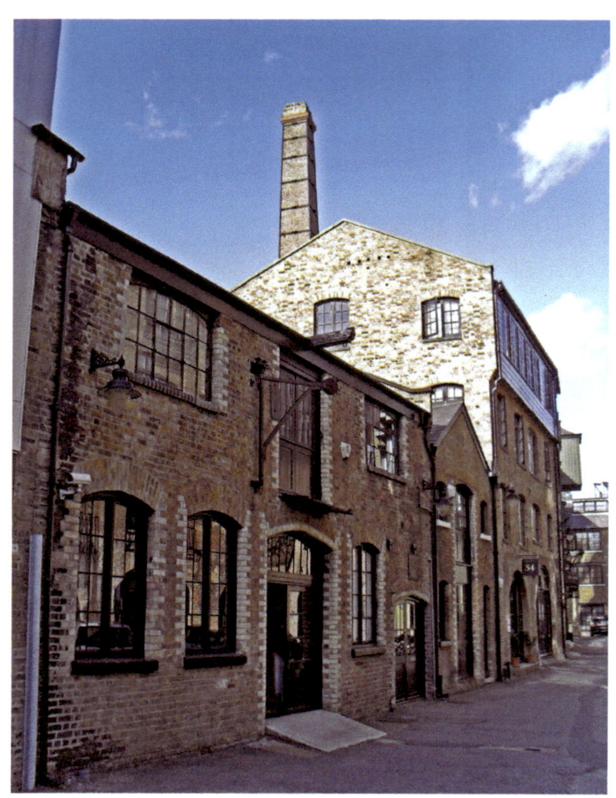

**Sarson's Vinegar Factory, 1985**
Vineyards have always flourished here and continued to do so when Slee & Company bought an old vinegar works in 1812. Later they amalgamated with Champion's, then with Sarson's. The huge vats have disappeared, to be replaced with housing, but some of the old factory survives in the guise of apartments. On a warm day those with a good sense of smell can detect the faint aroma of vinegar still emanating from the brickwork. (1985 photograph © Debra Gosling)

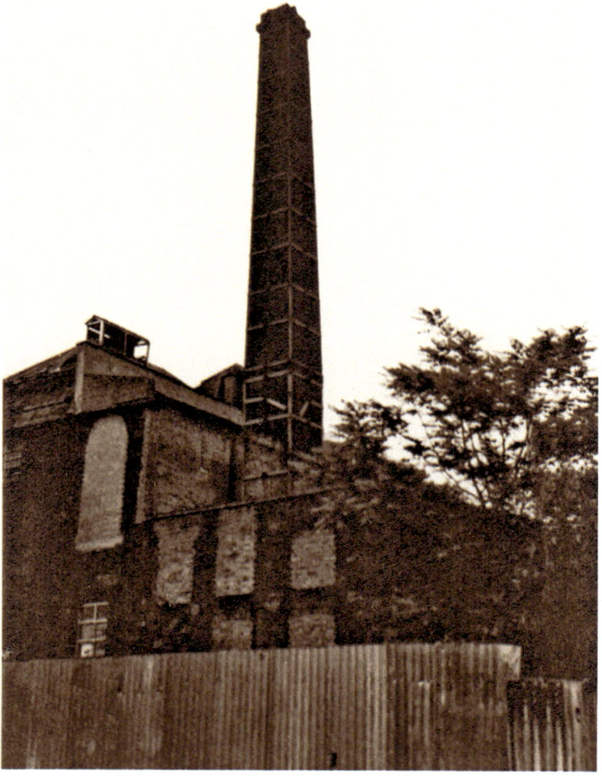

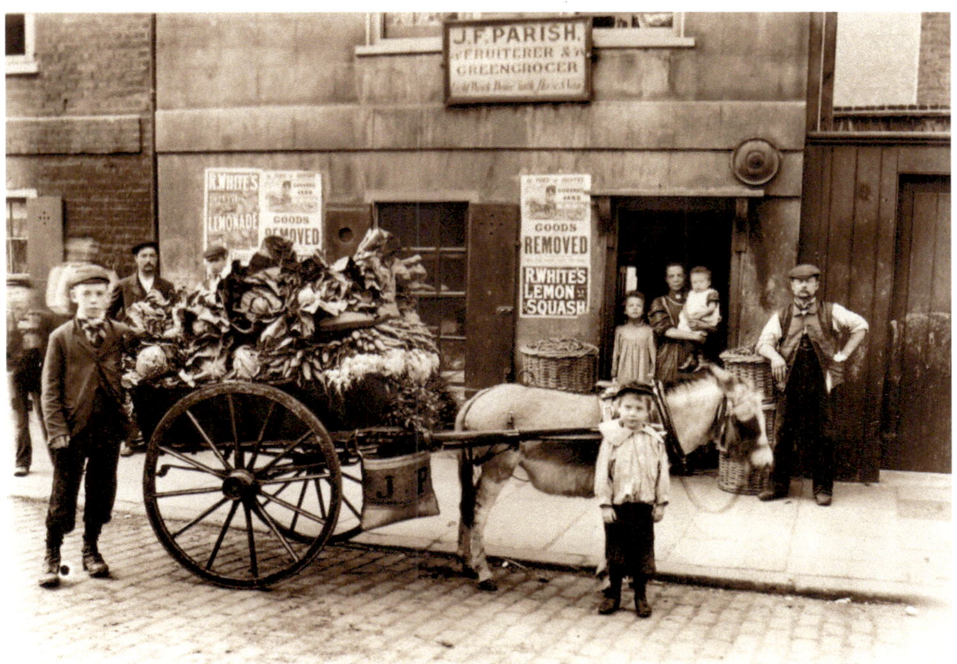


## Parish Greengrocer's, Tanner Street, 1900

The man on the right is Mr J. Parish. His family ran this shop for many years at 36 Tanner Street. He has a typical costermonger's barrow, loaded up with a tempting display of cabbages, carrots and onions, ready to be made into a hearty stew by his customers. The shop has disappeared into the pages of history, with only Sainsbury's nearby for today's vegetable-seekers! (1900 photograph © Kathryn Parish)

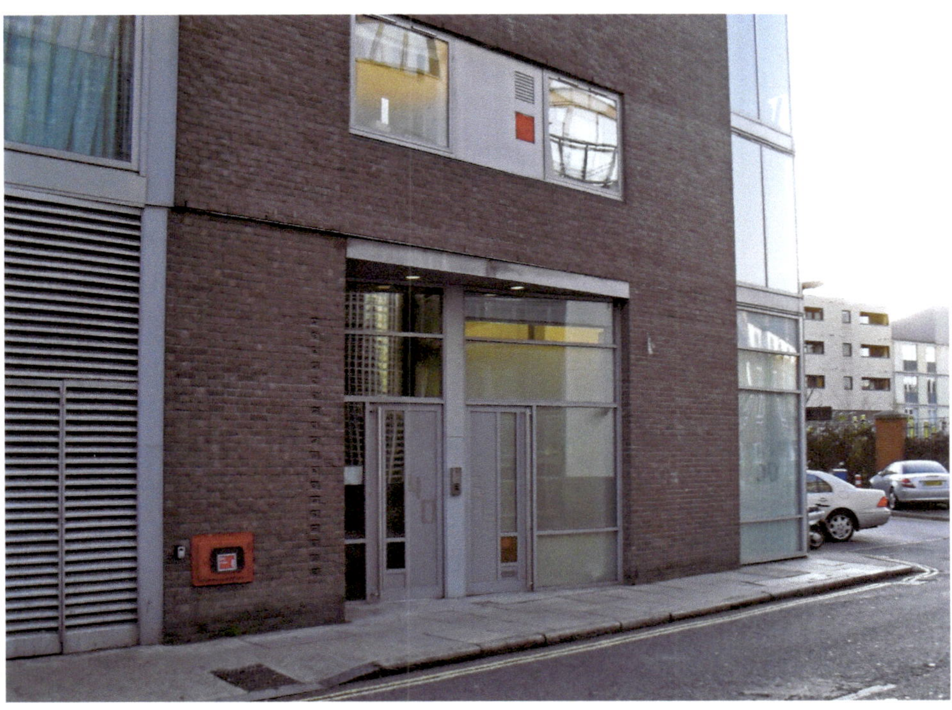

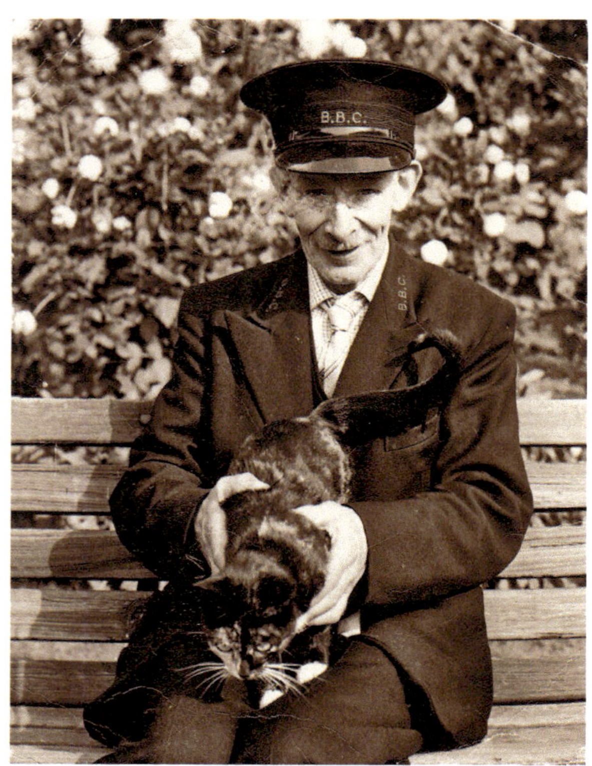



**Tanner Park, 1950s**
Parkie Albert Young bandaged knees, chased off suspicious old men and generally kept order. He proudly wore his Bermondsey Borough Council uniform and was a figure of authority. Were he to return today, he would only recognise St Olave's Tower, once atop the church of its namesake. The tower was relocated here in the 1920s but now stands forlorn and unloved, like Wilde's Canterville Ghost, ignored by the children and mothers in the swing park. (1950s photograph © Tony Young)

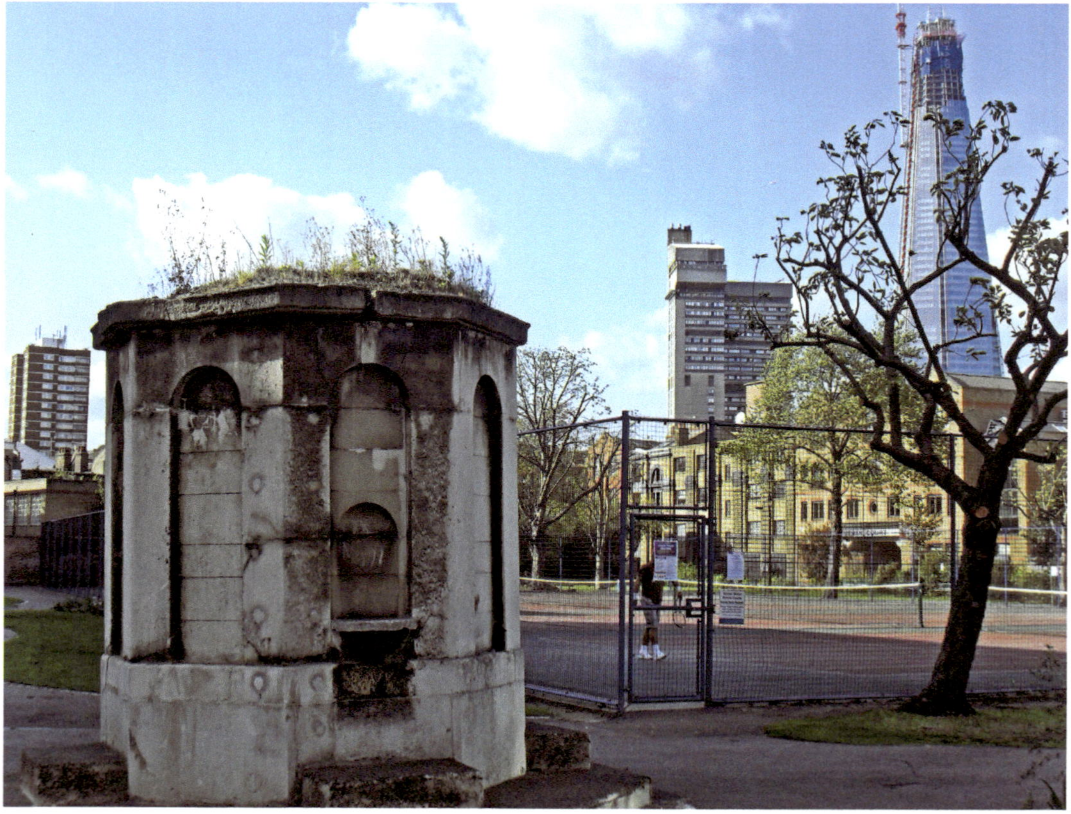

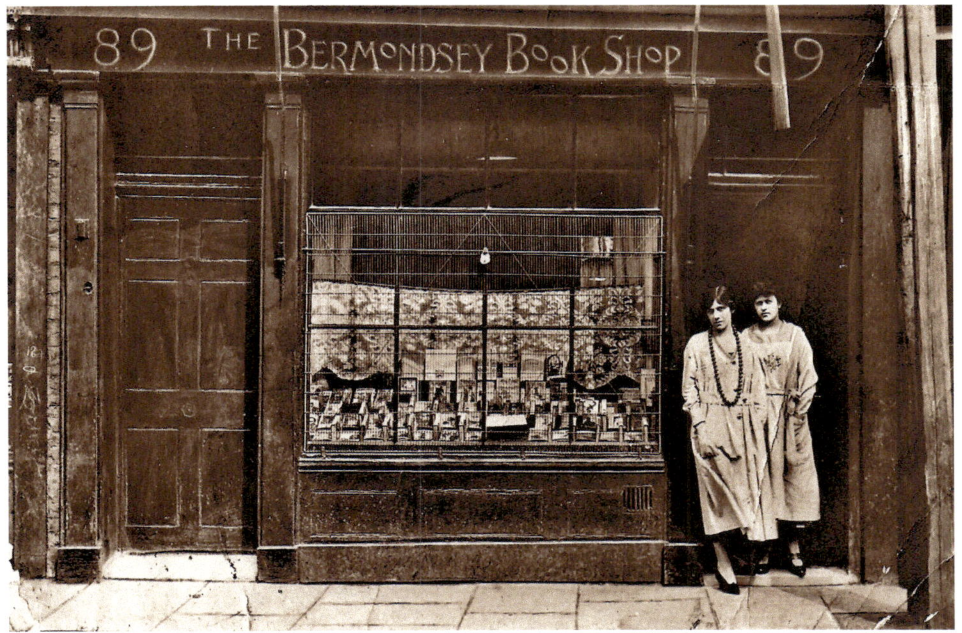

## Bermondsey Bookshop, 1921

Ethel Gutman (left) set up a bookshop amid the tanneries with husband Sidney. She held regular social evenings at the shop, with high profile guest speakers such as Alfred Noyes, the poet who penned the epic 'The Highwayman'. Sadly Ethel did not see her bookshop flourish, dying young in March 1925. Five years later the bookshop had closed and the space is now occupied by another businesswoman, Zandra Rhodes, with her Fashion and Textile Museum. (1921 photograph © Debra Gosling)

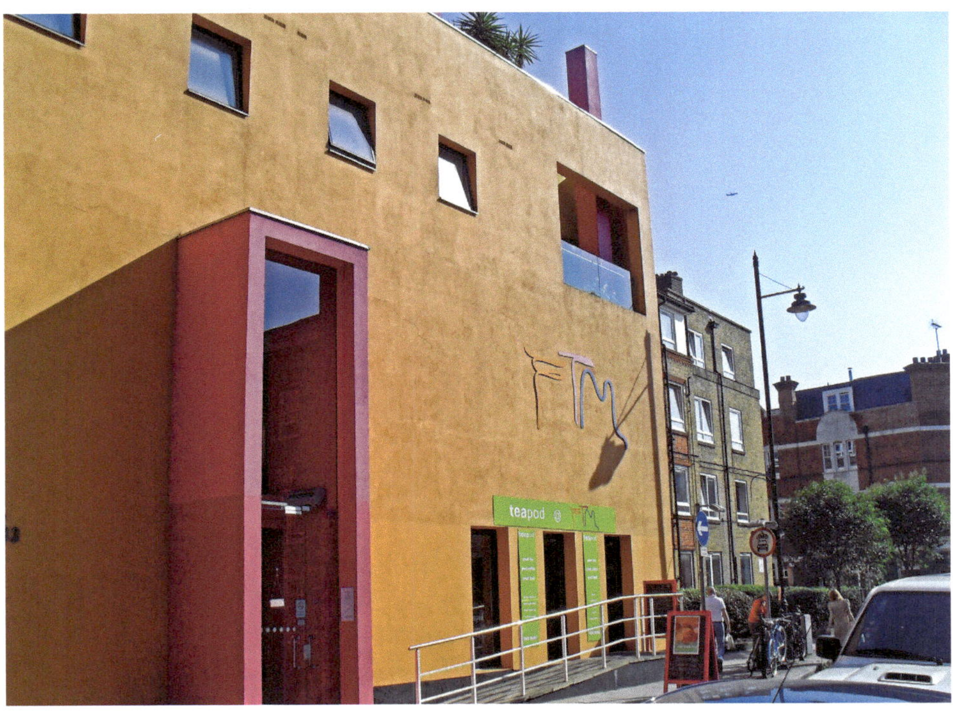

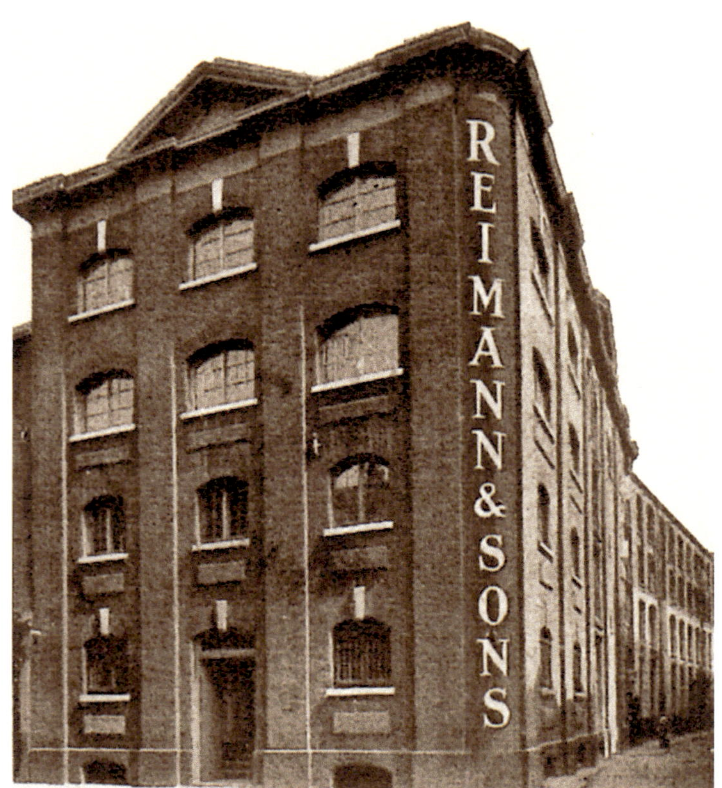


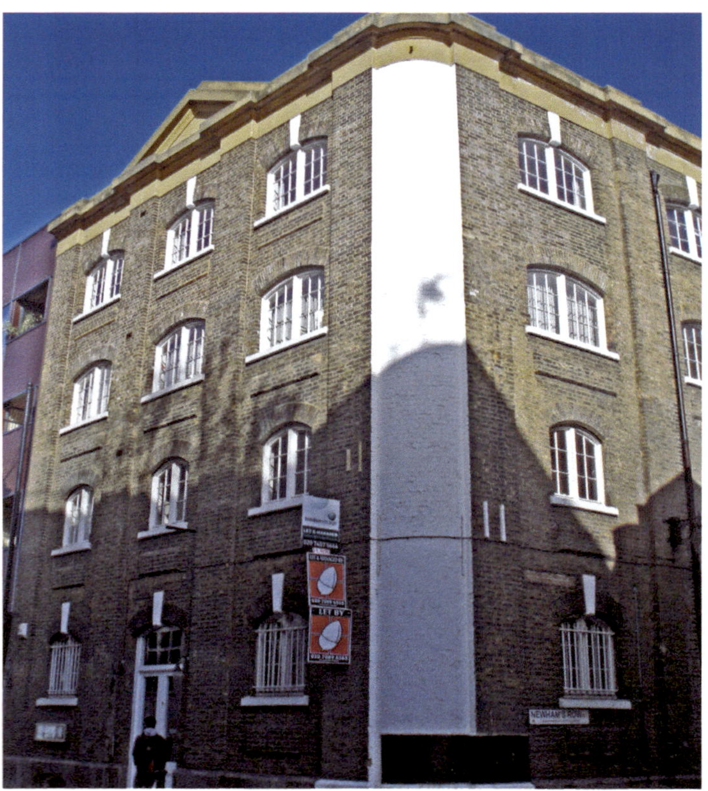

**Reimann's Clog Factory, Bermondsey Street, 1920**
Reimann & Sons manufactured industrial wooden clogs with leather uppers and were one of the many satellite industries that stemmed from the skin trade. Established in the nineteenth century, Mr Reimann and his family occupied various shops in Bermondsey Street before settling here. To the side of the building was Newham's Row, where famous hat manufacturers Christy's had one of their two factories. Reimann's exhibited at the 1929 British Industries Fair, advertising their clogs, laces and waterproof aprons, the sort of kit needed to work in the mucky industries typical of Bermondsey at that time. Once these industries disappeared, the clogs followed. The building now has multi-purpose live/work units.

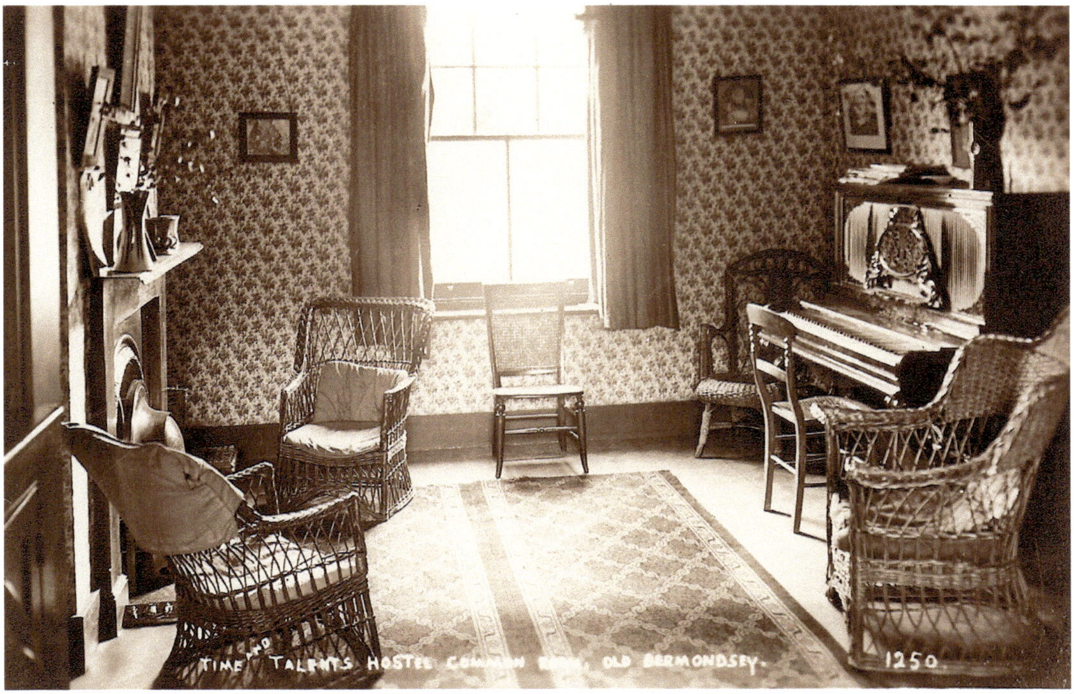

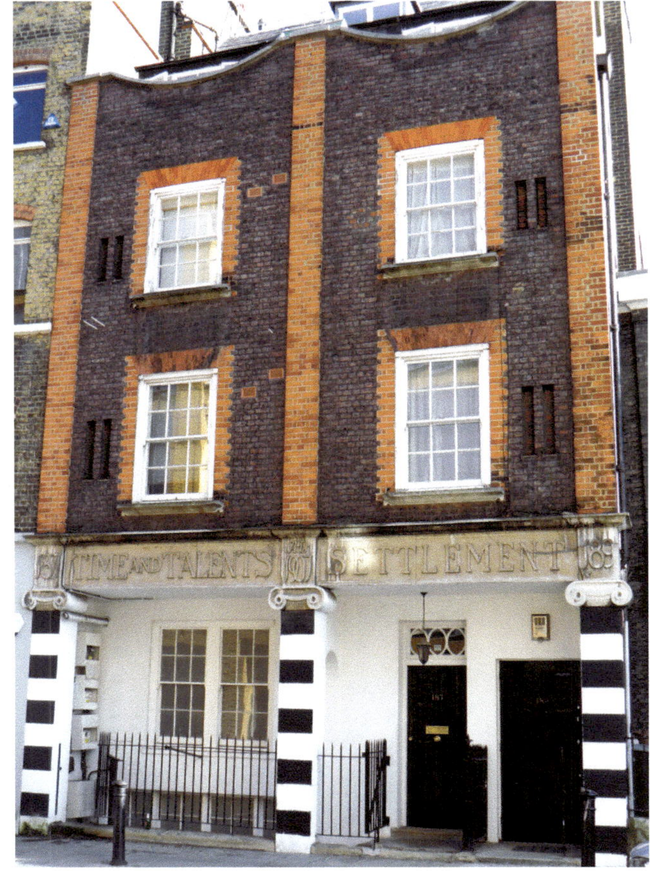


## Time & Talents, Bermondsey Street, 1909

With a name like Minna Gollock she was destined to do something amazing! Minna tackled the social issues of the underclasses by going out and getting her hands dirty. Working for the YWCA, she wanted the aristocracy to see that outside of their cosy, fragrant homes, women of their own age were working twelve hours a day in dirty, noisy and downright dangerous factories to earn a pittance. In 1907 this new building was erected over a ramshackle old tailor's shop, where the common room gave factory girls a place to sit and read, take tea in a proper china cup and look out over the peaceful churchyard. There is still a flourishing T&T at the Old Mortuary in Rotherhithe.

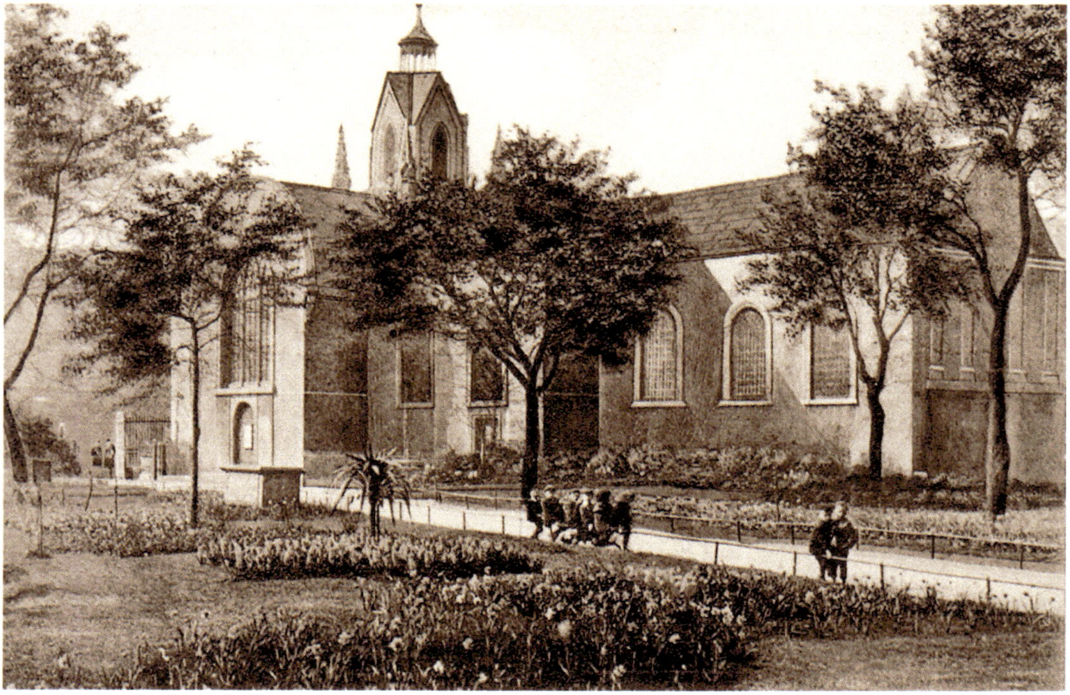

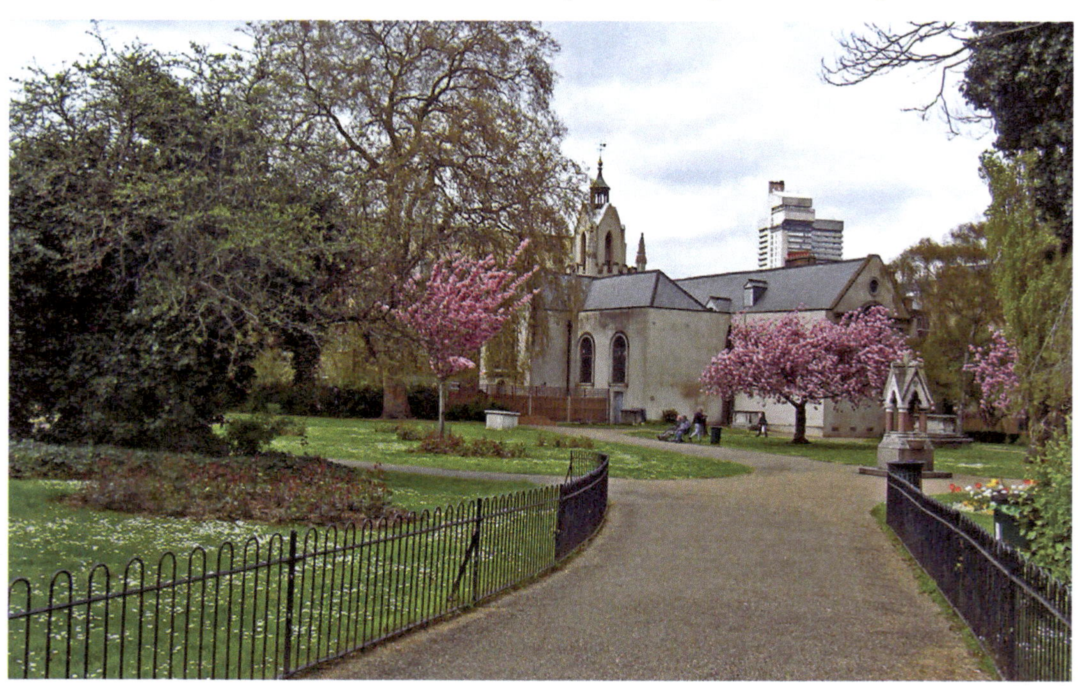

## St Mary Magdalen Church, 1900

The rumbling traffic and blocks of flats along Tower Bridge Road belie our rich heritage, for beneath the tarmac exist the foundations of one of medieval England's most important churches: Bermondsey Abbey. The lay church, St Mary Magdalen, is now the only surviving part above ground. The church has been constantly re-fashioned and its present castellated façade is the work of Victorian romanticism. Here you will find memorials to woolstaplers, wharfingers and cowkeepers.

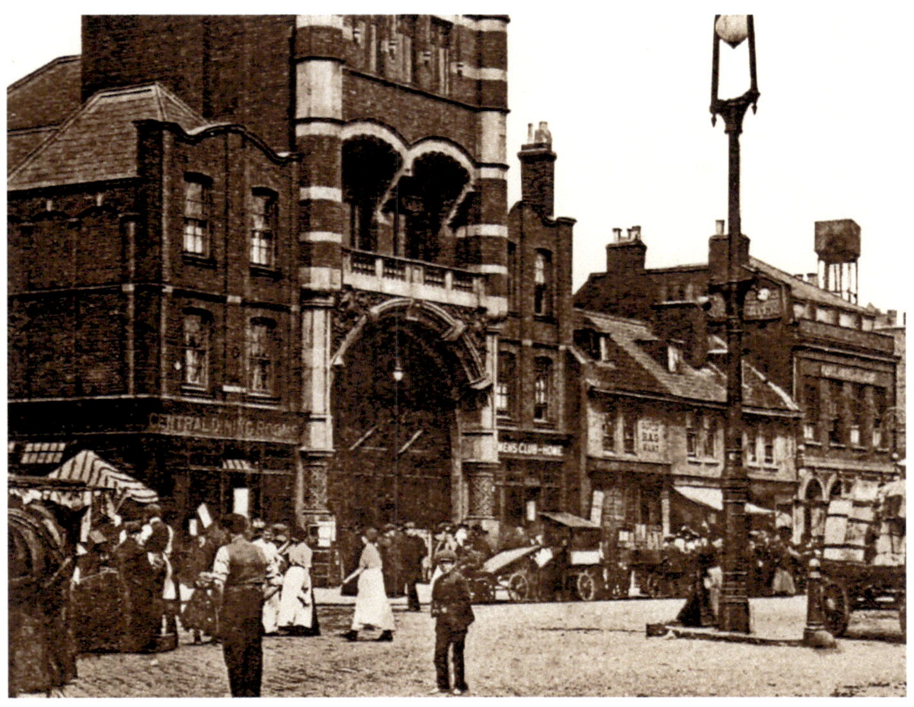



## Bermondsey Central Hall, 1910

Methodist minister Reverend Henry Meakin identified this site as ideal for a new Methodist church. His community was a poor one, with much want and a need for spirituality and practical help – the boy in the foreground is barefoot. Now reduced in size, the church still plays host to a healthy congregation, all of whom, happily, own footwear!

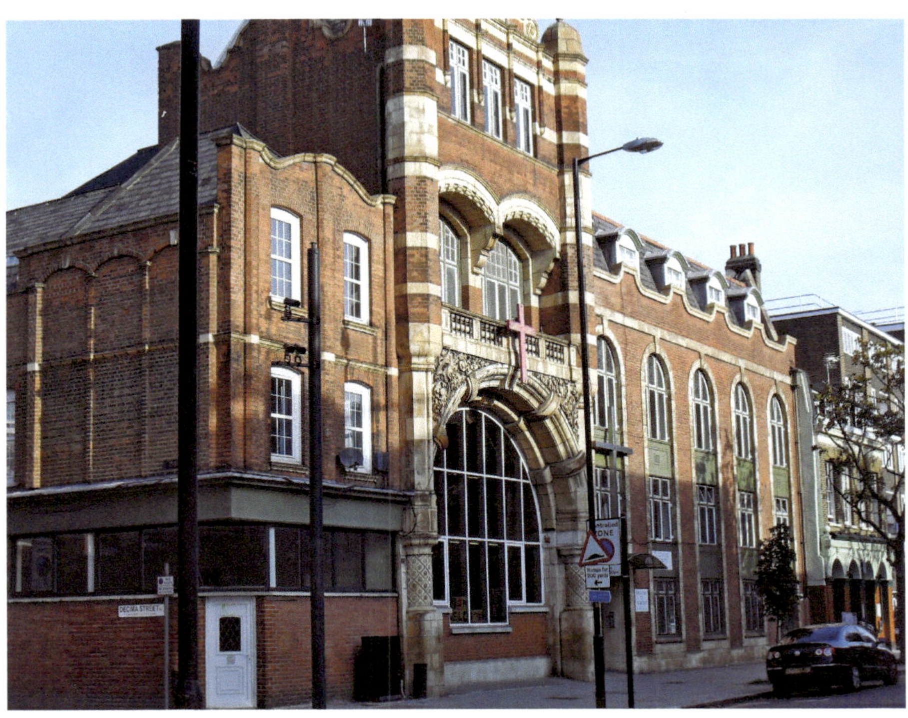

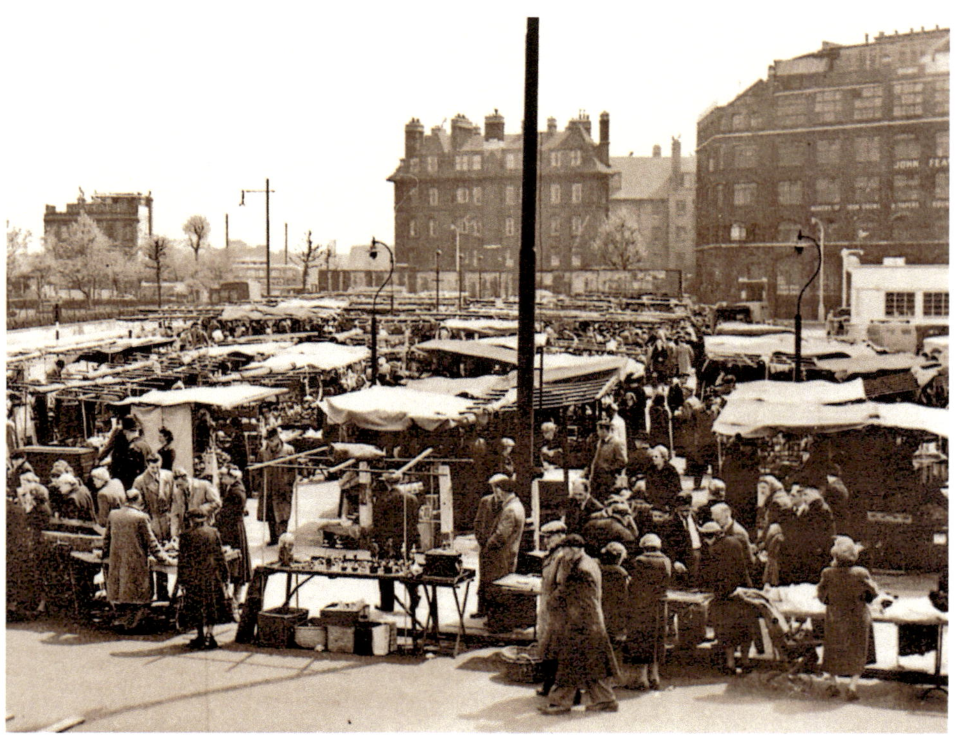

## New Caledonian Antiques Market, 1950

The 'Cally' arrived when the Second World War displaced it from Islington. Teeming with stalls, trading began around 4 a.m. It was the norm to see a policeman between parties sorting out ownership of anything from a stuffed bear to granny's knick-knacks! Until 1994 the medieval Market Overt law allowed a buyer entitlement over goods purchased between sunset and sunrise, effectively under the cover of darkness. These days such practices have disappeared, along with a significant number of stalls.

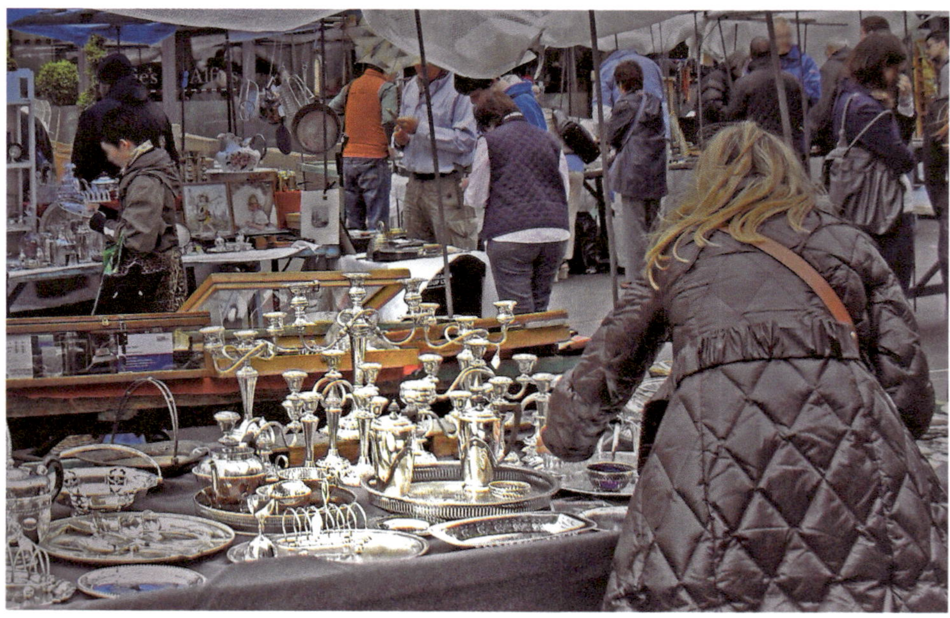

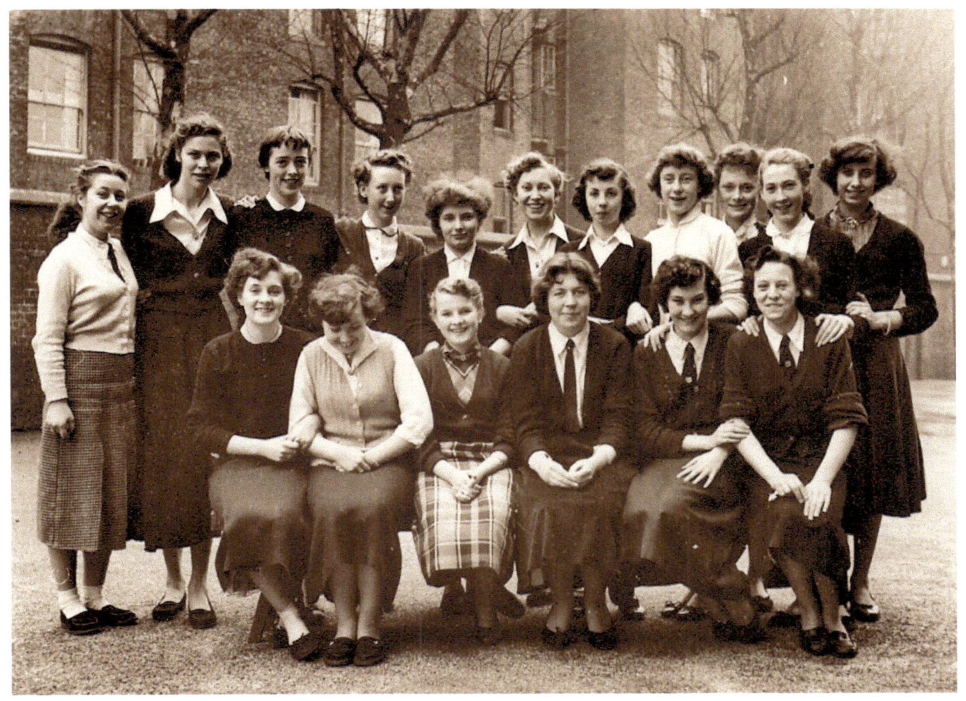

## Bermondsey Central School, 1954

Class 5G bravely face the elements to have a Christmas photograph taken. Behind them are old tenements that looked out onto the Old Kent Road. Now the buildings have been demolished, class 5G are pensioners, the school is gated luxury flats and only the trees remain in their original form! (1954 photograph © Mary Gosling)

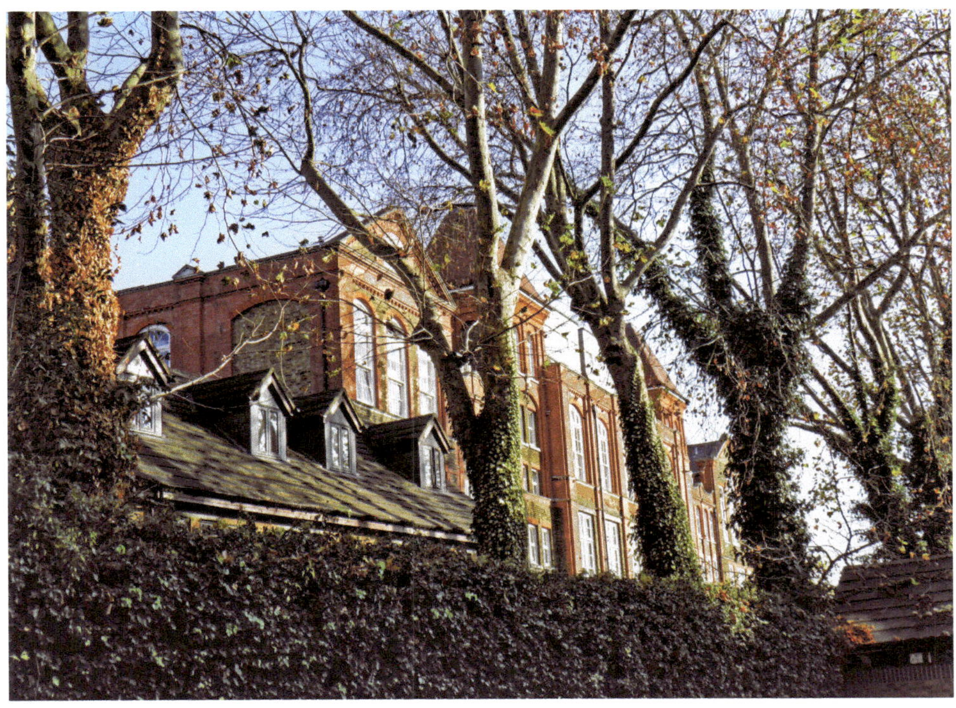

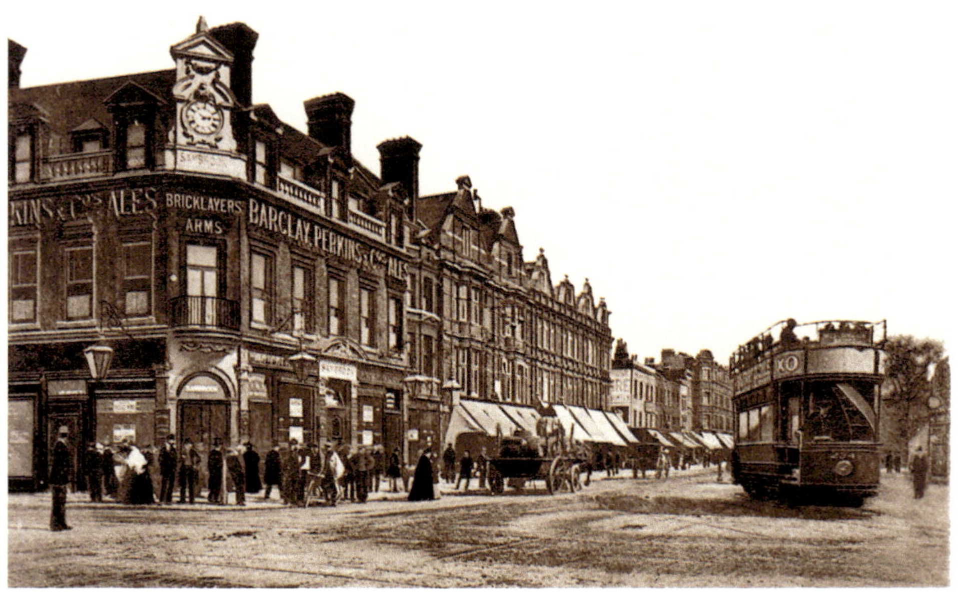

## The Bricklayer's Arms Public House, Old Kent Road, 1905

The 'Brick', as it was called, is now the hideous flyover junction where four main roads converge, but it got its name from the pub, the Bricklayer's Arms. There was a pub of this name on site for hundreds of years. Lord Horatio Nelson frequented it and local legend suggests that he was a customer of Edgington's, the sailmakers further along the road. The red-brick buildings to the right are original but have undergone extensive re-modelling.

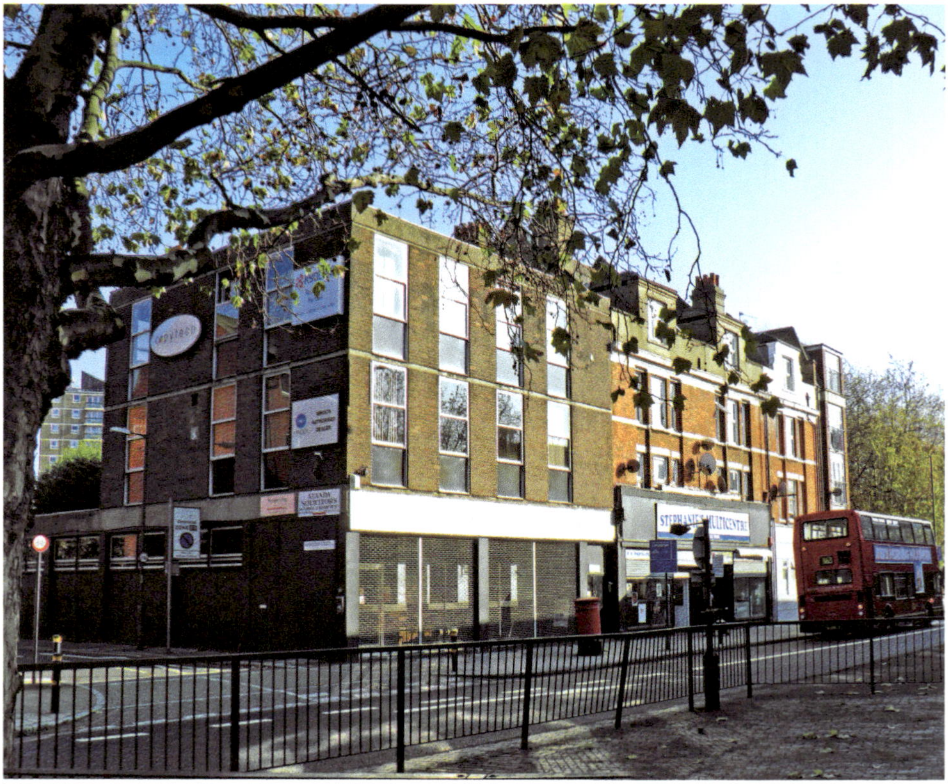

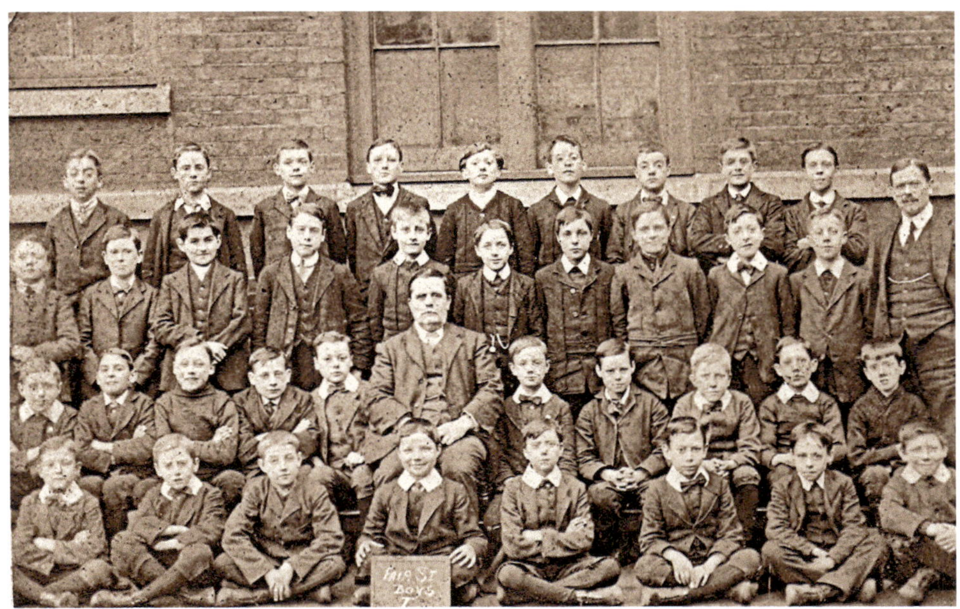

## Fair Street School, 1920

These boys are on the verge of starting work. These are no ragamuffins; almost all of them sport a smart starched collar and the boy in the middle even has a pocket watch and chain. Renamed Tower Bridge Primary, it now resembles a fortress with a high ornate fence, CCTV at every angle and locked, caged doors. However, the schoolkeeper's house, now a private residence, has this wonderful, cheery display every Christmas to lighten the mood. (1920 photograph © Debra Gosling)

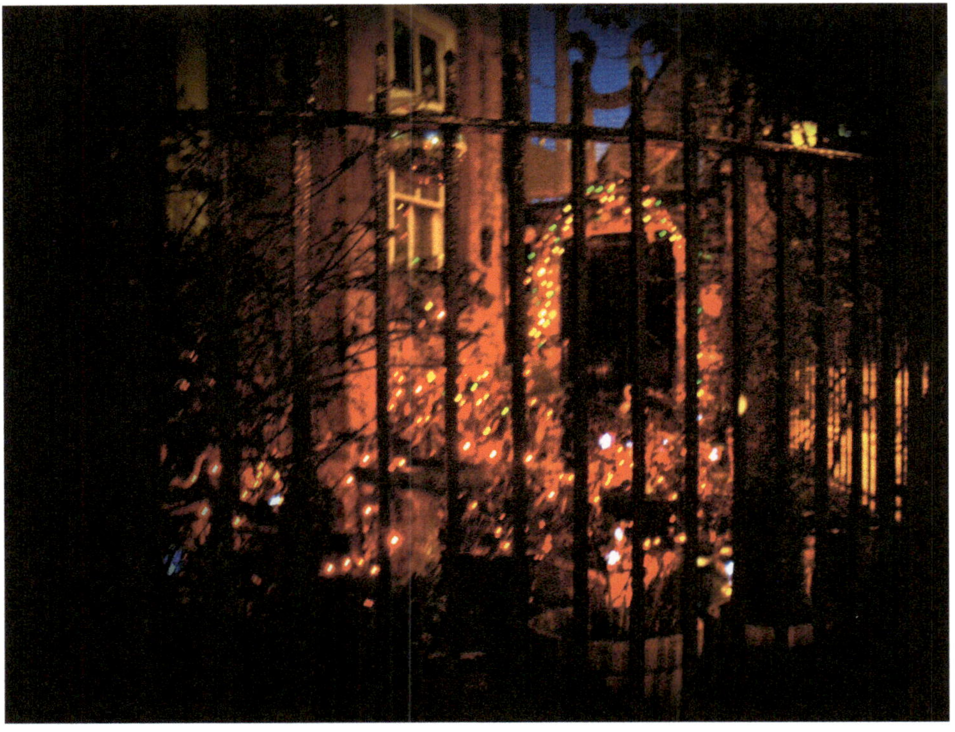

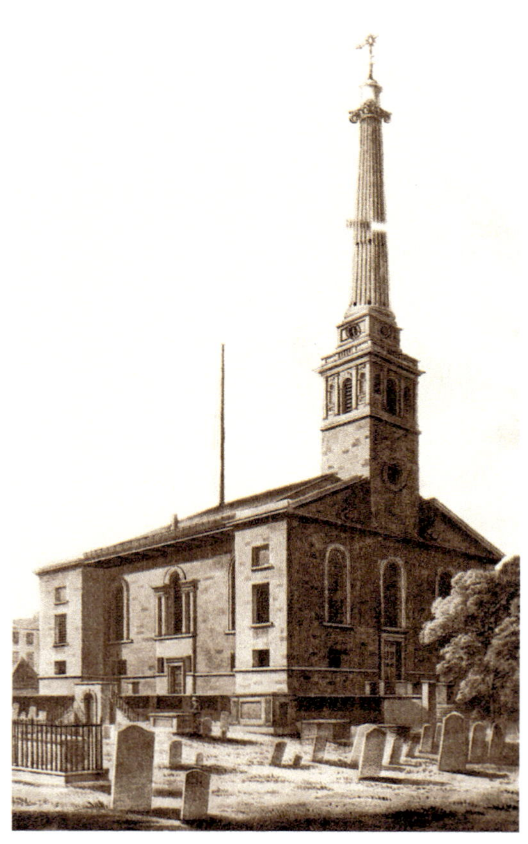



**St John's Church, Horselydown, 1740**
Built in 1736, St John's with its fine white stonework stood picturesquely in the fields of old Horselydown. Over 200 years later the Luftwaffe wrecked it. In perilous ruins, full of stray cats and tramps, it took on an air of Gothic romance. The London City Mission stands upon its foundations, which are now listed.

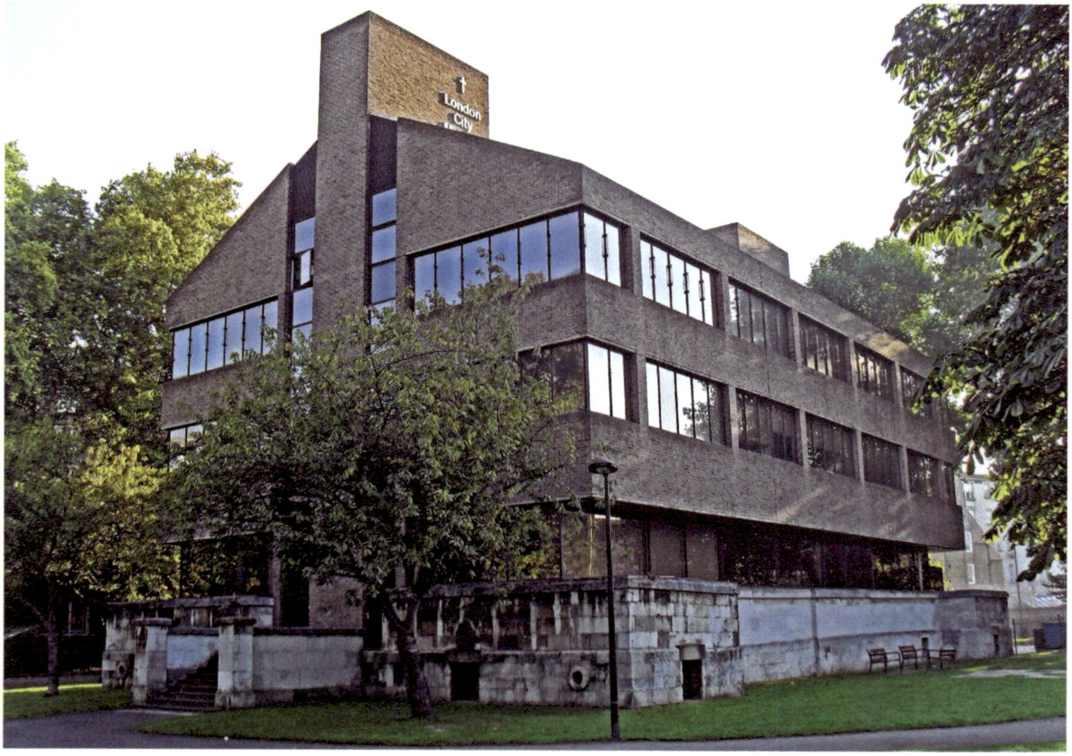

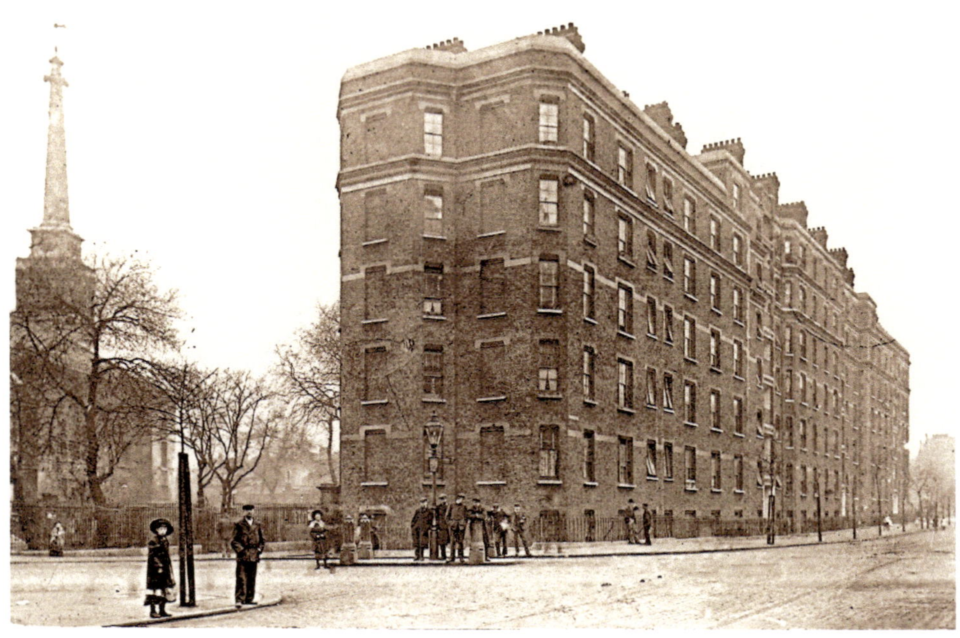

### Devon Mansions, Tooley Street, 1910

These rather swanky tenements were originally Hanover Buildings. Built in 1875, they retained their name until the First World War, when anything remotely Germanic was erased from the streets of England. It was at this point that the flats were renamed Devon Mansions. Ironically, a whole wing of the buildings further along the road was destroyed by enemy action and rebuilt after the war. St John's can be seen in the background.

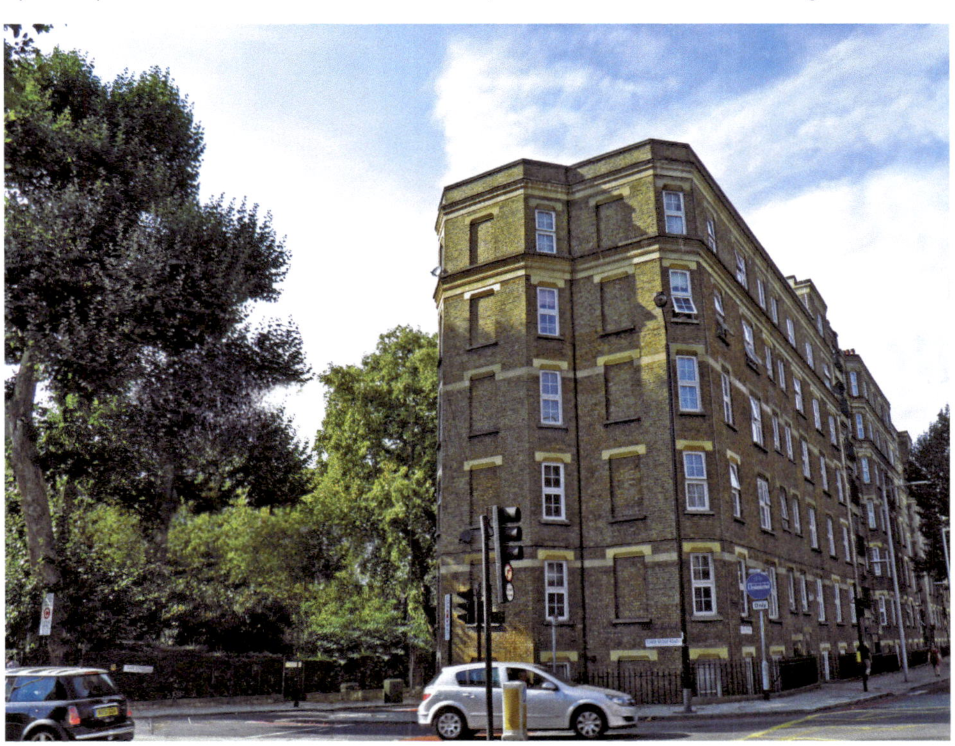

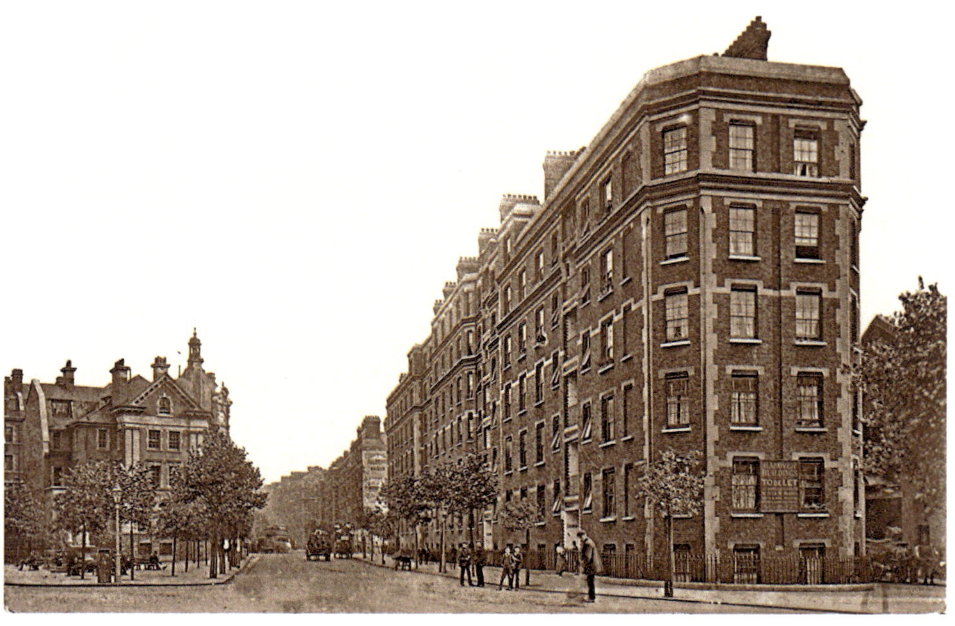



**Devon Mansions, Fair Street, 1910**

Buses and coaches aside, this view has barely changed in over a hundred years. The flats have not changed at all, save for the addition of a raised flower bed on the corner of Fair Street. Southwark council's gardeners do a good job of keeping the flower bed looking smart and this display of a Loch Ness monster type of creature must surely be one of their best to date.

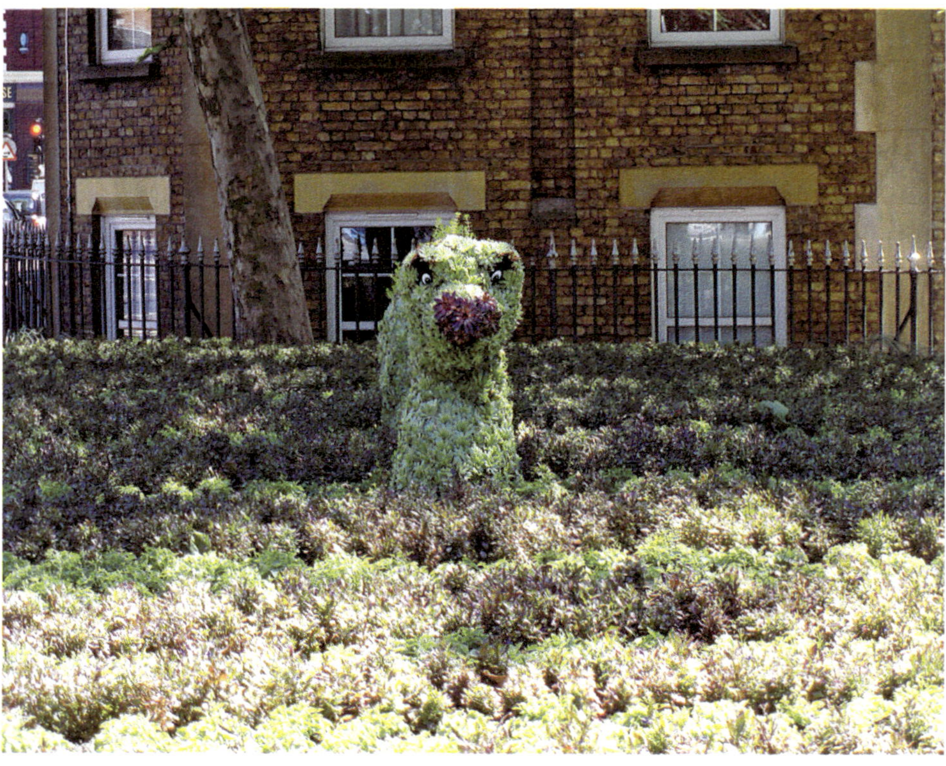

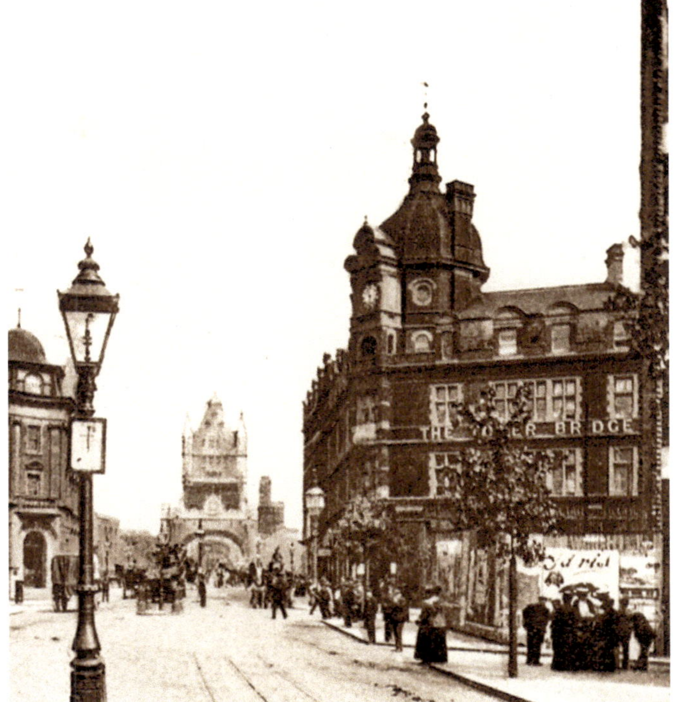

**Tower Bridge Hotel, 1900**
Another building that has barely changed. The hoarding behind the group gathered to the right of the picture was only removed in the last few years, to be replaced by a fire escape for the flats. Residents have made a feature of it, with luscious green pot plants climbing up the steps. When the bridge opened, the hotel provided board for tourists. It is now a rather large public house, which has kept many of its original features.

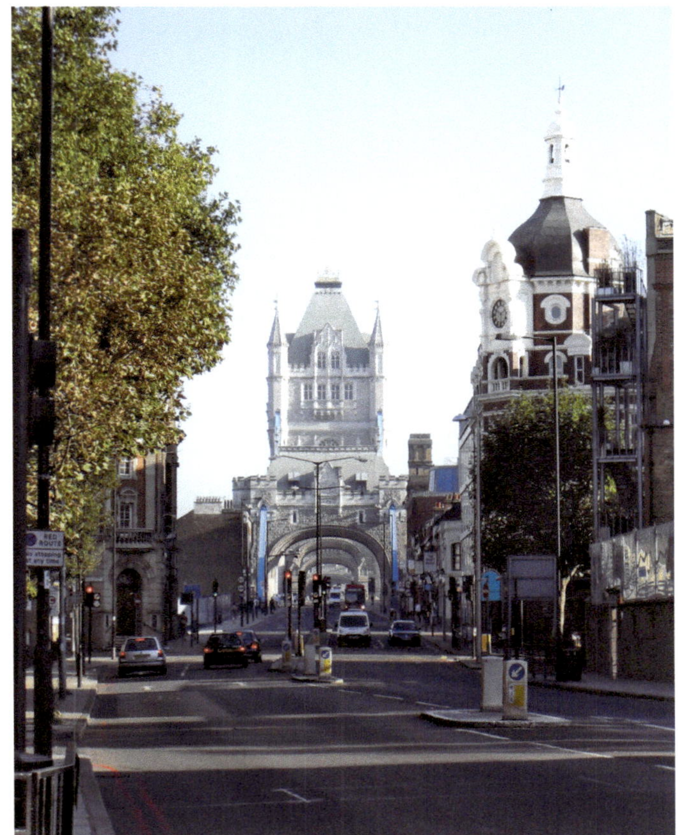

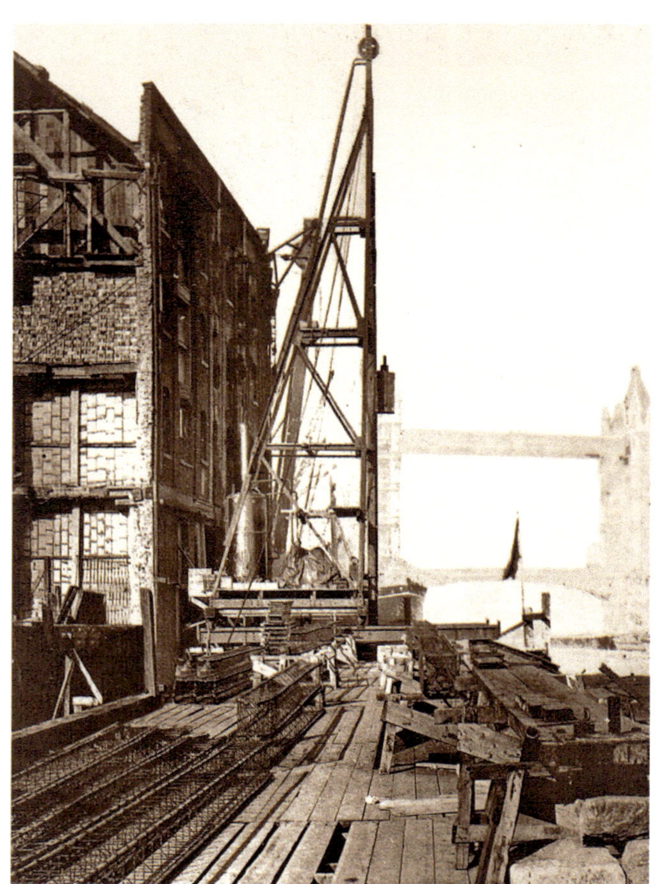

## Butler's Wharf, 1948

The wharf has undergone an amazing transformation in the last thirty years. Terence Conran is the man who saw the potential to socialise, eat and drink while overlooking the river along this terrace. It may have changed beyond all recognition but the wharf crane and the mast of Greenpeace's *Rainbow Warrior 3* could have been made in this same factory, seventy years apart.

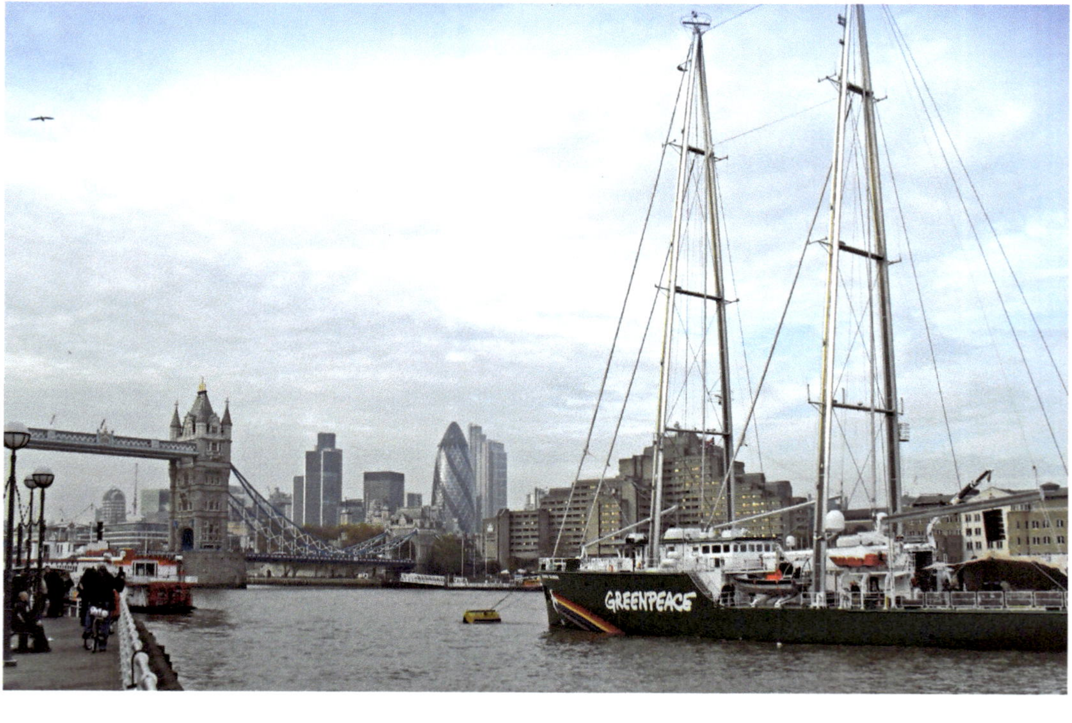

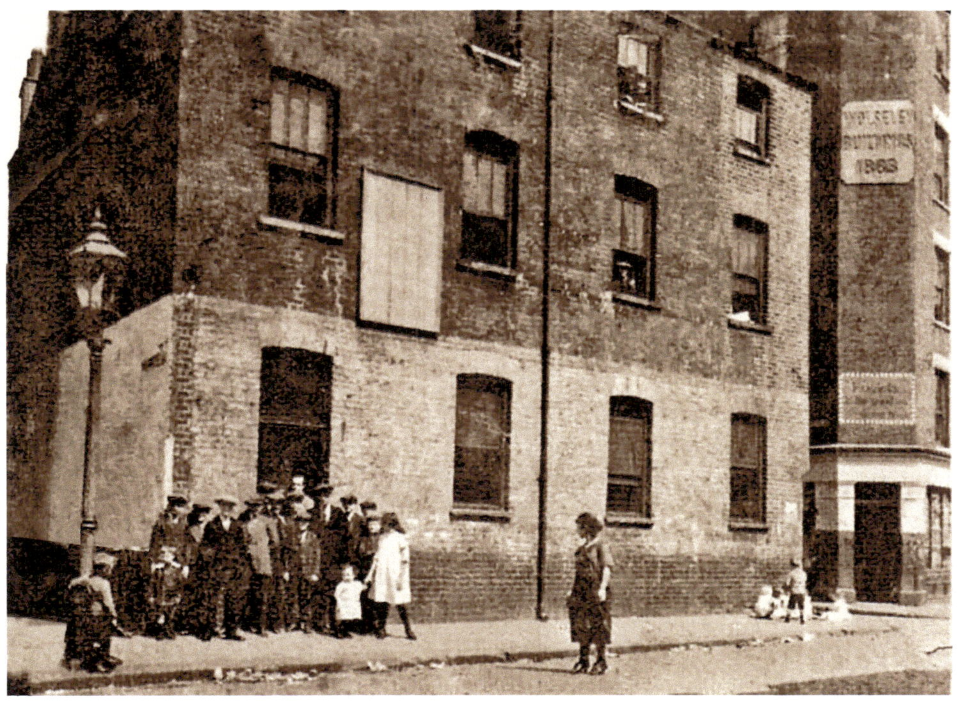



## Farthing Alley, Dockhead, 1910

Farthing Alley, parallel to Halfpenny Alley, describes perfectly this poverty-stricken area where overcrowding, disease and crime were once rife. By 1910 it was much improved, thanks in part to the Bermondsey Gospel Mission, which took over this building to educate, feed and give spiritual guidance to youngsters. Today, only Farthing Alley remains and in name only.

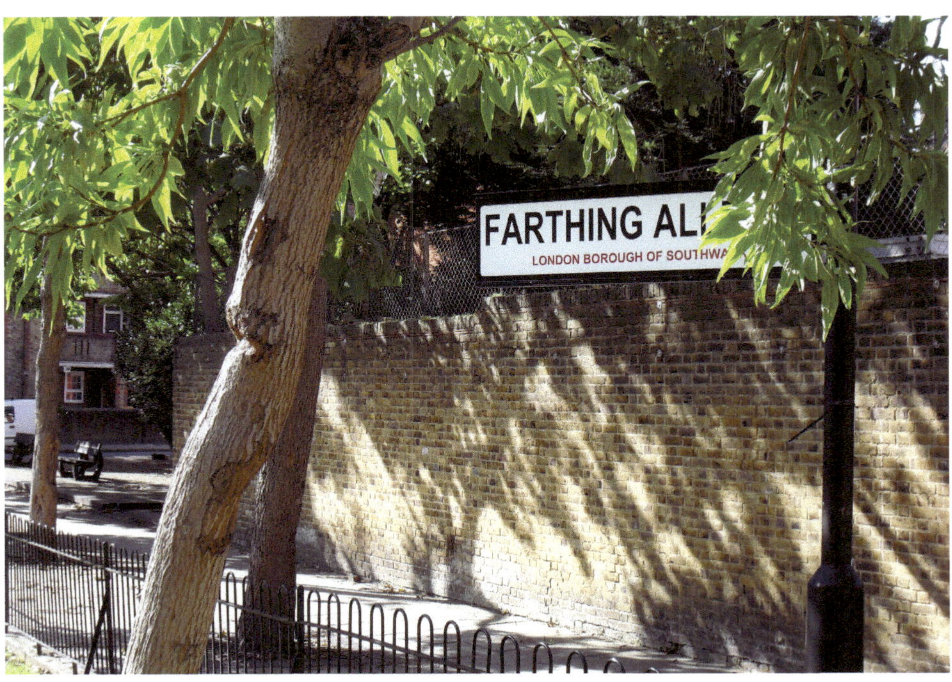

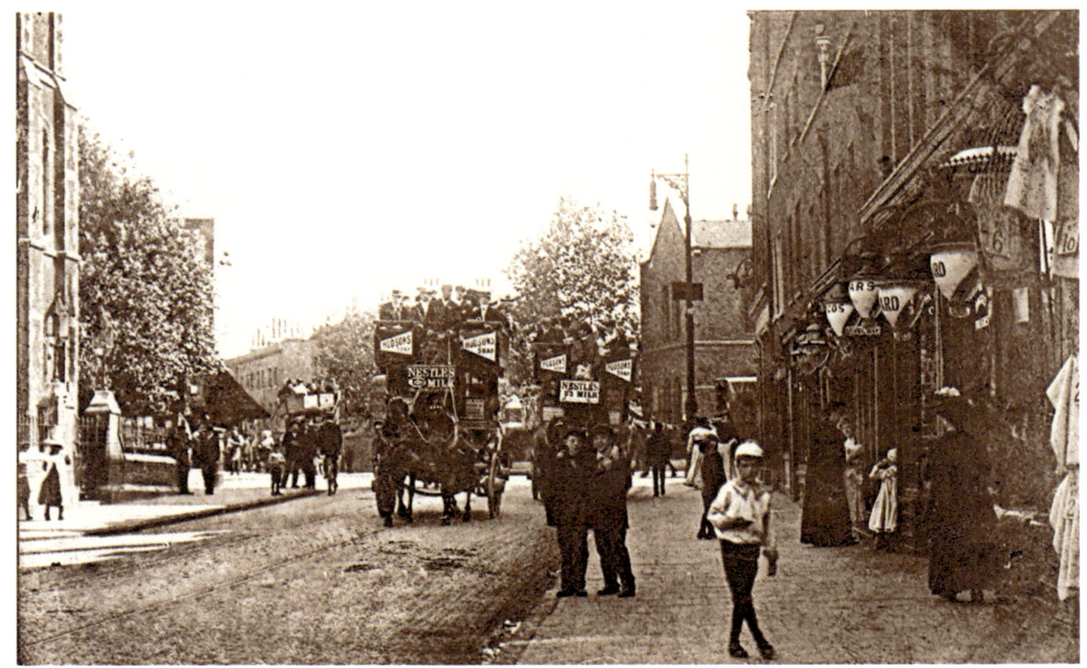

### Parkers Row, 1910

This street scene disappeared in the Jamaica Road redevelopment of the late 1960s. To the left is Christchurch and on the right is Marriott the bootmaker with the large advertising lanterns outside. In the window a promotion for Nugget Boot Polish can just be seen. Beyond the shops runs Abbey Street with the old Drill Hall in the background. (1910 photograph © Debra Gosling)

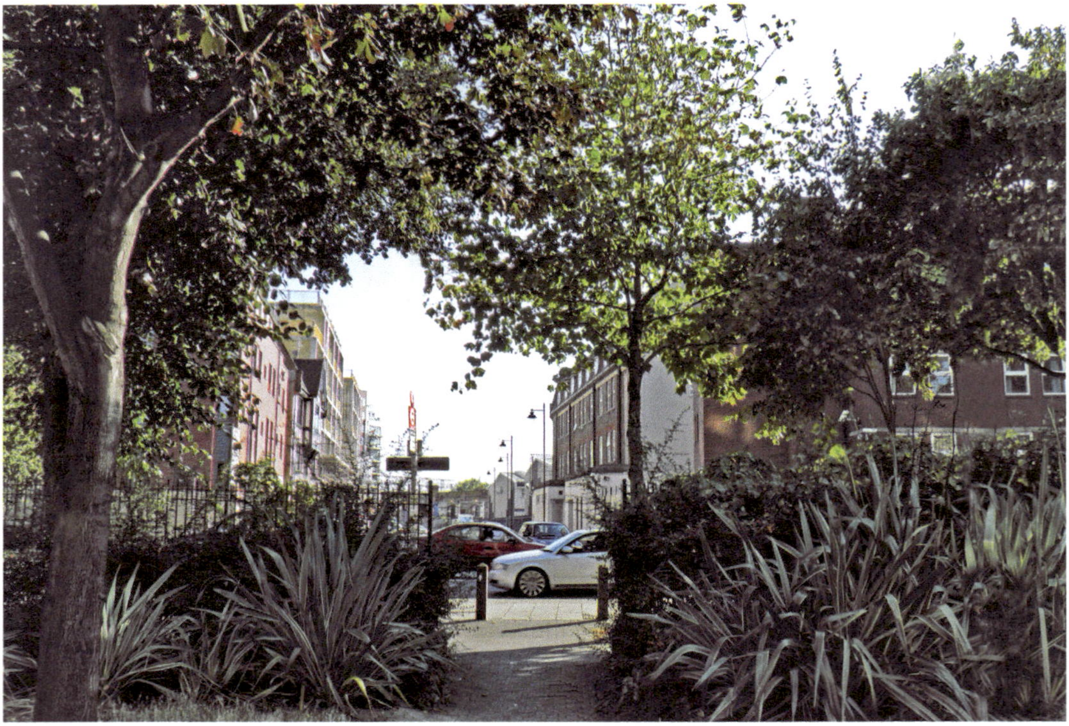

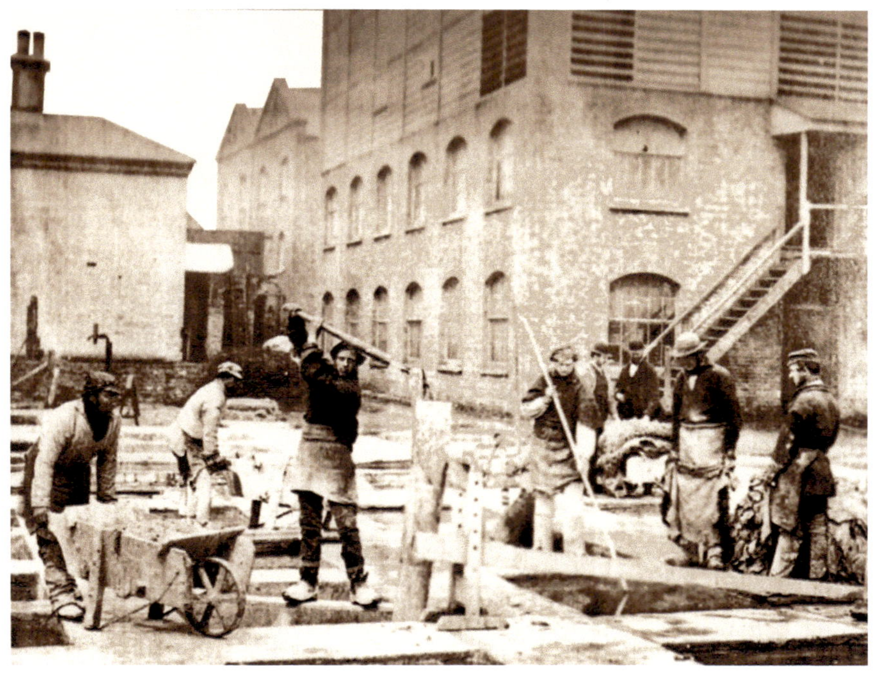

## Neckinger Mills, Abbey Street, 1880

Named after the local river, these mills were originally used to make paper before being converted to a tannery. Bevington's, one of the largest leather firms in Bermondsey, occupied them. The premises were extensive and hazardous places to be in. Here employees are working on the lime pits. Lime was used to de-hair carcasses ready for the tanning process. The work was smelly, dirty and, should someone slip, potentially fatal. They are now live/work units. (1880 photograph ©
Bevingtons & Sons)

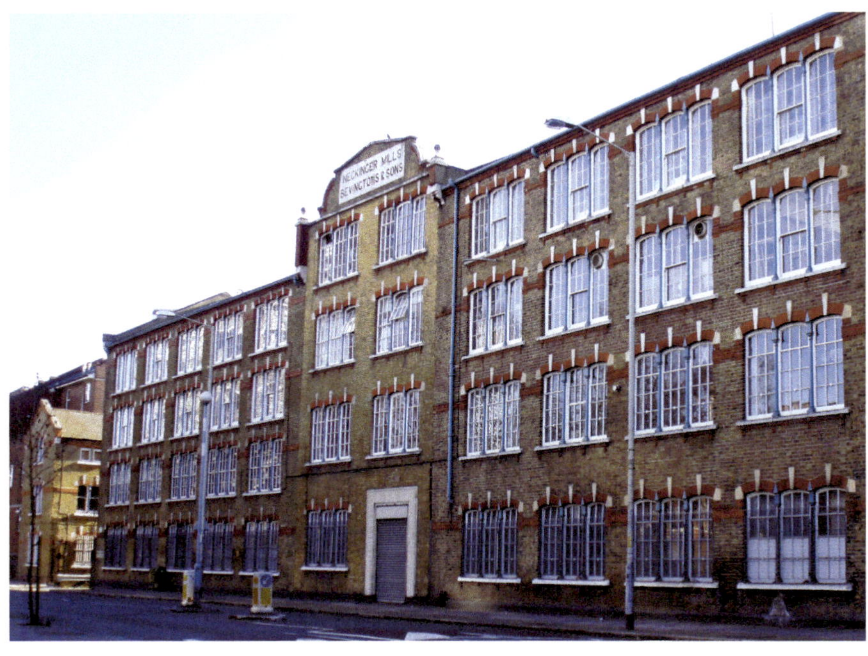

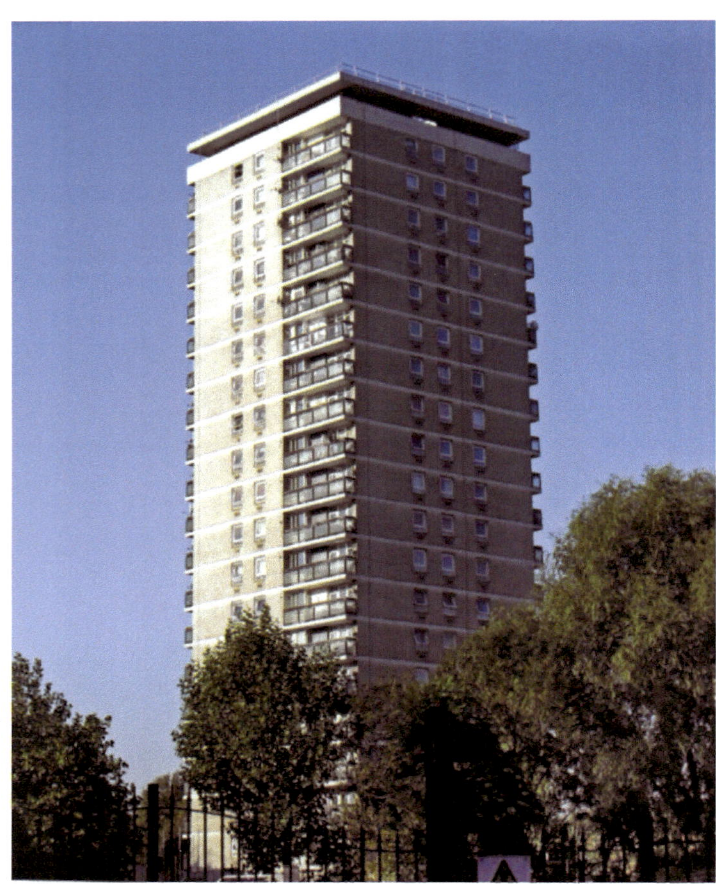

**Christchurch, Abbey Street, 1916**

The church was built in 1848 to cater for the growing community around Abbey Street, known as Bermondsey New Town. Enemy bombs rendered the foundations unstable and a great deal of the area was flattened. There was talk of raising funds to rebuild the church but the plans came to nothing and it was declared redundant in 1956. Ten years later it was demolished. Reaching up to the heavens itself, Lupin Point stands close to the site of the church.

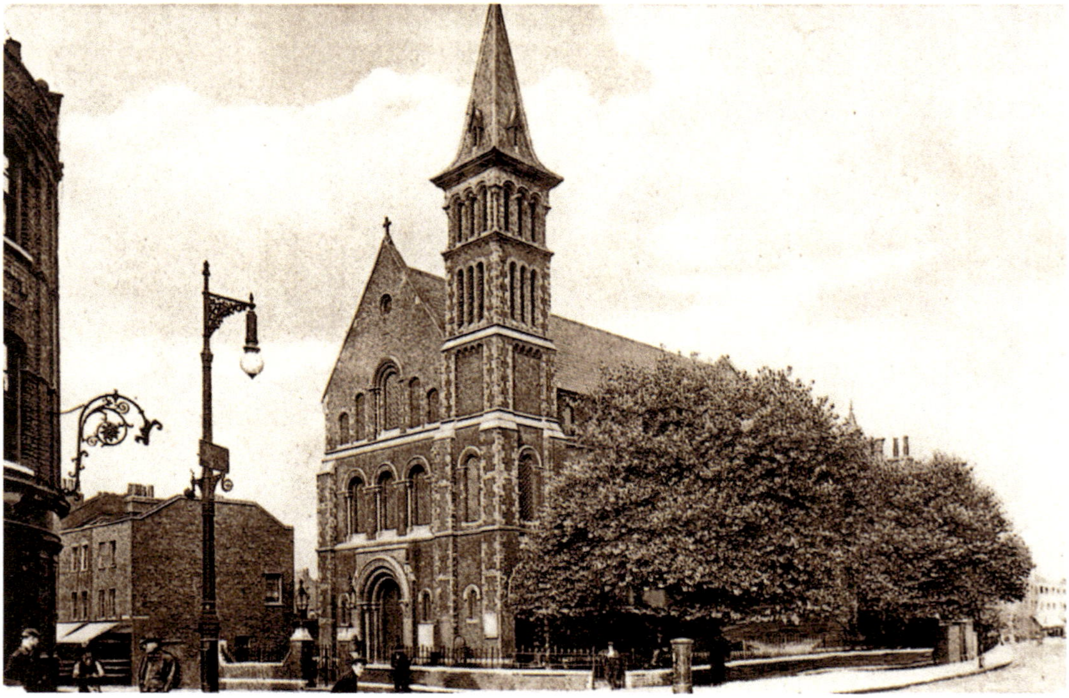

## Chambers Wharf, 1963

Before the cold stores were built, this piece of land leading down to the river was covered by mills and granaries, causing a high percentage of rodent occupation. The cold stores arrived and froze the little chaps out in the 1930s. During the Second World War, human residents sheltered in the basements and it was local legend that gold bullion was stored here. Now the cold stores are gone and redevelopment has been put on hold while a super-sewer is installed.

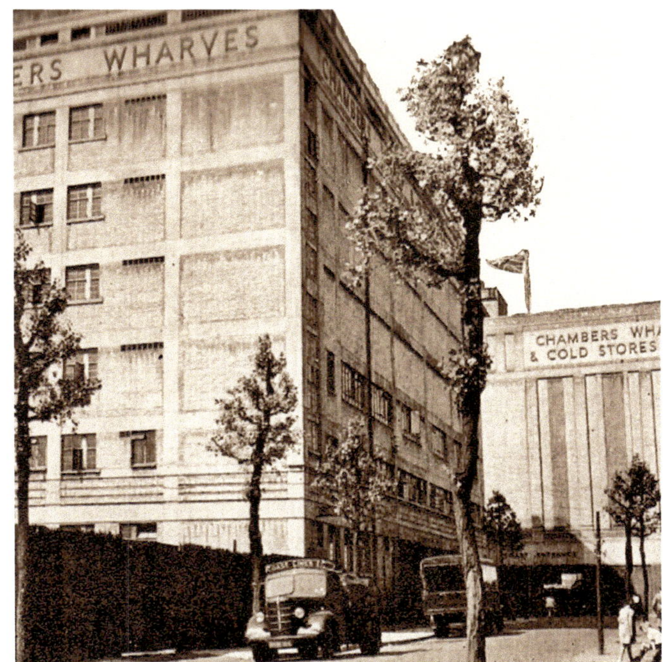

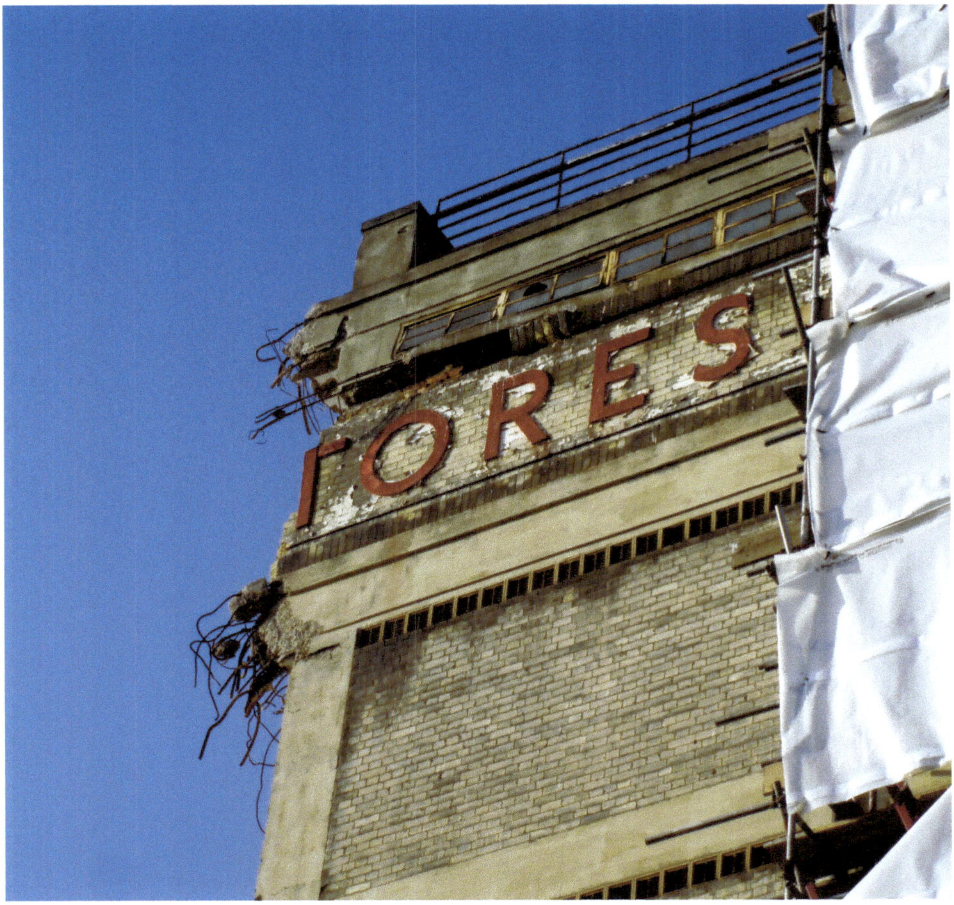

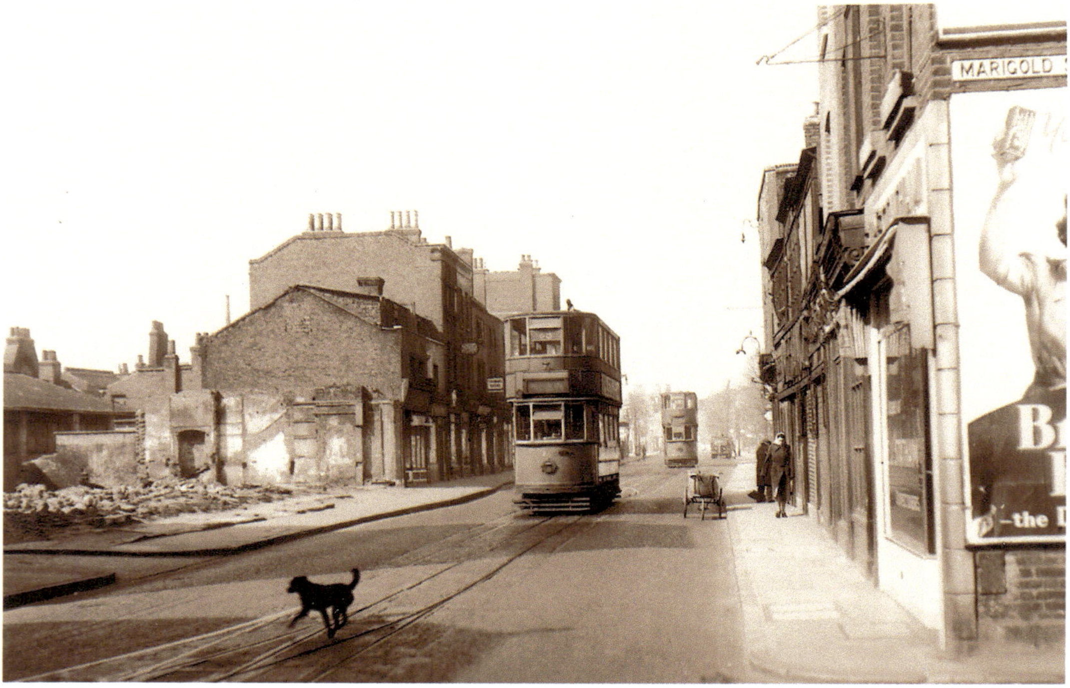

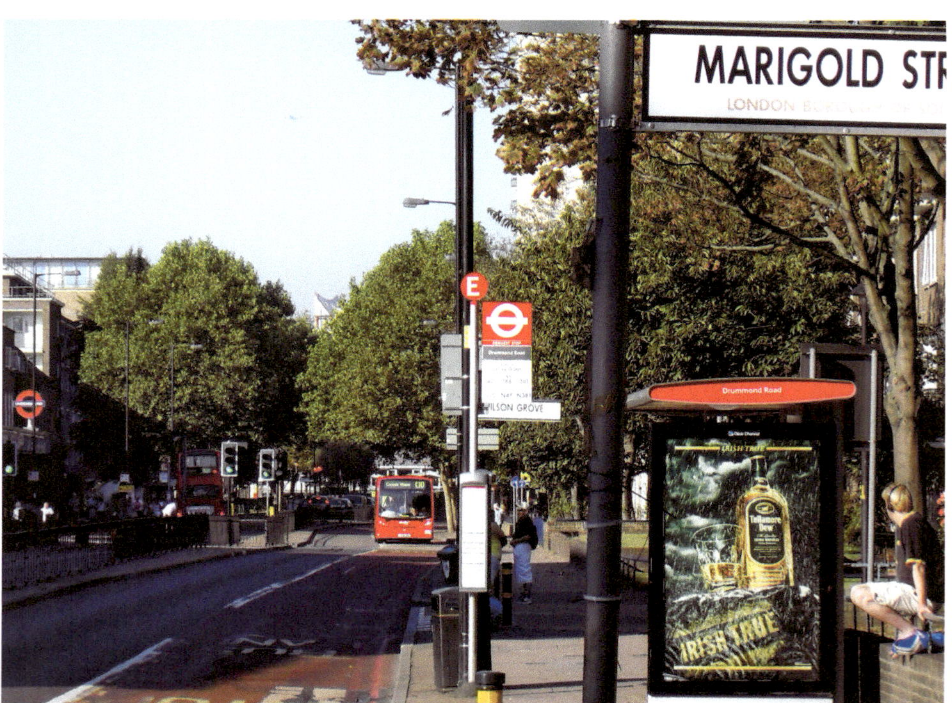

## Jamaica Road, 1950

How clear the roads were, with just a couple of trams and a council truck in the distance.
This is before the road was widened to resemble a motorway. Now this junction is a
changeover for travellers, with a choice of buses and trains. Bermondsey Tube Station
stands roughly where Boots the chemist stood.

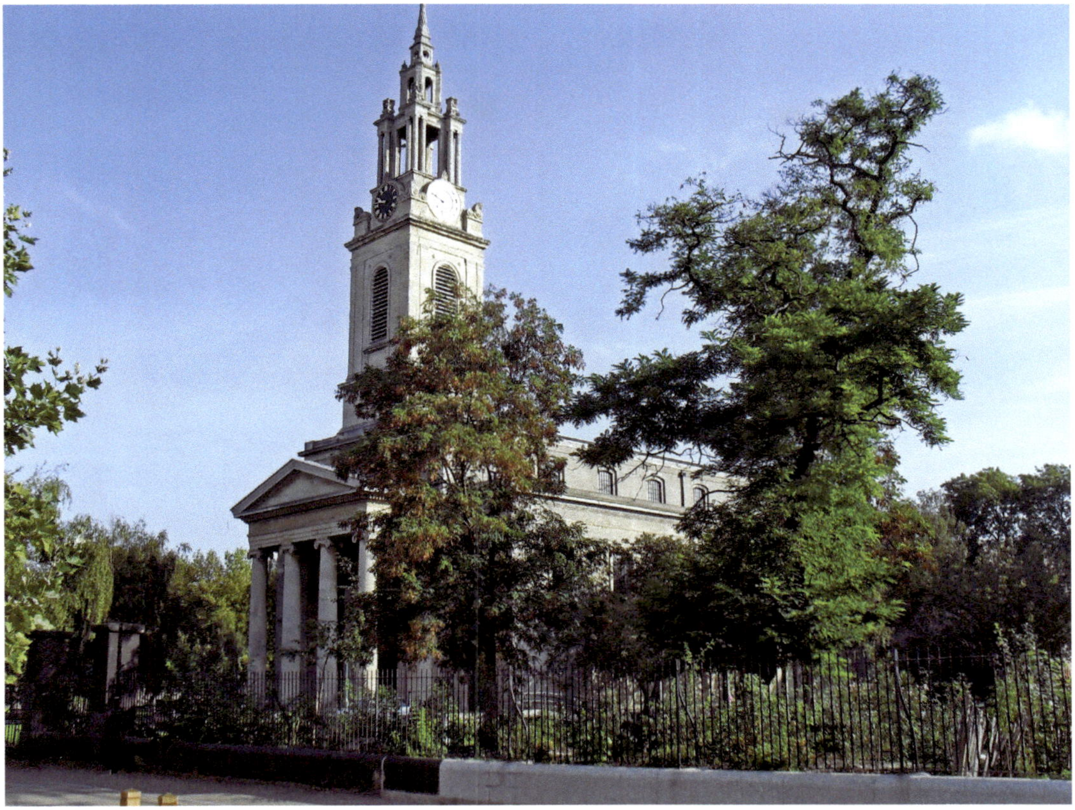

### St James' Church, Thurland Road, 1920

St James' is a real gem, with its elegant stonework and graceful chiming clock. A Waterloo church of 1829, it houses bells made from captured cannon. Of particular note is its gold dragon weathervane, which can be seen clearly from any passing railway carriage. Being so close to the river, the churchyard holds some interesting tombstones informing us of mariners and ship disasters. The trees in the old picture are just saplings, but now they are mature and magnificent.

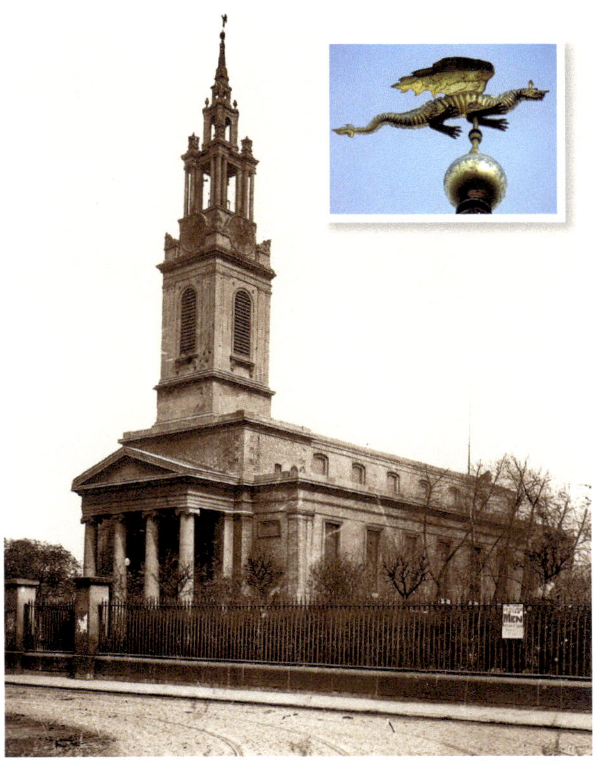

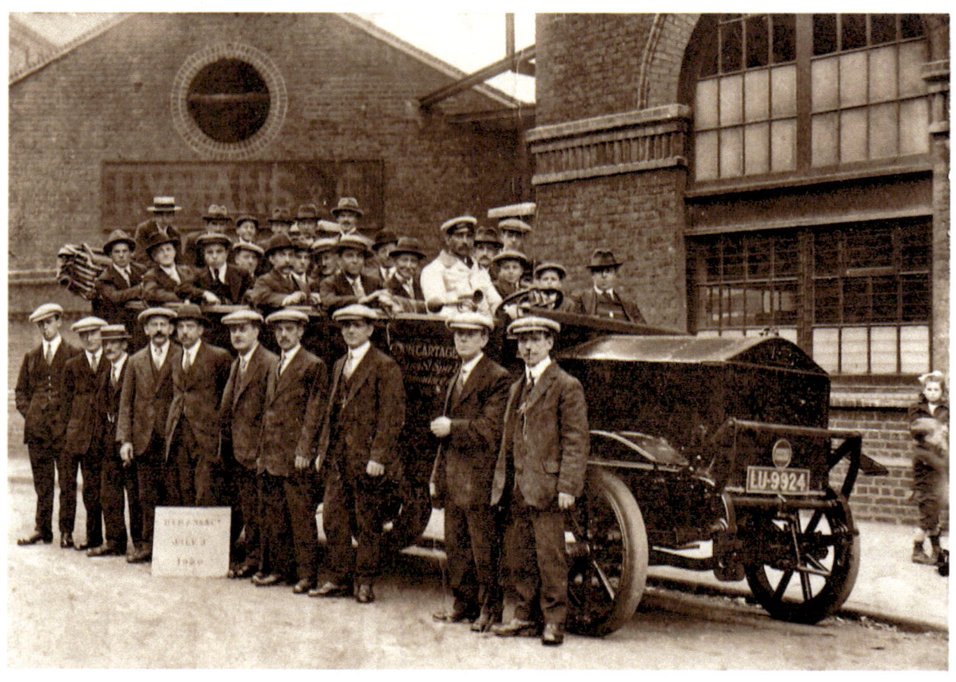

## Hyman's Leather Firm Beano, Dockley Road, 1920

The workers, kitted out in their best suits and cheesecutter caps, wait for the off. Second to the left in front, is Henry Roden, a leather finisher, who later worked for Bevington's after Hyman's was reduced to rubble in the Blitz. At the very top of the picture you catch a glimpse of the railway, which attracted so many attacks in the Second World War. New flats are now on the old site, but the gateposts are still to be seen. (1920 photograph © F. Low)

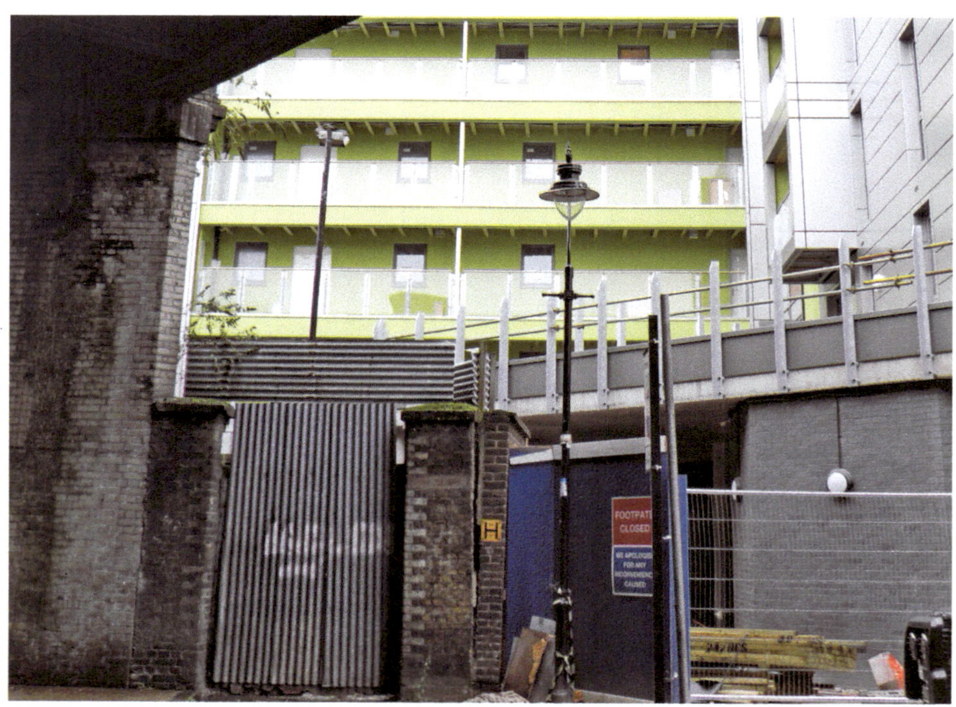

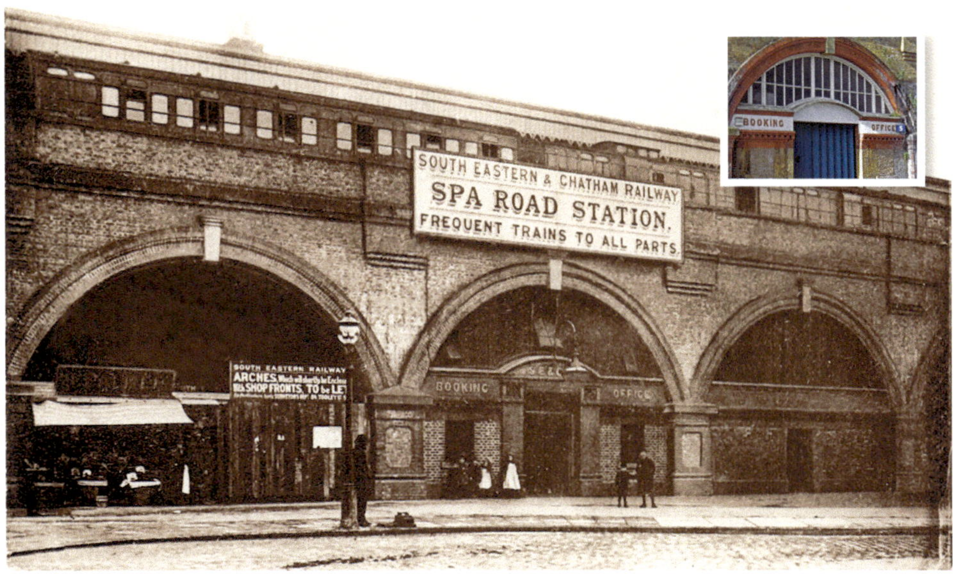

## Spa Road Booking Office, 1920

When the London & Greenwich railway opened in 1836, Spa Road Station was the first terminus. However, once the track was extended to London Bridge, it became obsolete. Today, railway passengers can glimpse the old platforms as the train whizzes past, along with a good view of St James' Church, the old Peek Frean's biscuit works and Tower Bridge. Were they still permitted to alight here they could also see this photographic reproduction set into the arch. History repeats itself!

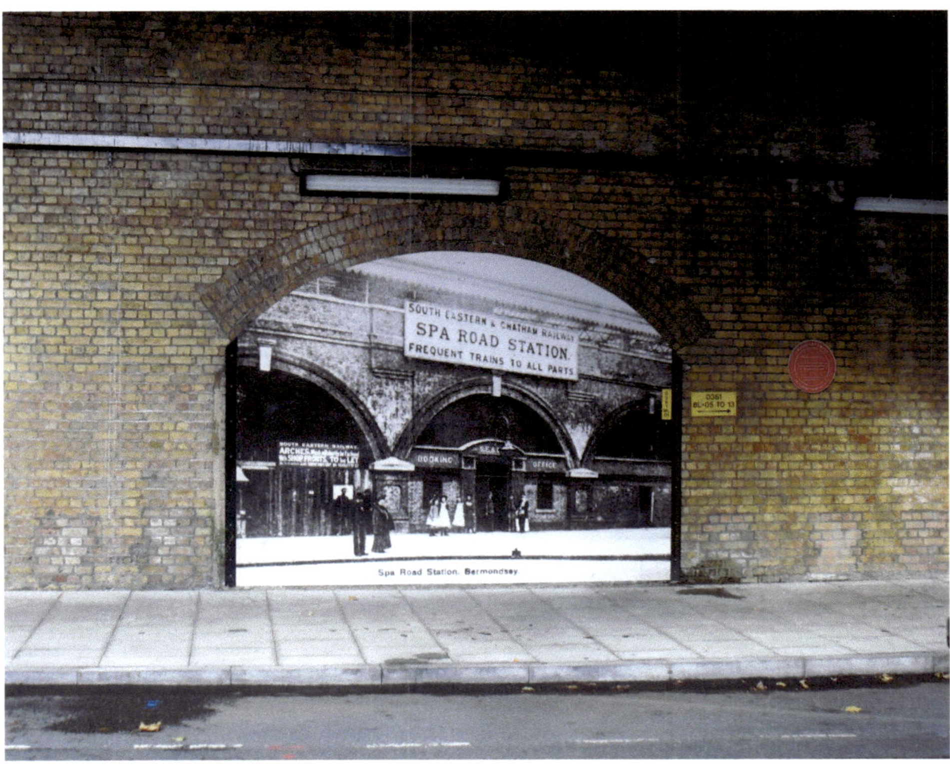

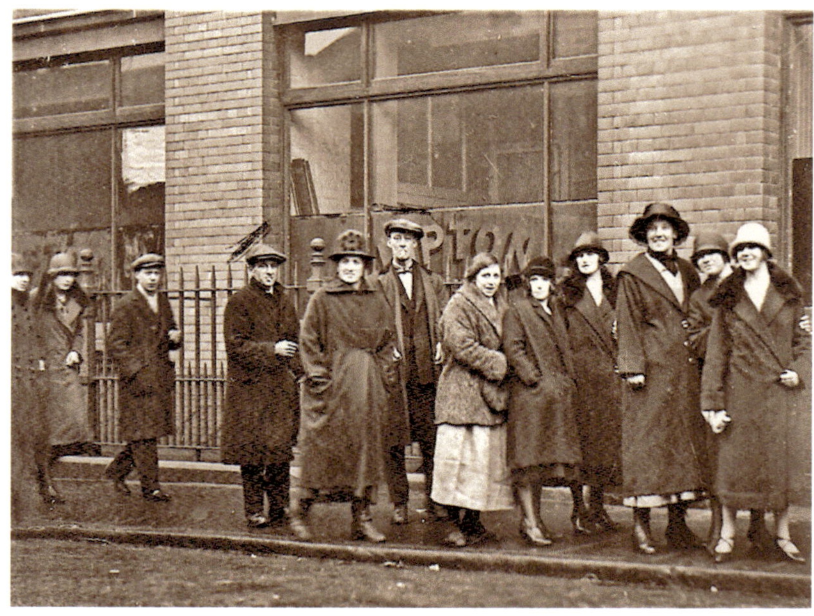

## Lipton's Factory, Rouel Road, 1928

Damaged but surviving the Blitz, Lipton's factory continued producing tea, jam, jellies and cooked meats until the late 1970s. Many Bermondsey people spent their whole careers working there and, as this picture demonstrates, a real sense of community prevailed. The Evelyn Lowe Estate was built over the Lipton's site, reducing the size of Rouel Road by half. (1928 photograph © M. Padbury)

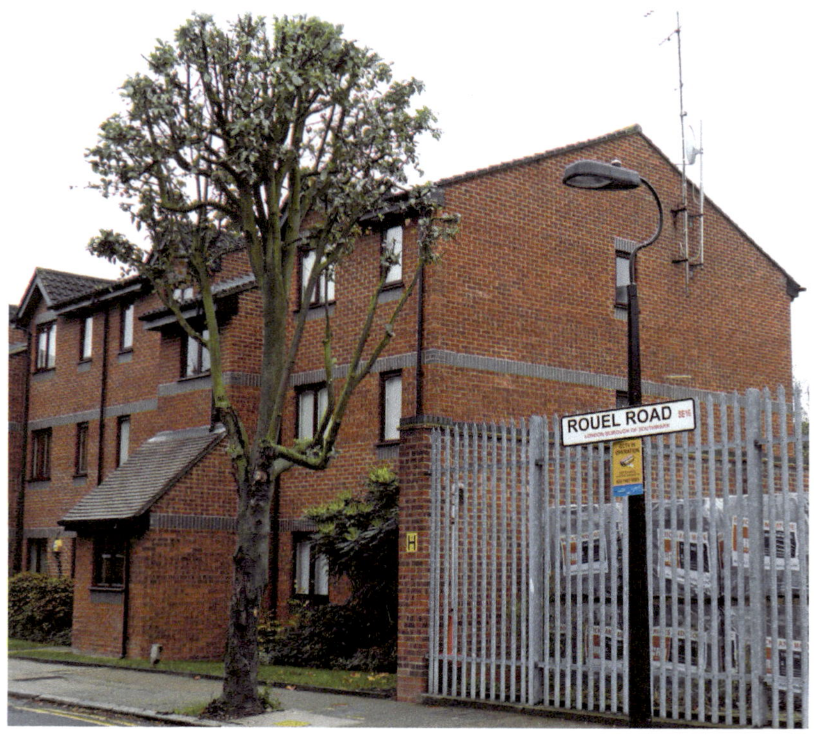

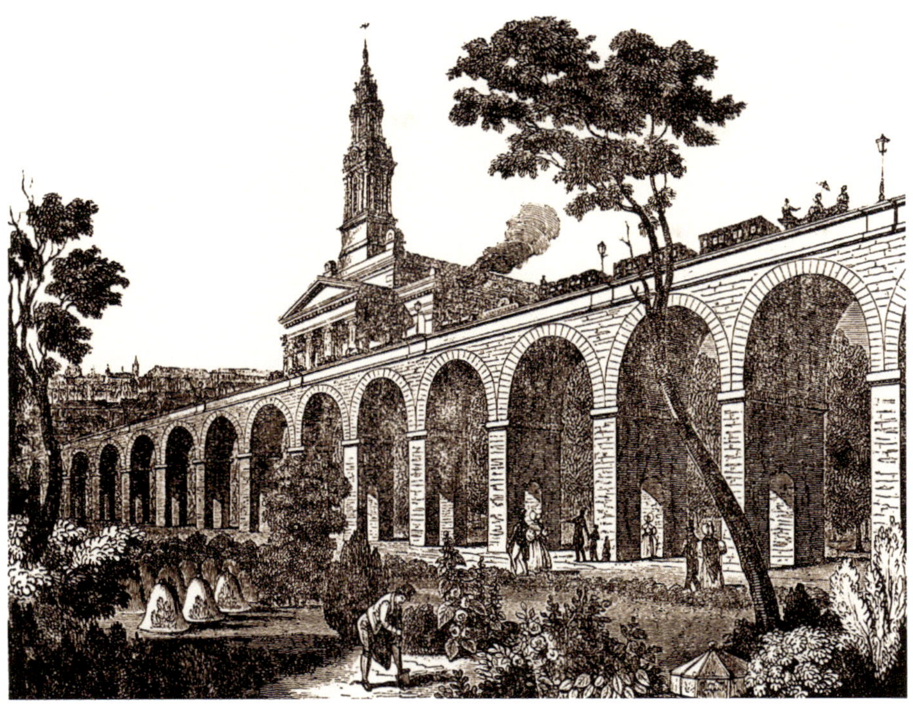

## London & Greenwich Railway, 1836

The railway's four-mile viaduct was built across many disgruntled residents' properties, rendering them homeless. The resulting rubble was sold to buy the bricks and cement required for the arches – all 878 of them! It is recorded that when the first stretch of track was opened, the bells of every parish along those arches rang out.

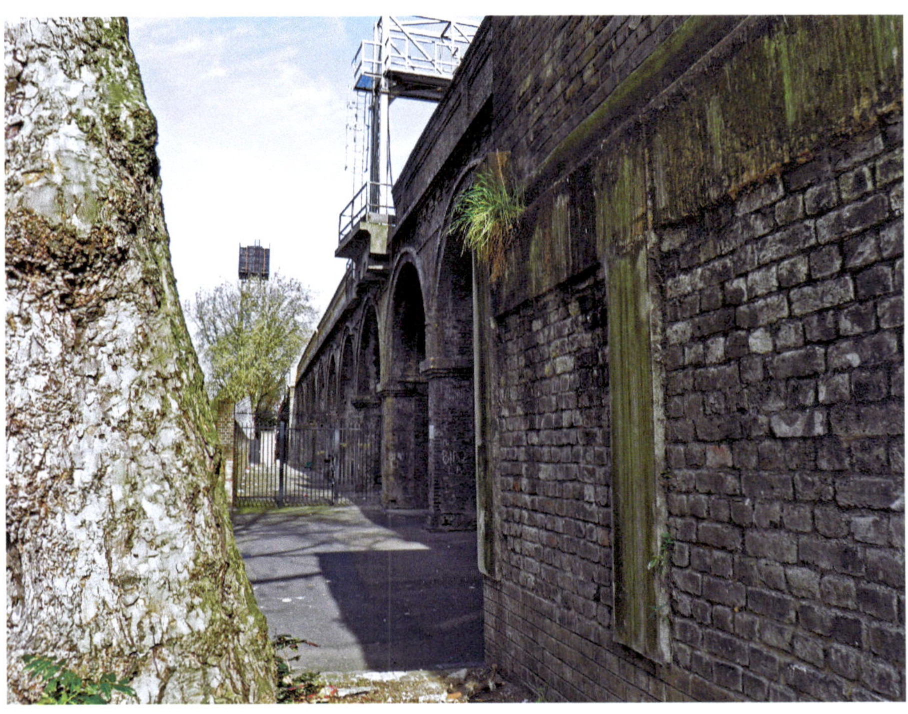

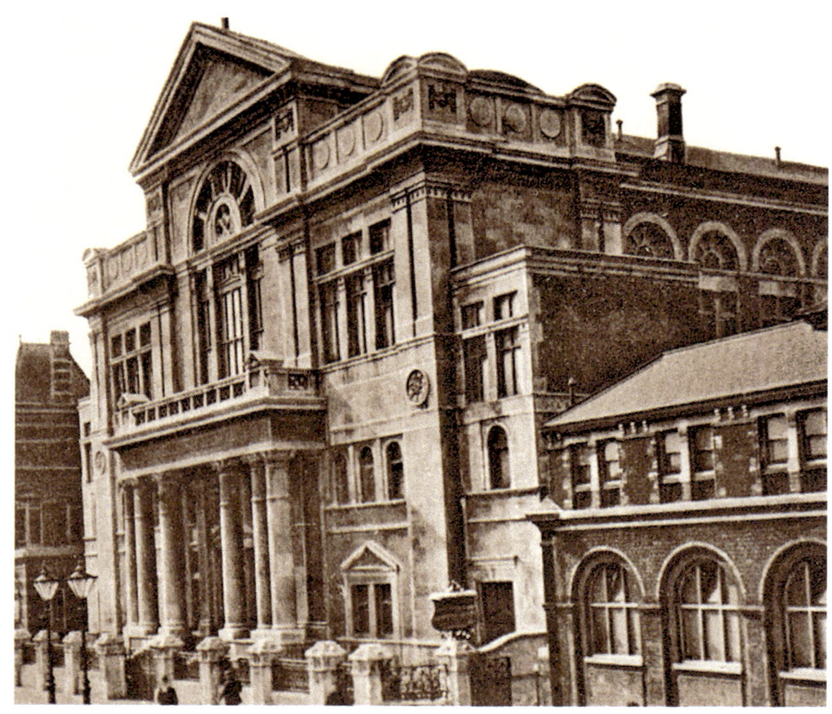



Built in 1880 on an old tan yard, the town hall held emotional memories for many people. Mayor Albert Henley was killed there in 1941 trying to extinguish fire bombs raining down upon the building. Later it was used as a builder's yard until finally, in 1982, it was fully demolished. The council's 'One Stop Shop' now occupies the site with the old gates remaining *in situ* as a poignant memorial.

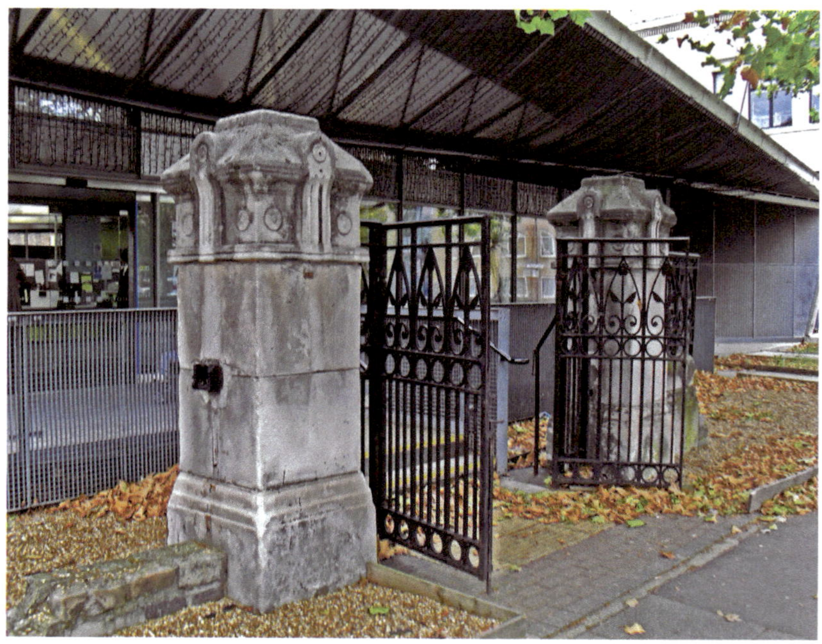

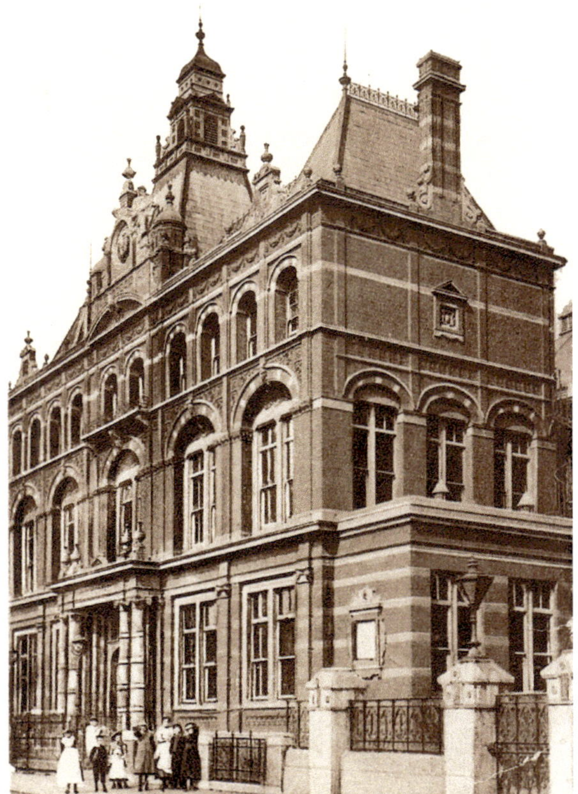

## Bermondsey Library, 1900

Now a Buddhist centre, this building opened in 1892 and boasted a lending library offering 100,000 books, with fifty newspaper stands holding eighty different news titles. The first floor had an extensive reference library while in the basement was a bookstore, coal cellar and a room for bookbinding. Today, libraries are noisy places with computers, coffee shops and televisions. Sometimes they even have books!

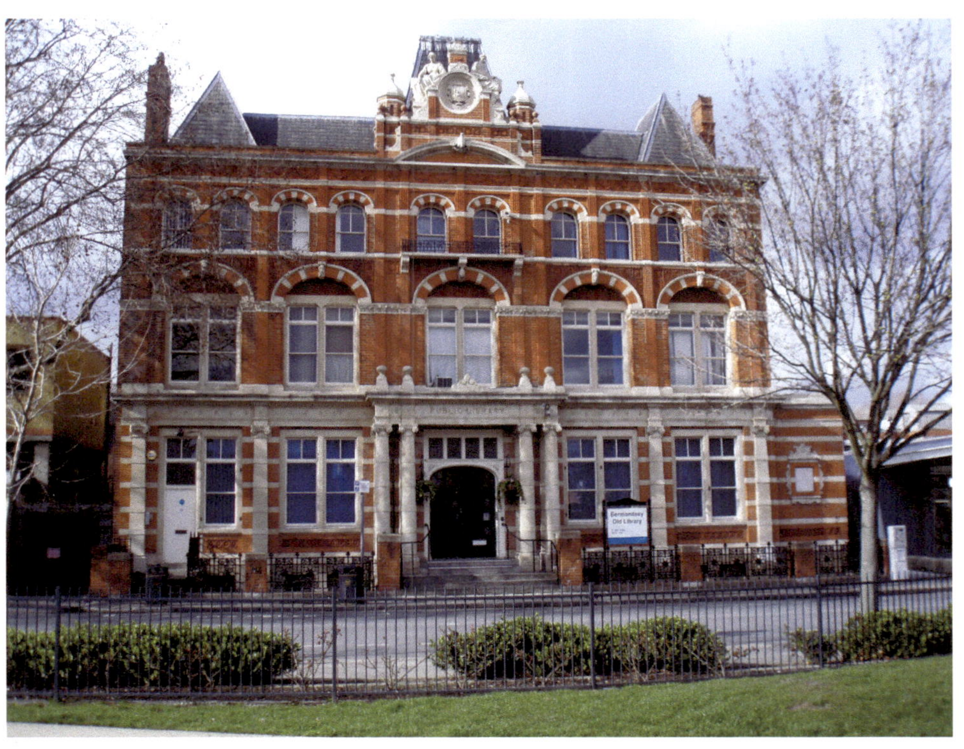

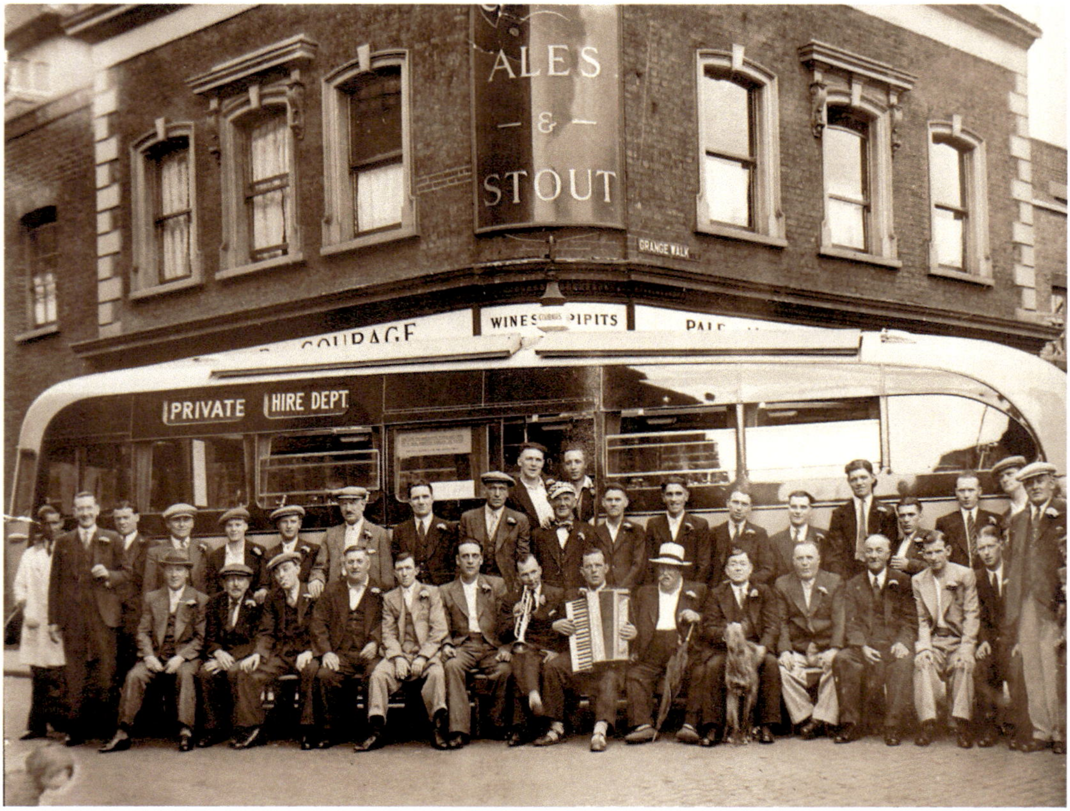

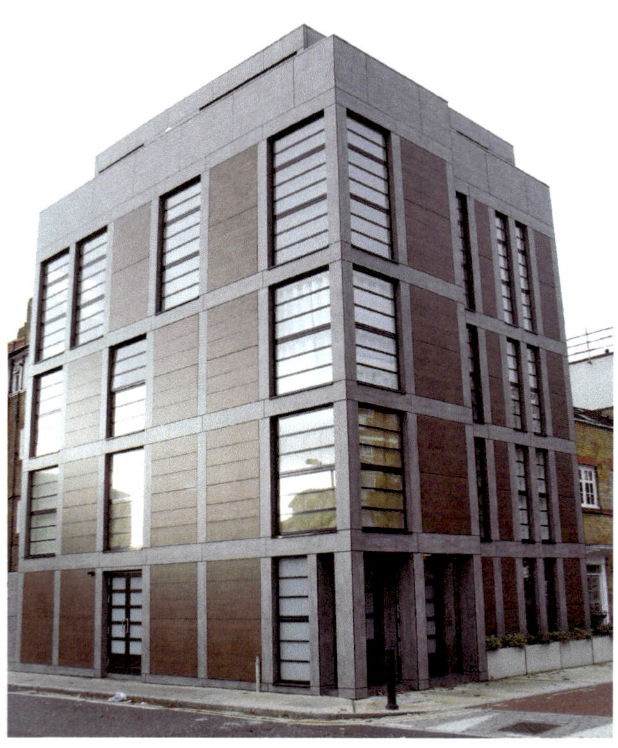



### The Red Cow Public House, The Grange, 1949

What a motley bunch setting out on a beano! One in a very loud hat, one with a trumpet, an accordionist bravely sporting socks and sandals and even one in slippers! He is taking no chances with the weather: Panama hat AND a brolly. Very British! No doubt a good time was had by all – and unlike today, no fights, no drugs and no drinking and driving. These classy apartments have replaced the pub. (1949 photograph © Pat McKenna)

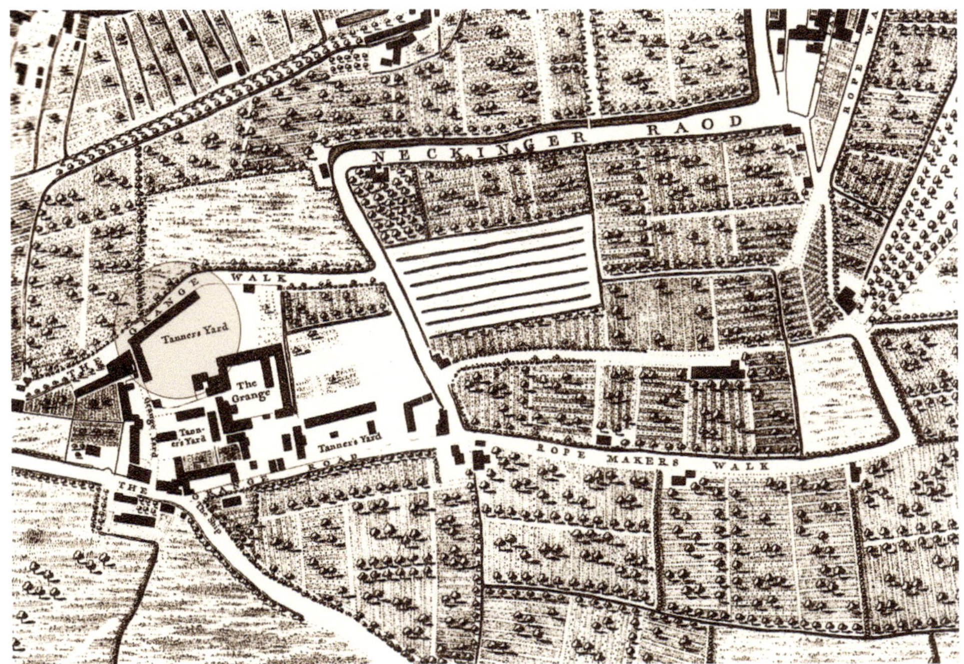


### Garnar's Leather Factory, The Grange, 1746

Roque's map shows that almost 300 years ago there was already a tannery on what became Garnar's leather factory. It specialised in chamois, supplying bookbinders, bootmakers and glovers, as well as Christy's hat factory, with this soft leather. One of the last to leave Bermondsey, Garnar's finally gave up in 1981 and the company was dissolved in 2007. The building, which took up a large part of the eastern end of Grange Walk, was demolished and now awaits redevelopment.

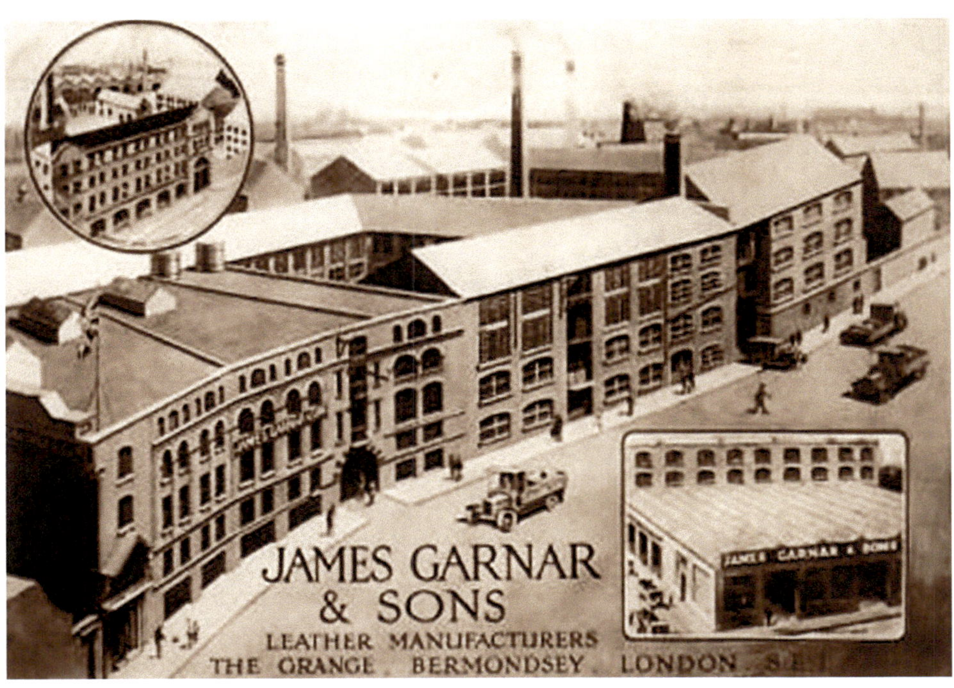

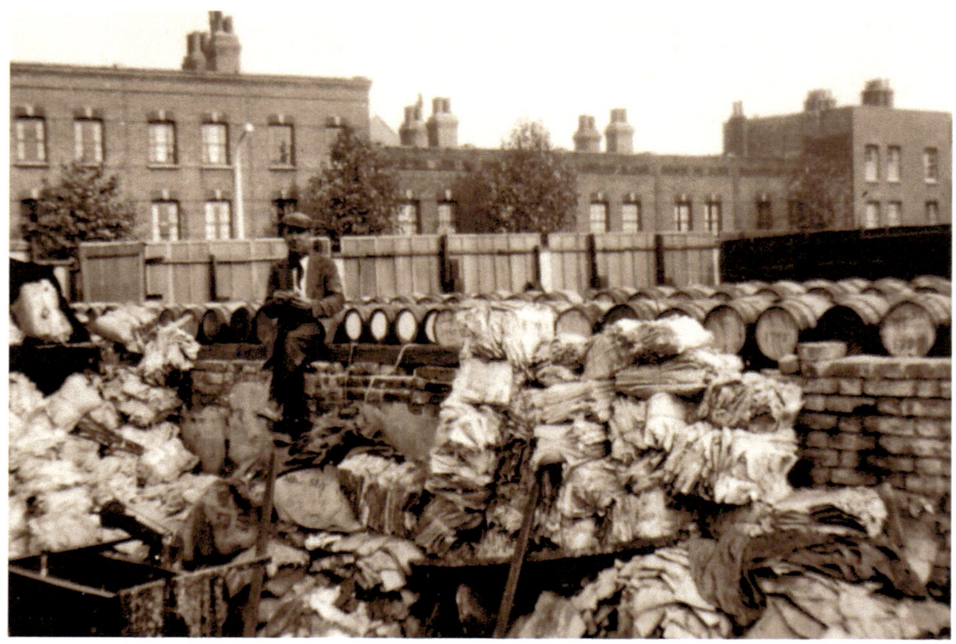

**Pages Walk, 1950**

This is Charlie Voss enjoying his lunch in his mate Cooksey's rag and bone yard. The site was used for storage after the houses that occupied it were bombed. Behind Charlie are stored Sarson's vinegar barrels, chosen for use in the pickled products of Messrs Crosse & Blackwell, who were based opposite the houses. The rag man has gone and now the site is fenced off, probably waiting for a few more luxury flats to be built! (1950 photograph © Peter Voss)

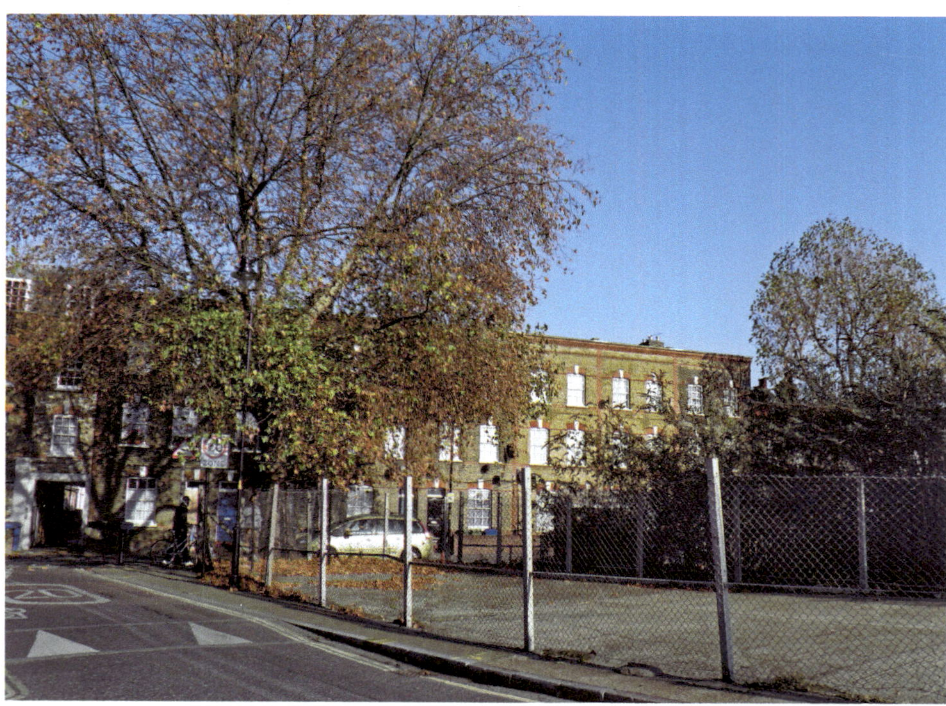

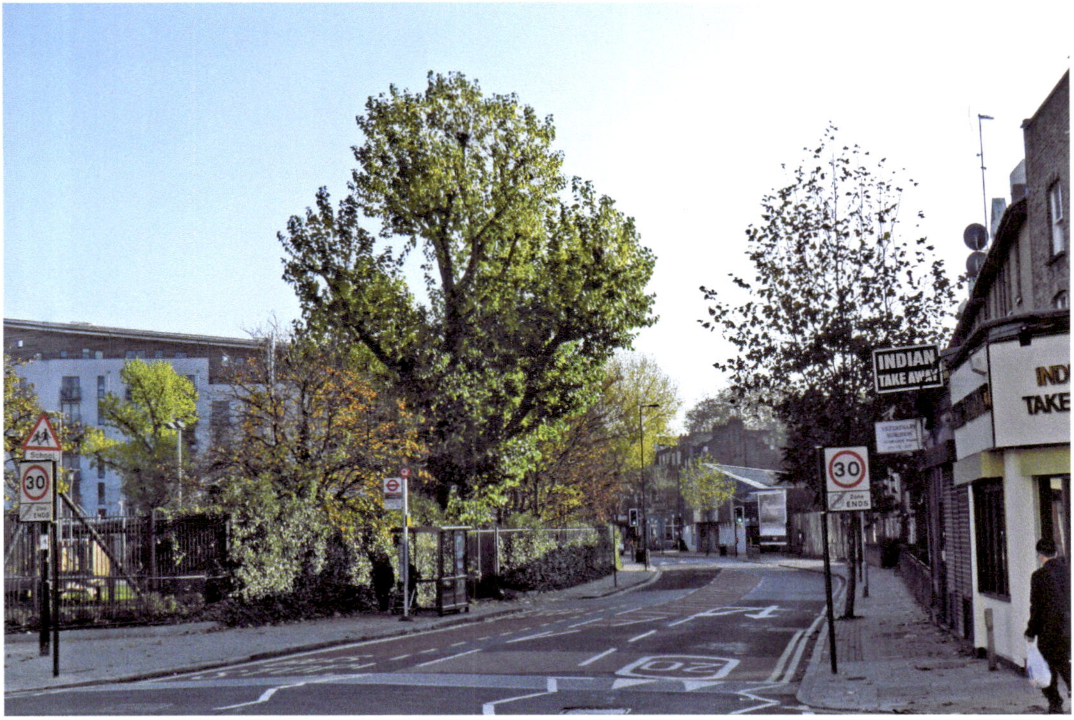

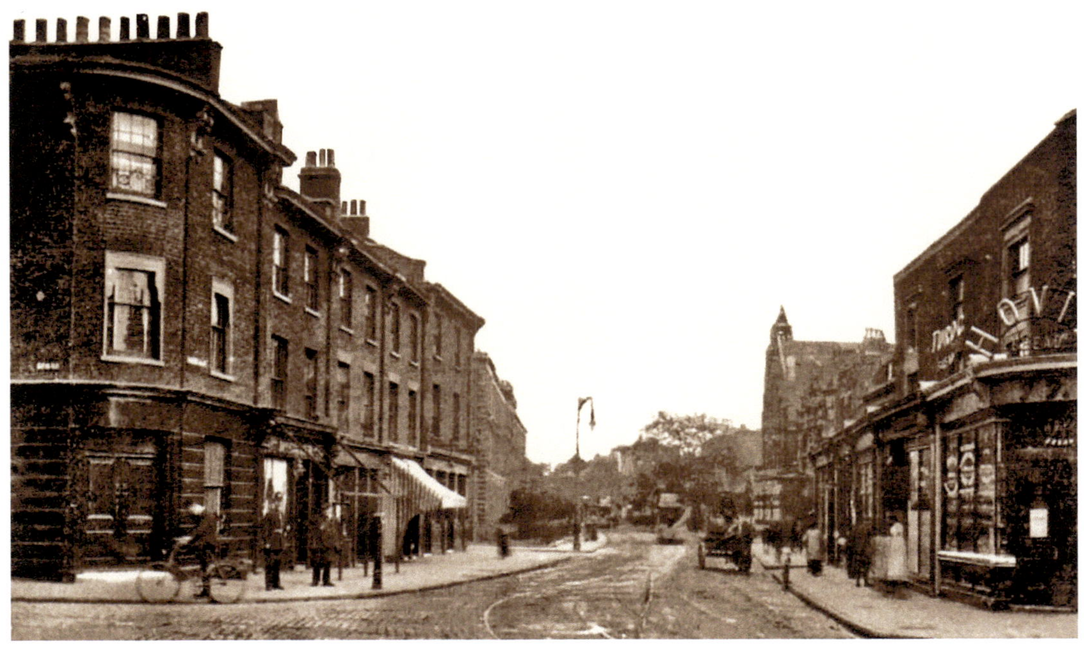

## Grange Road/Spa Road, 1915

The houses on the left were demolished in the 1960s. Spa Park behind them replaced more houses and is now re-landscaped. It was originally a pleasure garden with a natural spa, founded by artist Thomas Keyse in the eighteenth century. Aristocracy came from far and wide to take the waters and to watch the many firework displays, battle re-enactments and hot air balloon flights. Today, after dodging the constant traffic to access it, the park is a little green oasis.

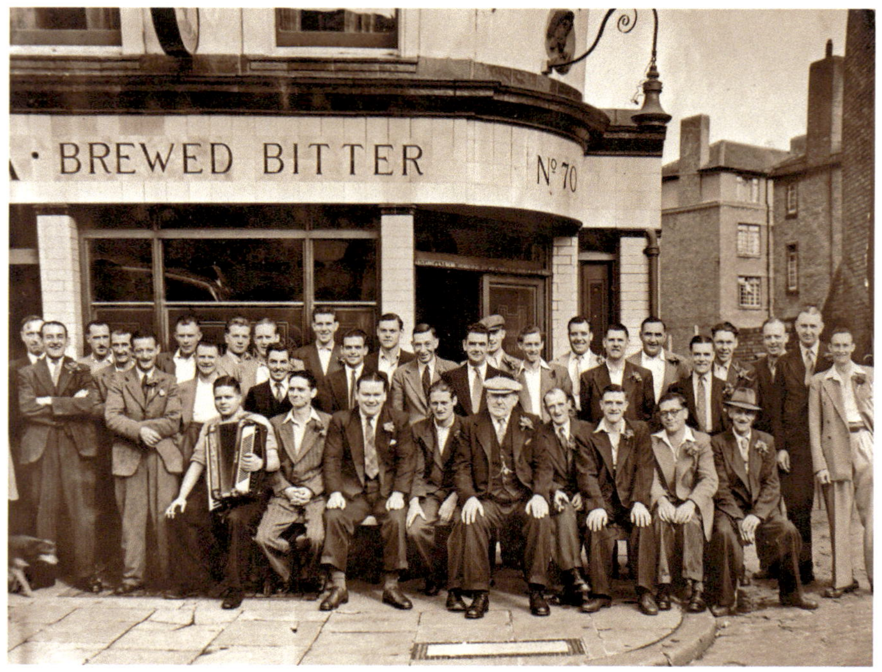

**The Victoria Public House, Pages Walk, 1950**

There used to be at least three pubs here in very close proximity but 'The Vic' is the only one still in business. It was built around 1880 for the railway workers on the nearby Bricklayers Arms Depot. Jim Gibbons, the licensee of the pub, sitting in the front row with the flat cap, was a formidable man, larger than life in both build and character, who took no nonsense from any loud, drunken punter! (1950 photograph © Pat McKenna)

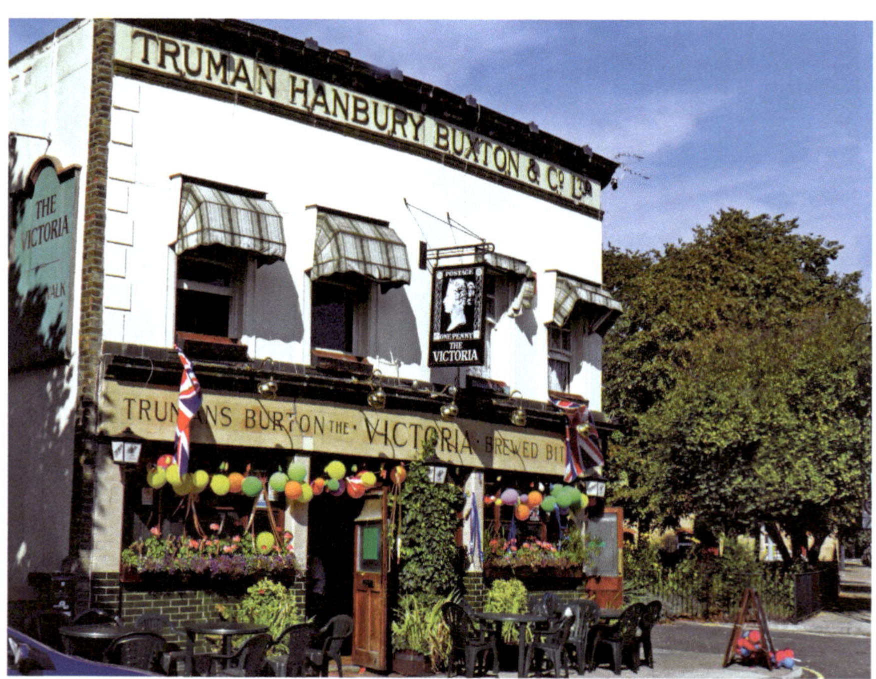

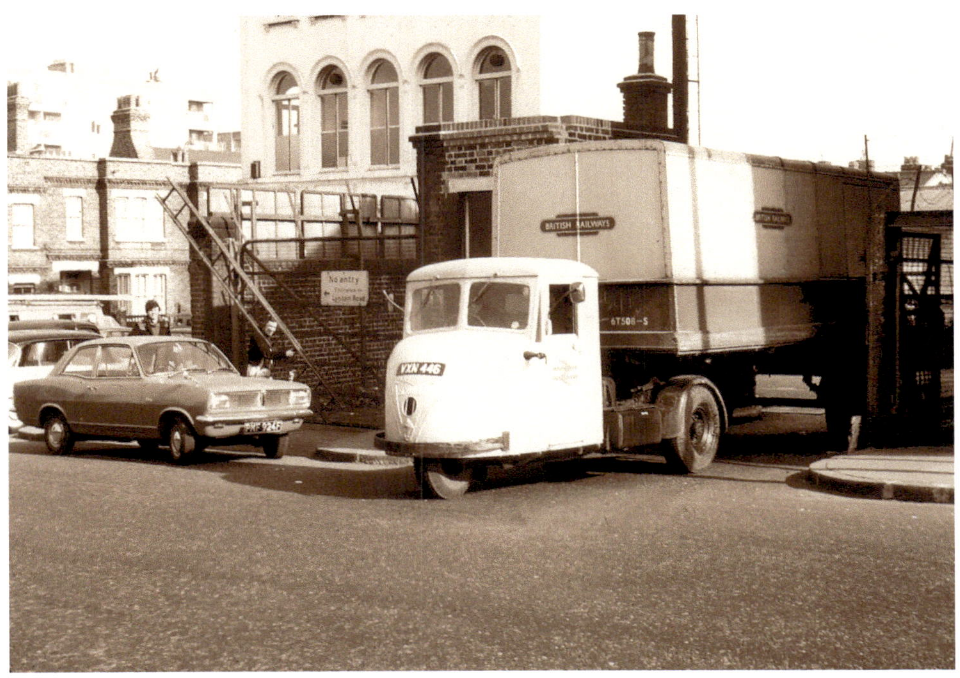

## Bricklayer's Arms Goods Yard, 1969

The railway depot occupied a sizeable chunk of Bermondsey until the 1980s. British Railways used these easily recognisable Scammell Scarab lorries to convey goods around. This one is just leaving the depot on the corner of Lynton Road. The white building to the left was the Anglo-Continental Container Services and before that was the Greyhound pub. (1969 photograph © Freddie Roll)

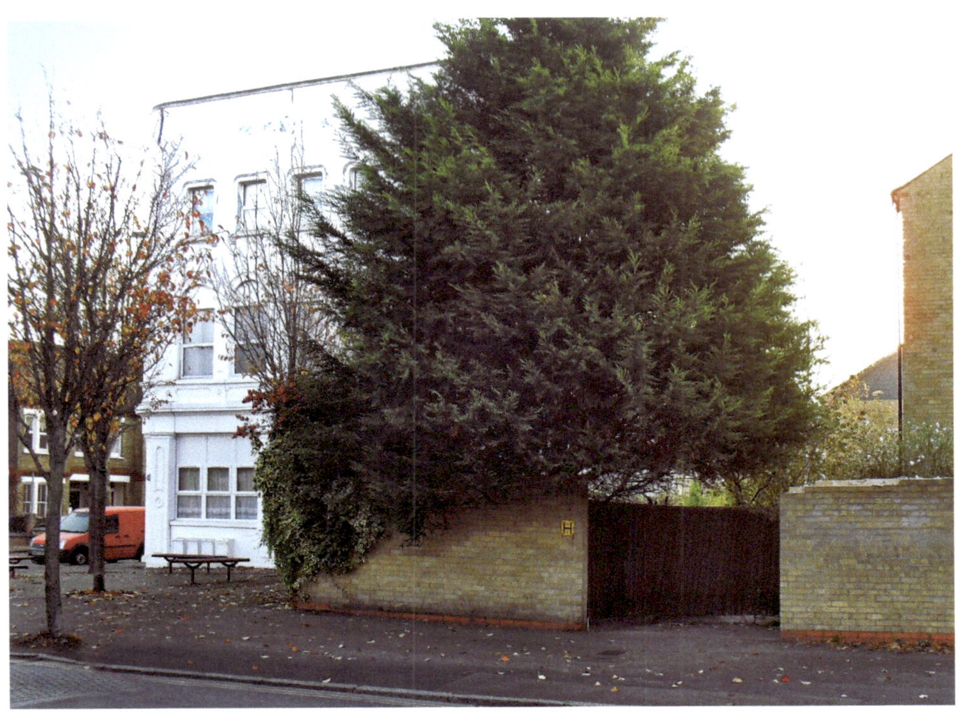

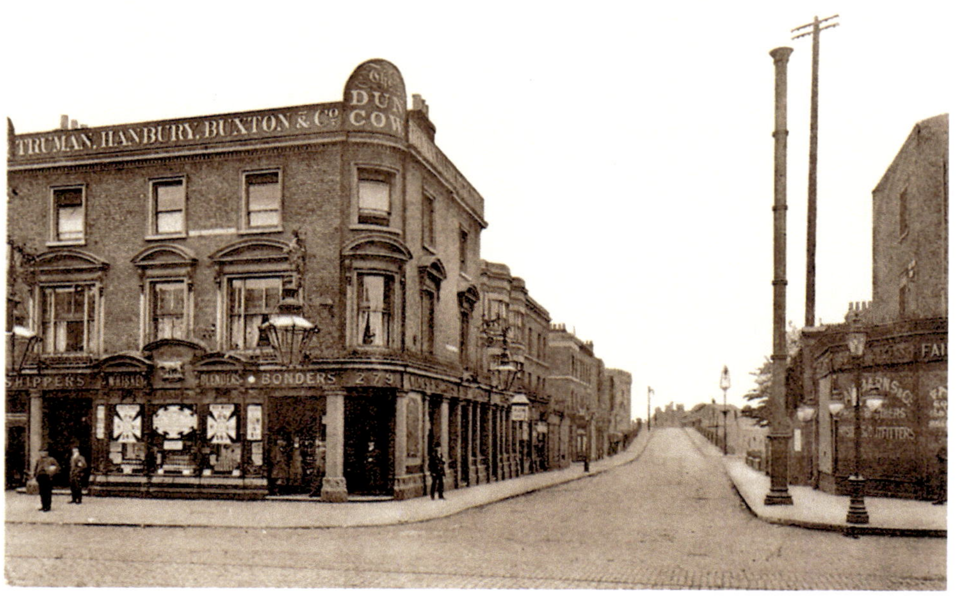


### The Dun Cow, Old Kent Road, 1918

The Dun Cow dates back to medieval times, but it has been repeatedly rebuilt. This scene depicts a picture of serenity, compared with the ominous place it is today. Until 1918 the land upon which the pub stood was owned by the Rolls family, of Rolls-Royce fame. In the old picture Dunton Bridge can be seen, which carried people across the Bricklayers Arms Goods Yard that lay below. The two houses around the corner from the pub remain today, although the pub is now a doctor's surgery.

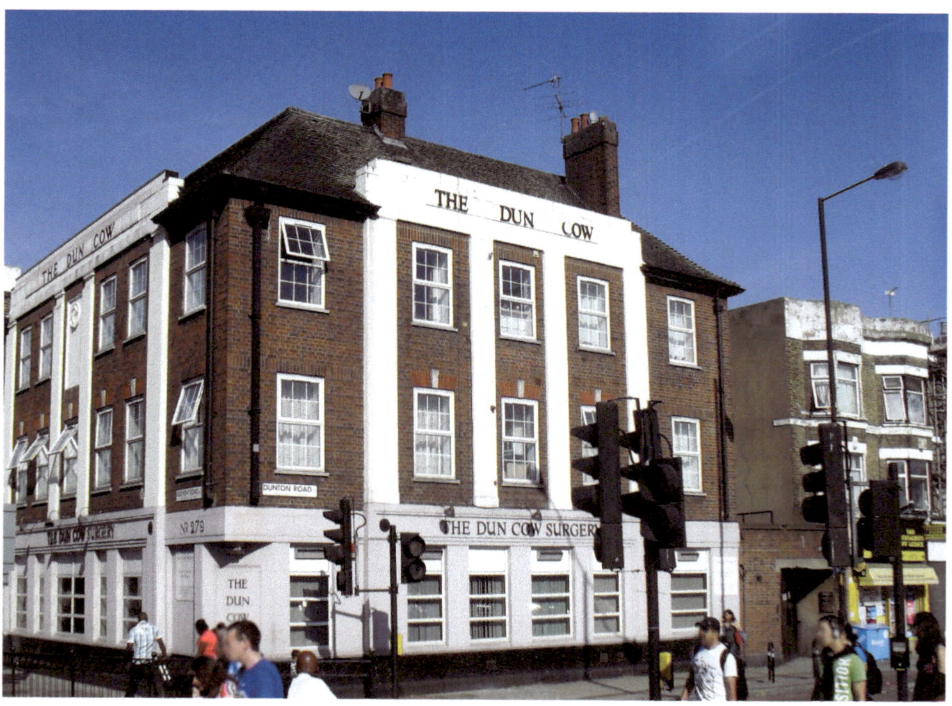

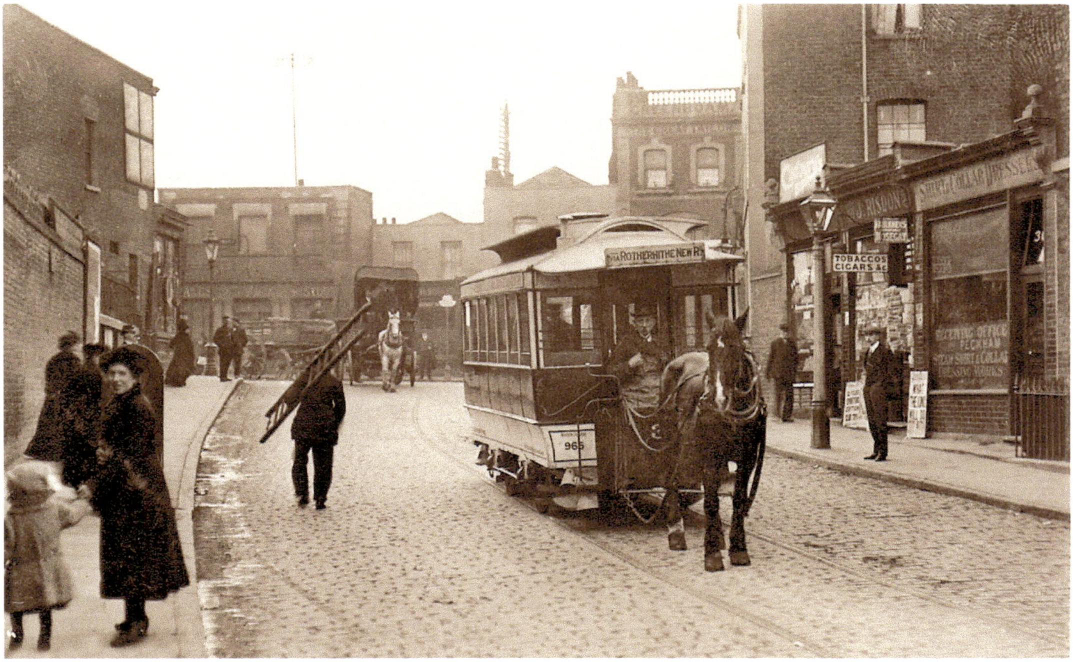

## Canal Bridge, St James' Road, 1910

The ha'penny bumper held twelve people and transported them around before buses and trams, but by 1913 it had ceased to be. The bridge ran over the Surrey Canal and is now a wide junction of frenetic traffic. However, there are still horses about. The 170-year-old Southern Railway stables are situated just around the corner from the old scene, presenting a little nostalgia and tranquillity (and free manure).

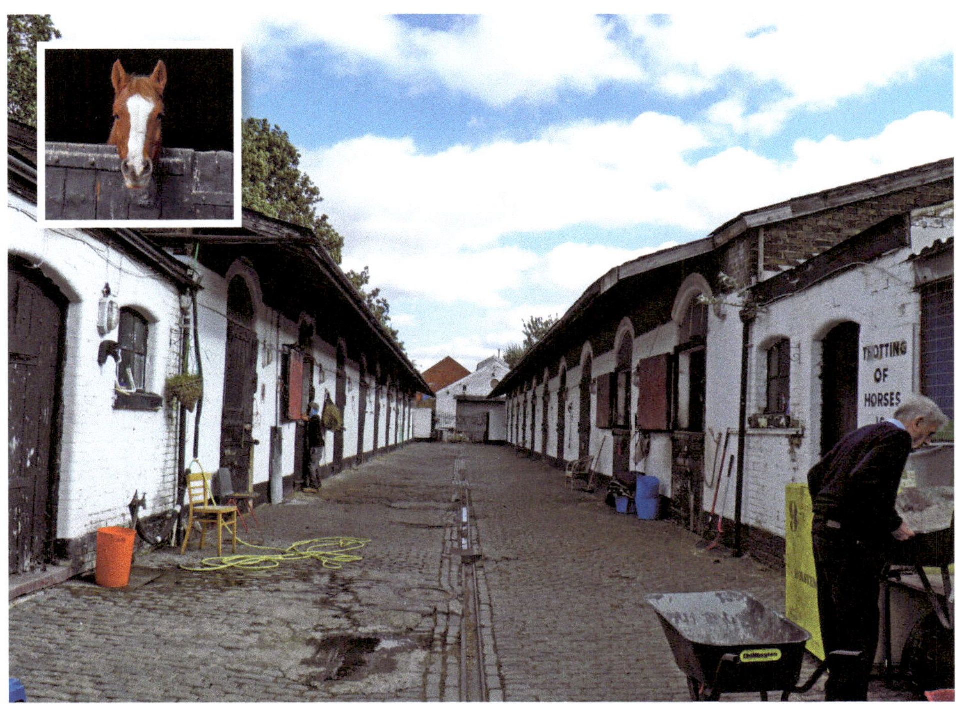

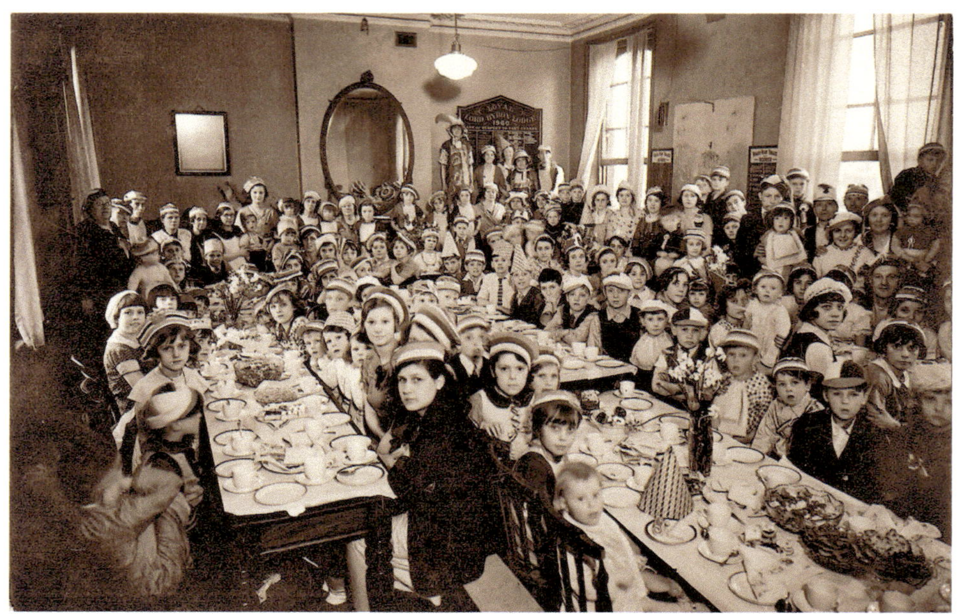

## The Sultan Public House, Lynton Road, 1935

This gathering appears to be the members of a mutual society, as the board on the wall reads Loyal Lord Byron Lodge. Unlike the freemasons, these kind of mutual societies collected 'dues' from their members, to be paid out in times of festivities or need. Members usually met in their local pub and here the number on the board is a lodge number, not the date. The Sultan was demolished a few years ago and these flats have replaced it. (1935 photograph © D. Toogood)

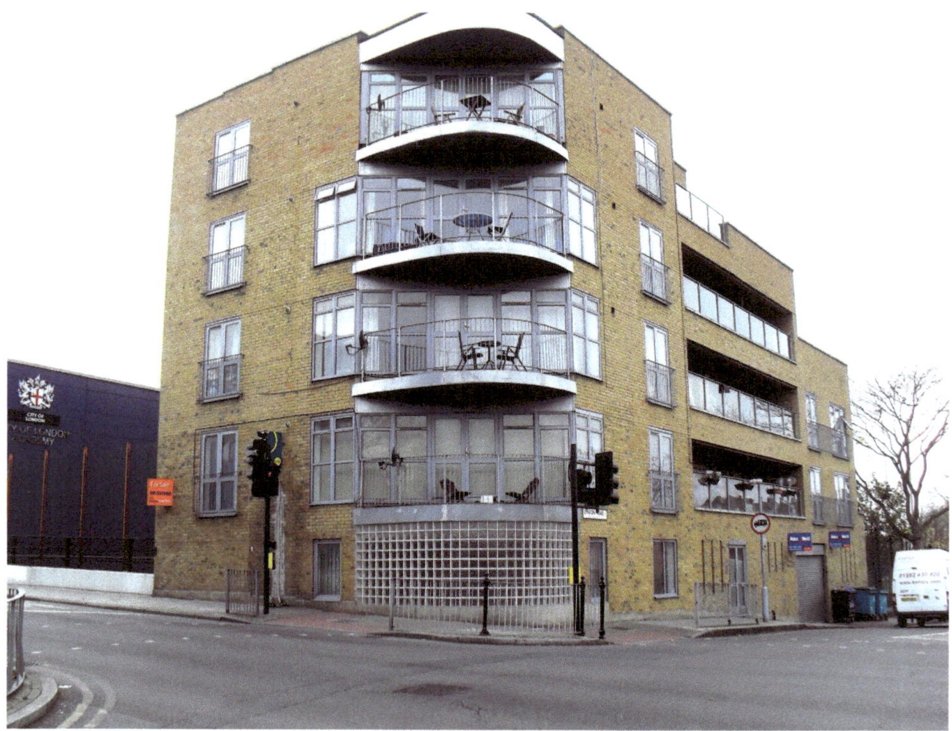

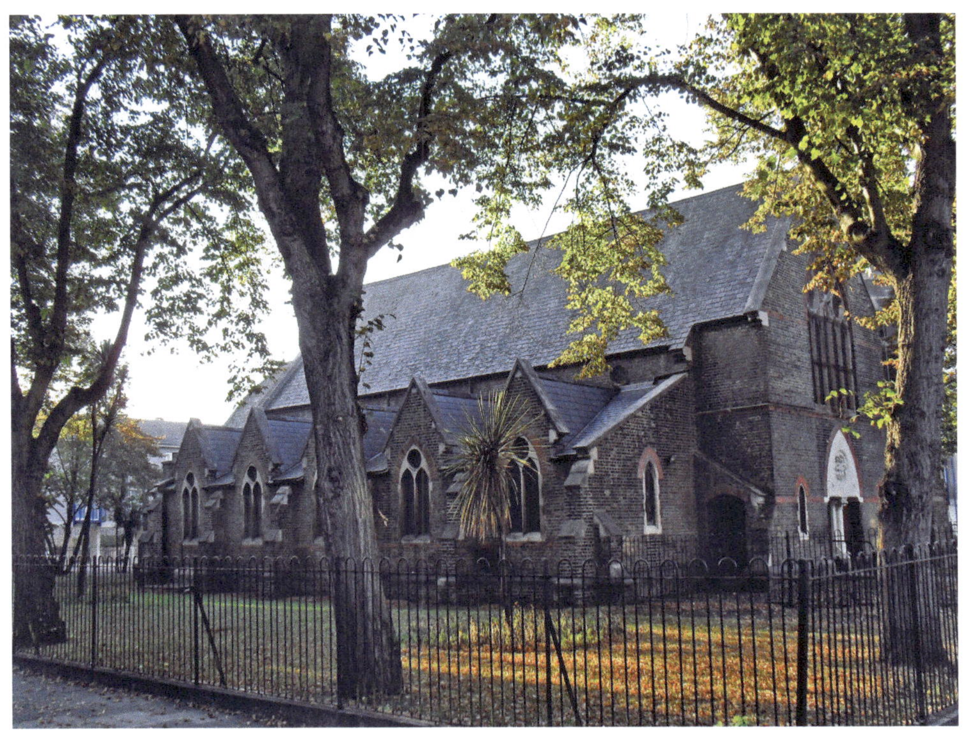

### St Anne's Church, Thorburn Square, 1925

Built in 1870, the church reflected the building of a new community. The streets surrounding the church were all built on the estate of the West family, wealthy landowners from Kent. In 1965 the houses in the square were demolished to make way for a new housing estate. Luckily the church survived this upheaval, looking as elegant and mature as the trees that surround it.

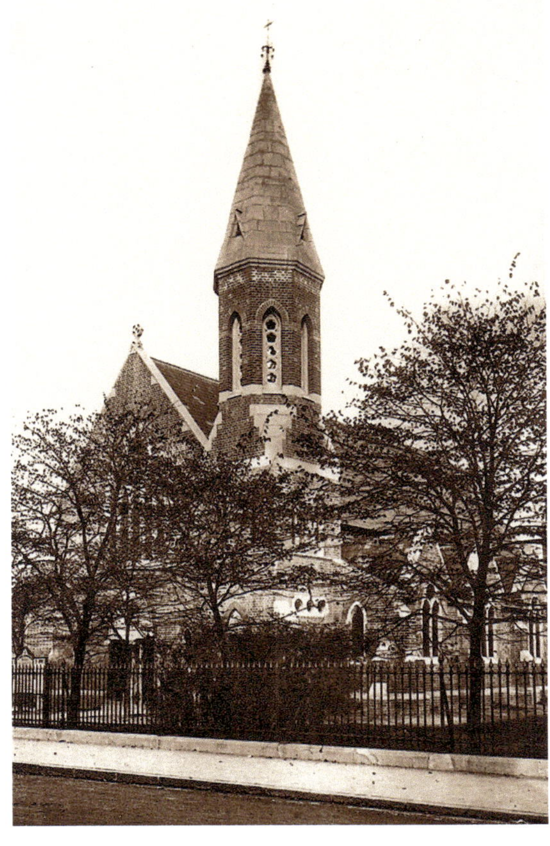

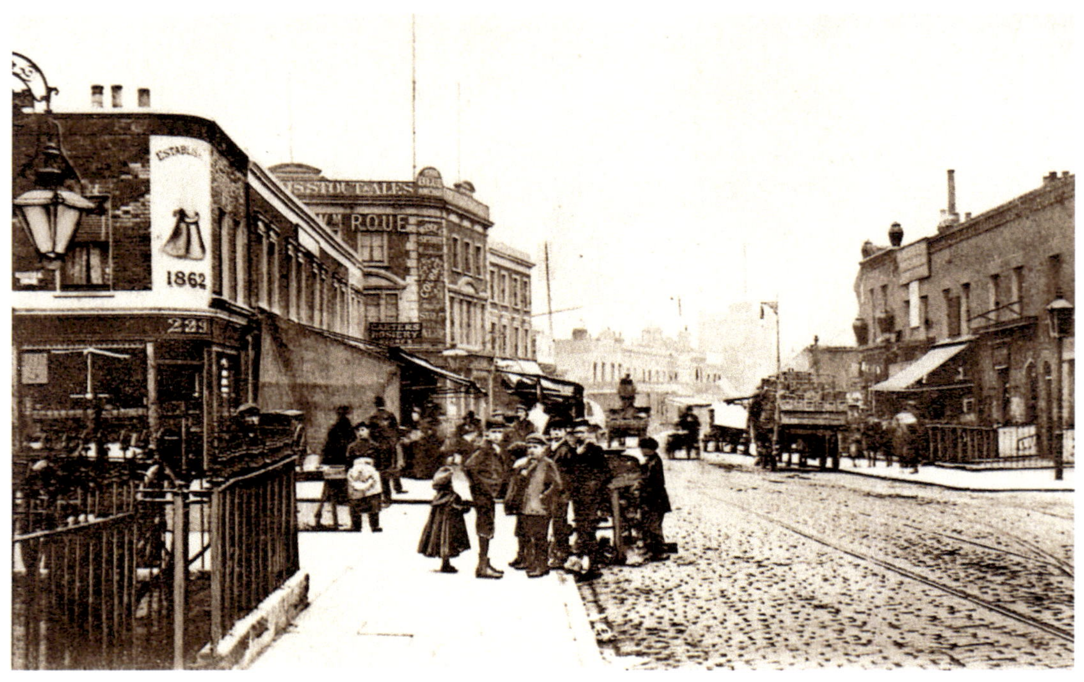



### The Blue Market, Southwark Park Road, 1900

When these children were posing for the camera there were over 250 stalls lining both sides of the road, selling everything from cotton reels and curtaining to jellied eels and tangerines. If you wanted it you could get it down 'the Blue'. All the costermonger patter, the shouts and hollers, arguments, laughter and jokes – it was one big cockney kasbah! Today, all that is left is a handful of stalls in a soulless concrete triangle.

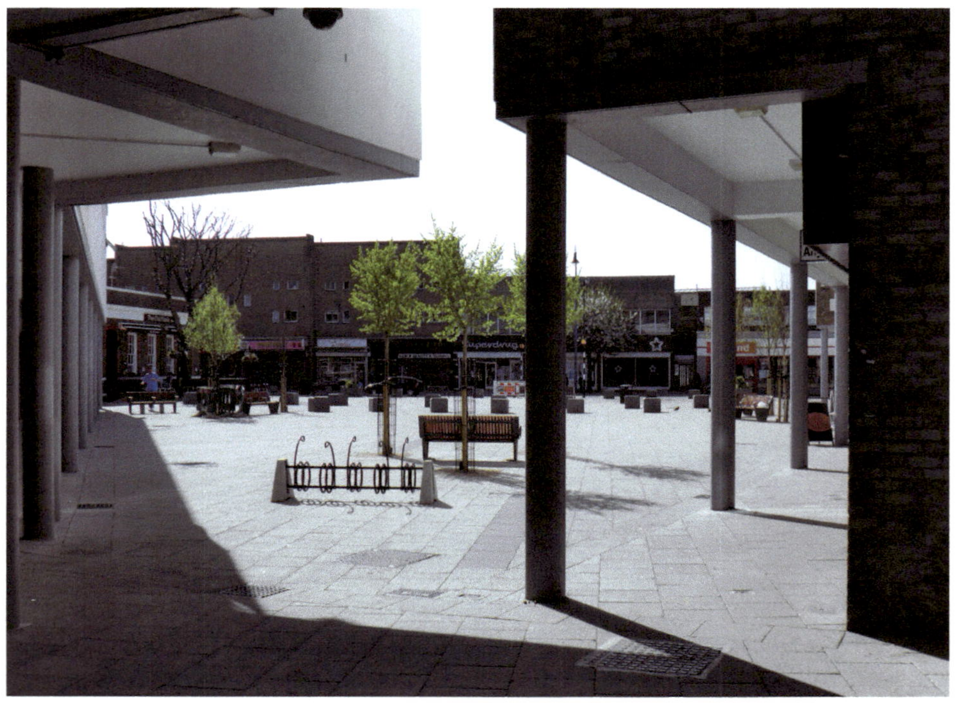

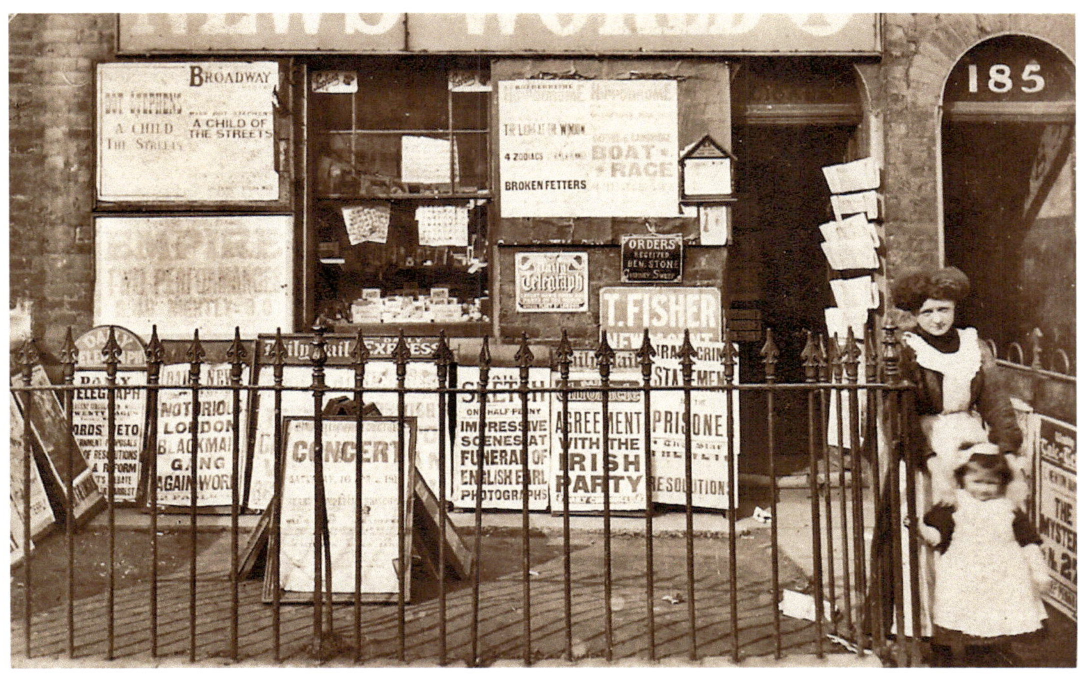


## Fisher's Newsagents, Southwark Park Road, 1910

Mrs Mary Burton poses here with one of her twin nieces. Mary and Lucy Fisher, born in 1908, grew up, lived and worked in this shop until 10 May 1941. At 11.15 p.m. the first sirens went off on what was later described as the worst air raid of the war. Mary and Lucy died when the shop received a direct hit. Nobody passing this vacant 1980s shop has any idea of the tragedy that occurred on this spot. (1910 photographs © Fred Low)

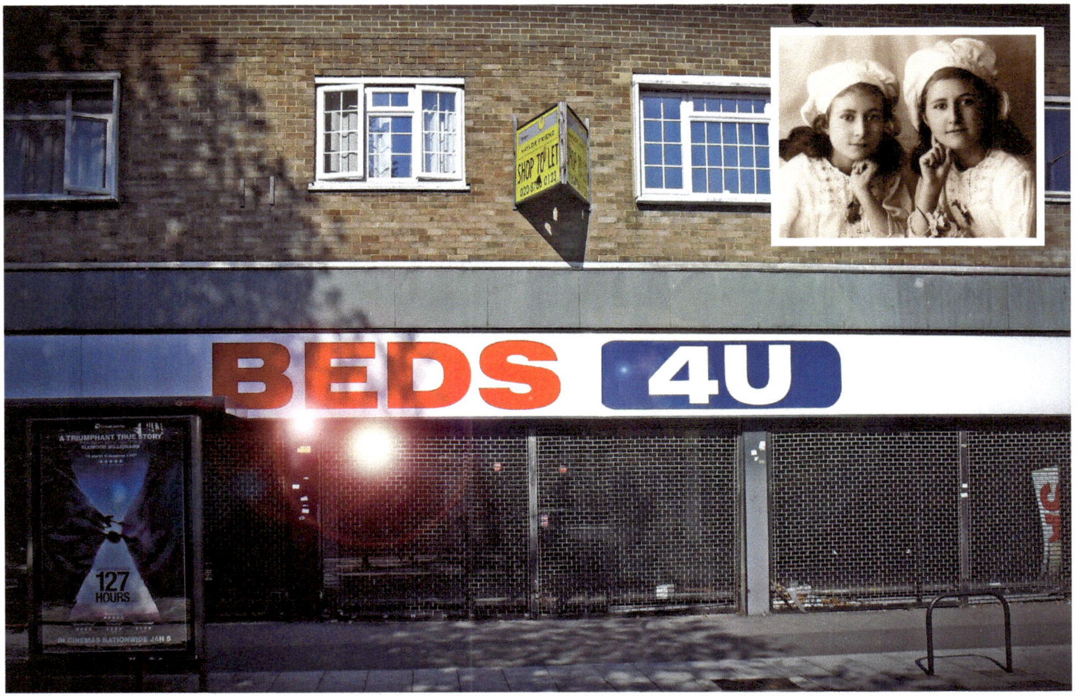

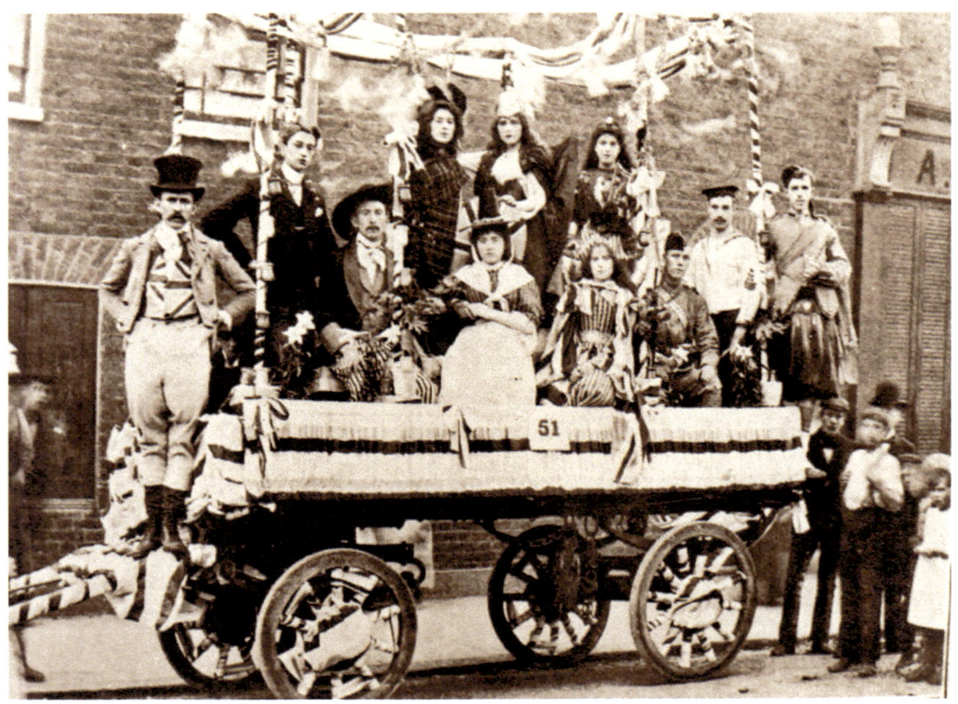



**Bermondsey Carnival, 1900**

The employees of draper Ambrose Pomeroy are ready join the first Bermondsey Carnival. Mr Pomeroy himself was on the committee that organised this fun day to raise cash for the families suffering hardship due to Boer War casualties. The Carnival is still going strong today, albeit on a less grand scale, raising funds for charity. These ladies are just heading towards the site where Pomeroy's emporium stood in their grandparents' time!

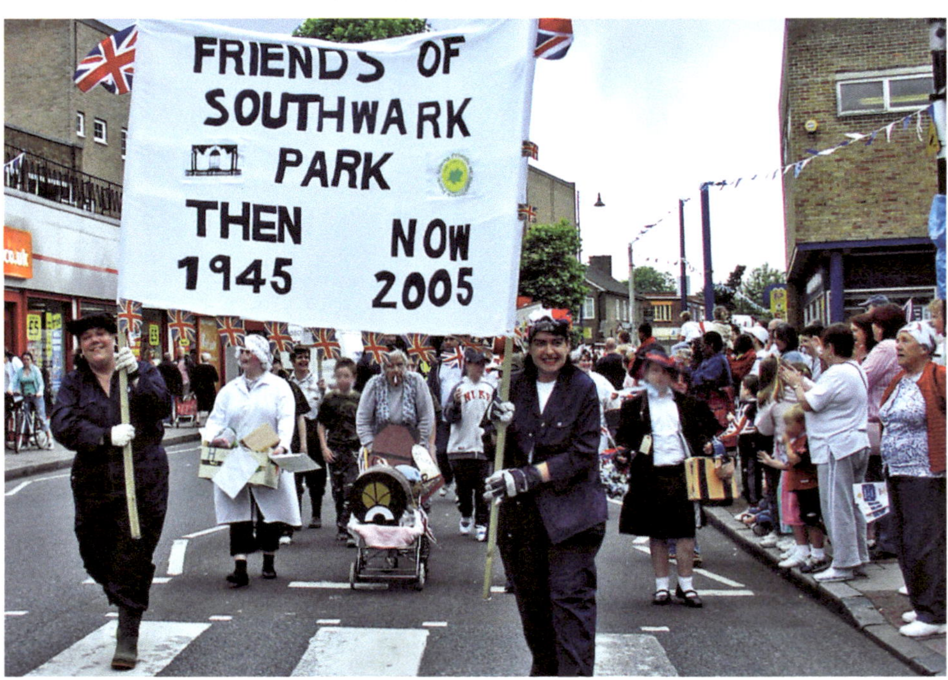

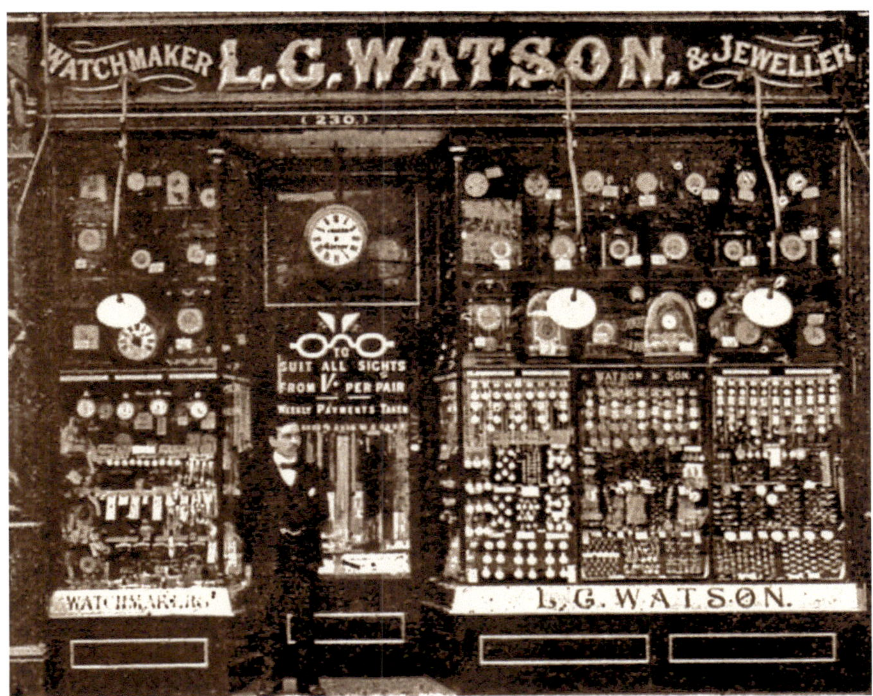


## Southwark Park Road, 1908

Bermondsey-born Leonard Watson proudly stands outside his shop to be photographed. He had taken over the business from William Sargent around 1898 and supplied pocket watches and spectacles of every description and for every budget. Delicate little *pince-nez* for the ladies and monocles for the men were to be found in his shop, with prices starting at a shilling. Leonard's shop was demolished and now Morgan's hairdresser's occupies the space.

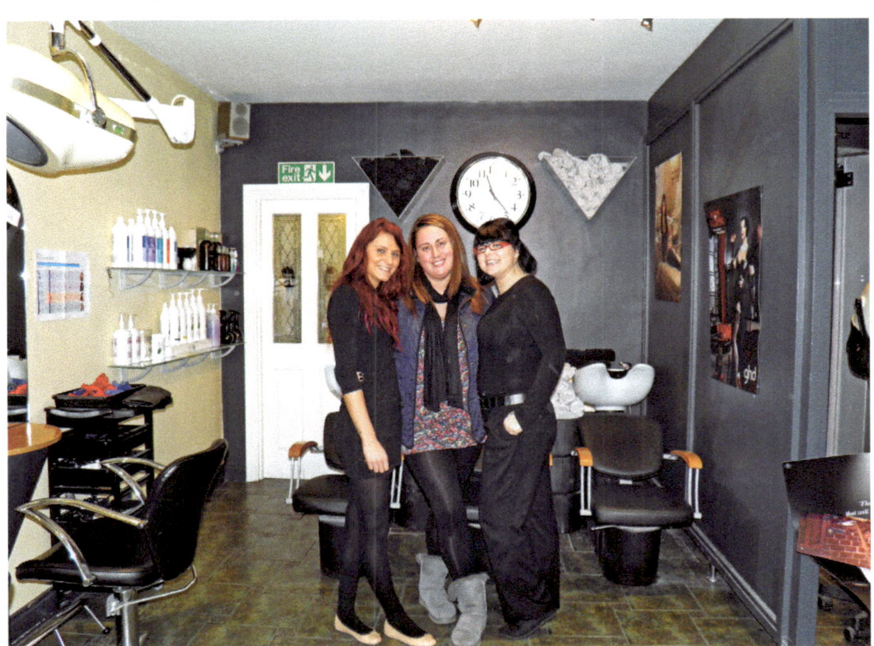

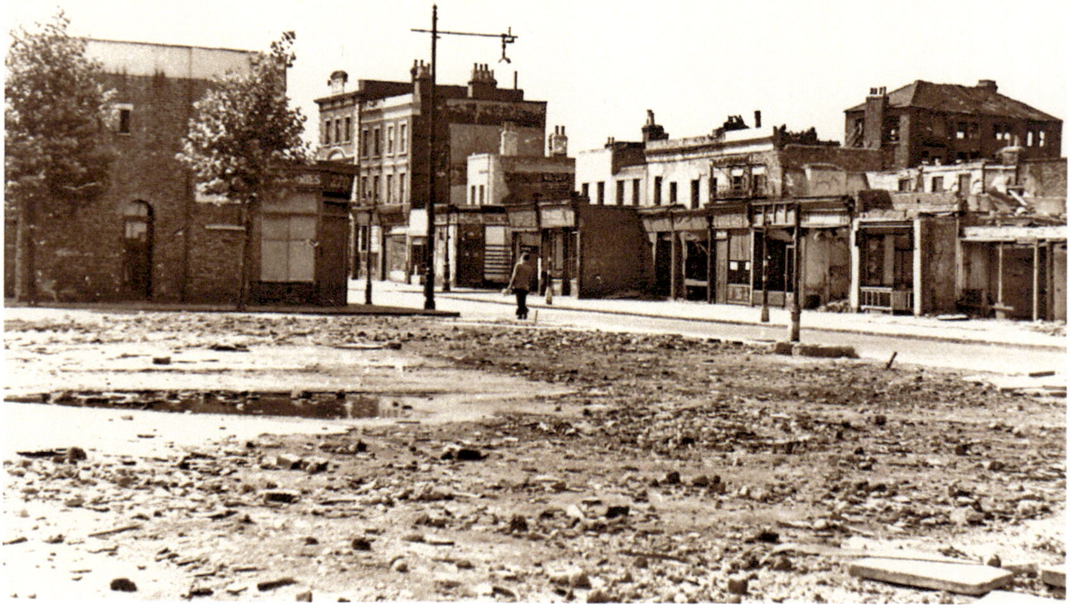

**Southwark Park Road Junction with Galleywall Road, 1946**
This shows the devastation caused by V2 bombing to this part of Bermondsey. Shuttleworth Park now covers the site. This junction is the approximate border of Bermondsey with Rotherhithe. (1946 photograph © Michael Holland)

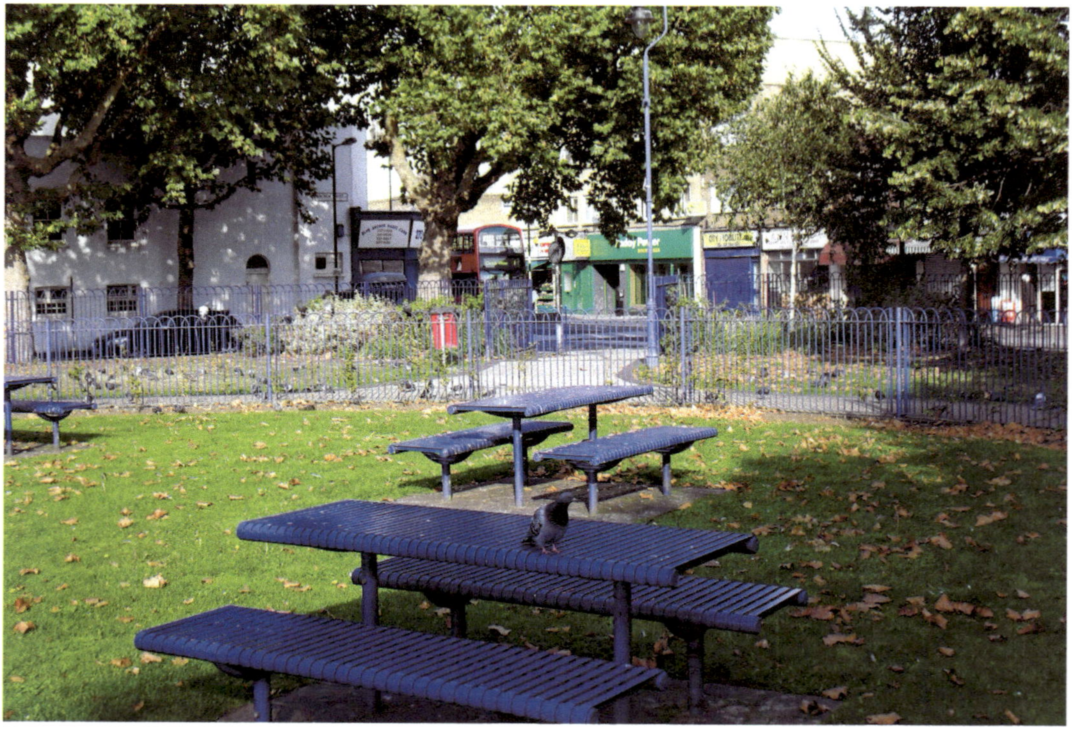

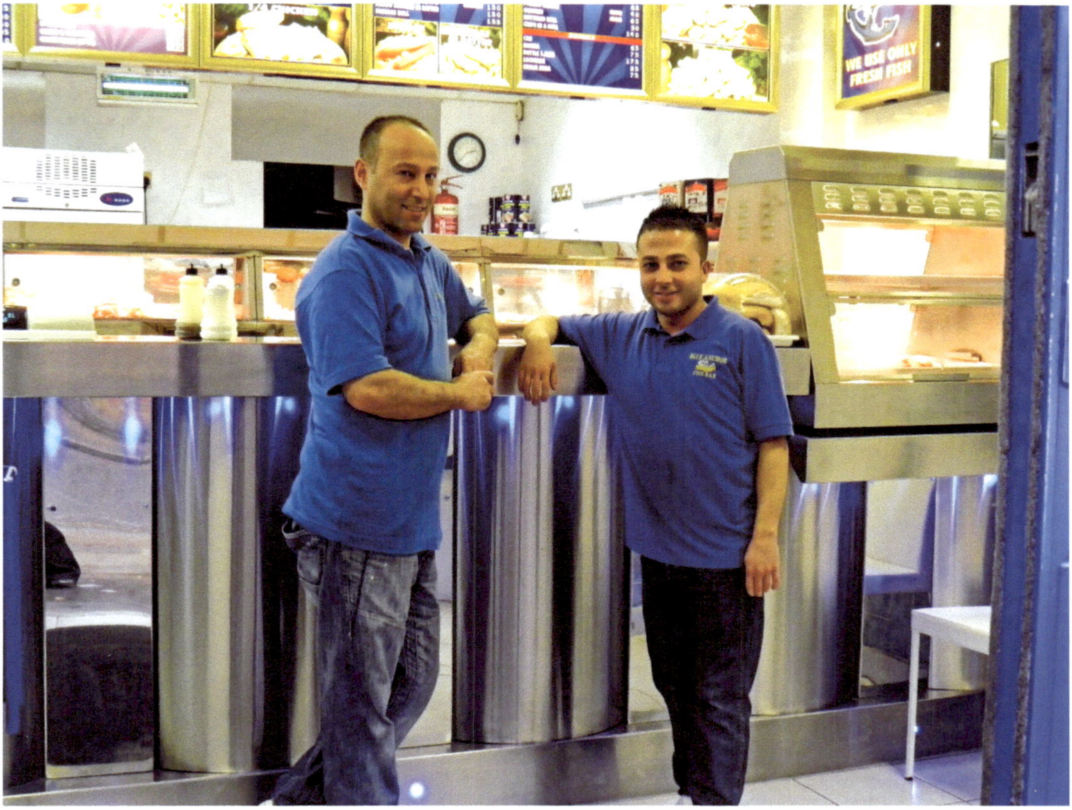

## Blue Anchor Fish Bar, 1960

Established in 1878, this old chip shop started life as a fishmonger's before converting to fried fish. Brothers Telemachus and Michael Evangelou arrived on a warship from Cyprus in 1945, pooled their savings and bought the Anchor Fish Bar. The family are still in the business but have moved on to Rotherhithe New Road. The Blue Anchor now has a new wave of happy fish fryers, but its usage remains the same, even after more than 130 years. (1960 photograph © M. Miltiadous)

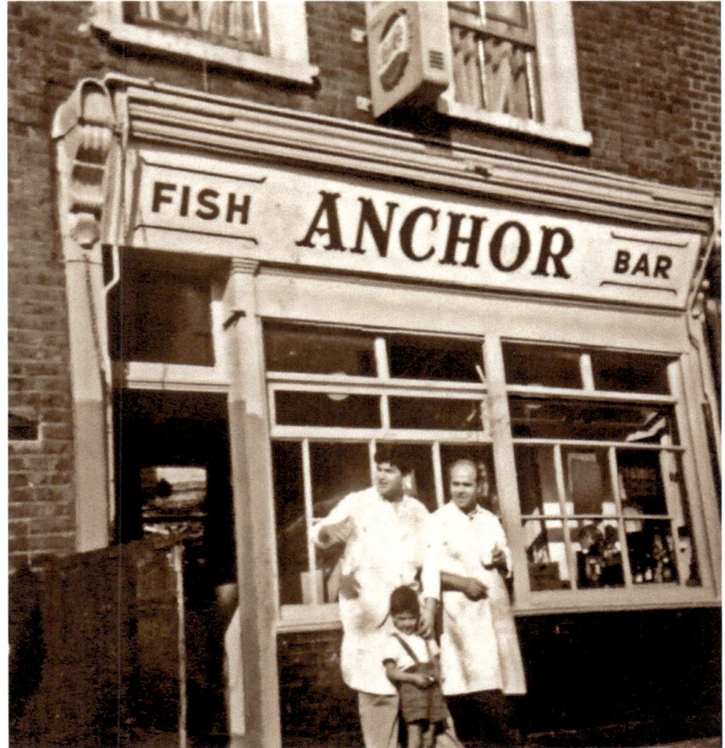

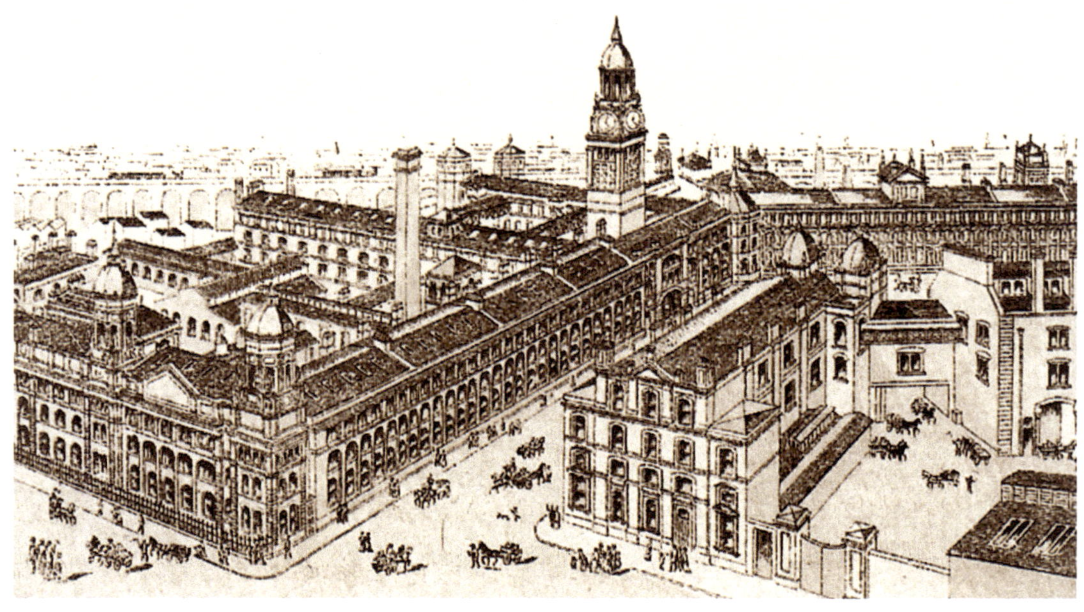

### Peek Frean's, Clements Road, 1880

Known as Biscuit Town, everyone in Bermondsey knows someone who worked for Peek Frean. Besides delicious biscuits, the factory had workshops, a fire brigade, a fleet of lorries, a packing plant and a shop on site. Aunts, mothers, sisters; they all worked at the biscuit factory in between the school day or even on a night shift. It really was the hub of the community. The factory has gone but the building survives as an industrial estate.

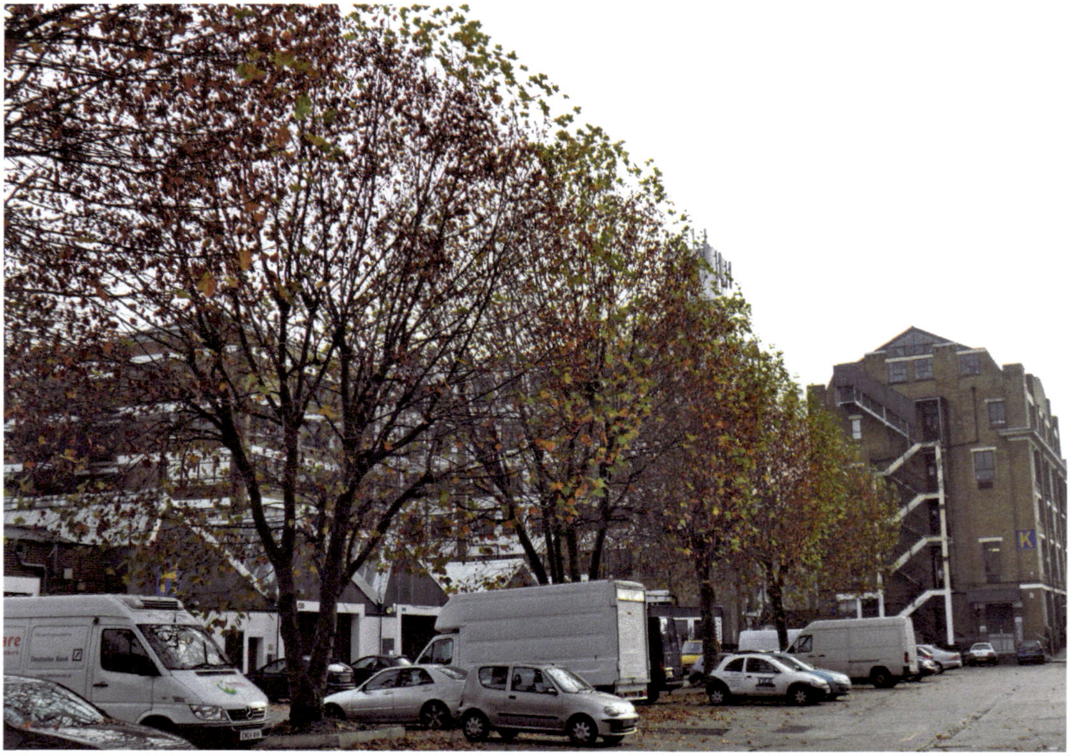

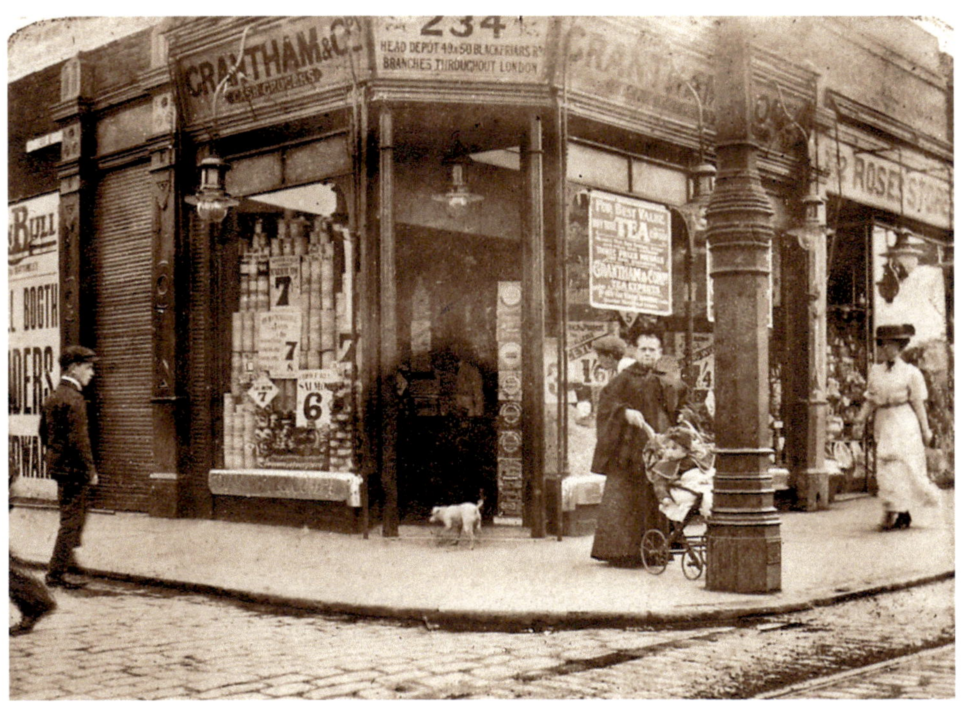


## Camilla Road/Southwark Park Road, 1910

The shopping area known as 'the Blue' had a myriad of haberdashers, drapers and food shops. Number 234 was situated on the corner of Camilla Road and occupied by Grantham & Co., a chain that sold everything you required for an afternoon tea. Ernie, the lad that took this old photograph, actually worked in the shop. Today, most of the old premises are gone but this rather striking mural brightens up the space, which leads into a residential area. (1910 photograph © D. Toogood)

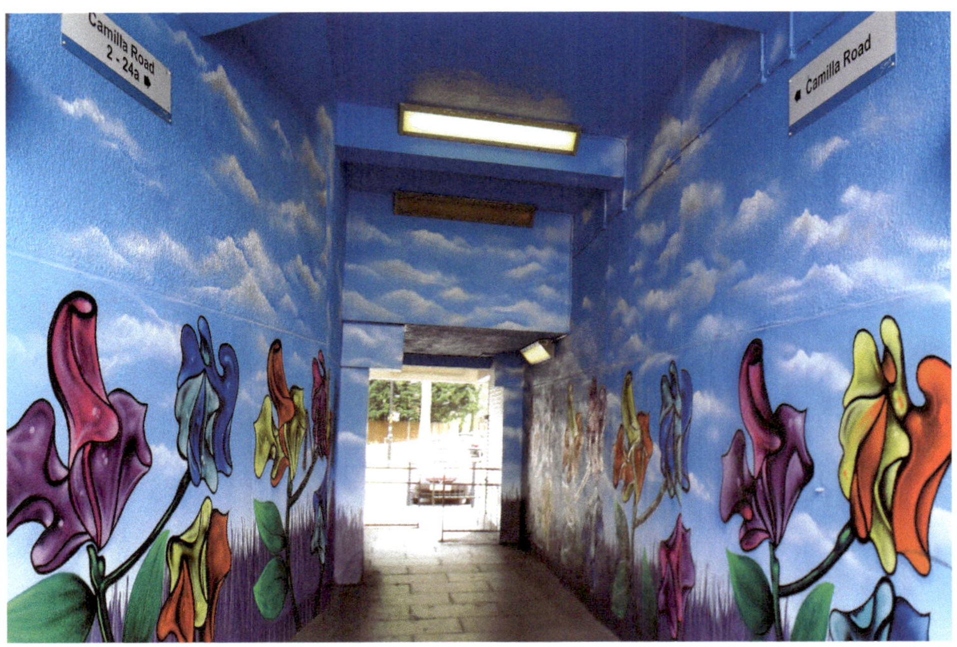

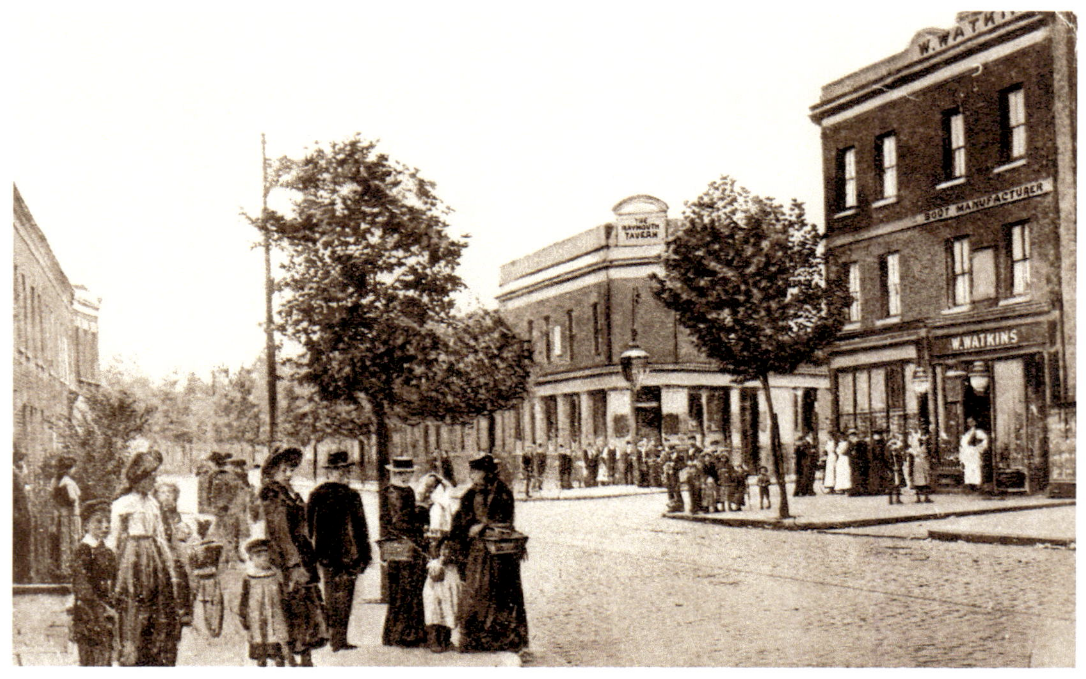

## Raymouth Road, 1900

Here is cobbler William Watkins at his door, a fixture for untold years, with his name above his shop for all to see from the railway carriages that passed over John Bull Arch. The shop has disappeared and its neighbour has lost a floor, probably when the arch was demolished by the V2 raids. However this end of Southwark Park Road remains a leafy residential thoroughfare. The Raymouth public house held on until the 1990s but is now flats.

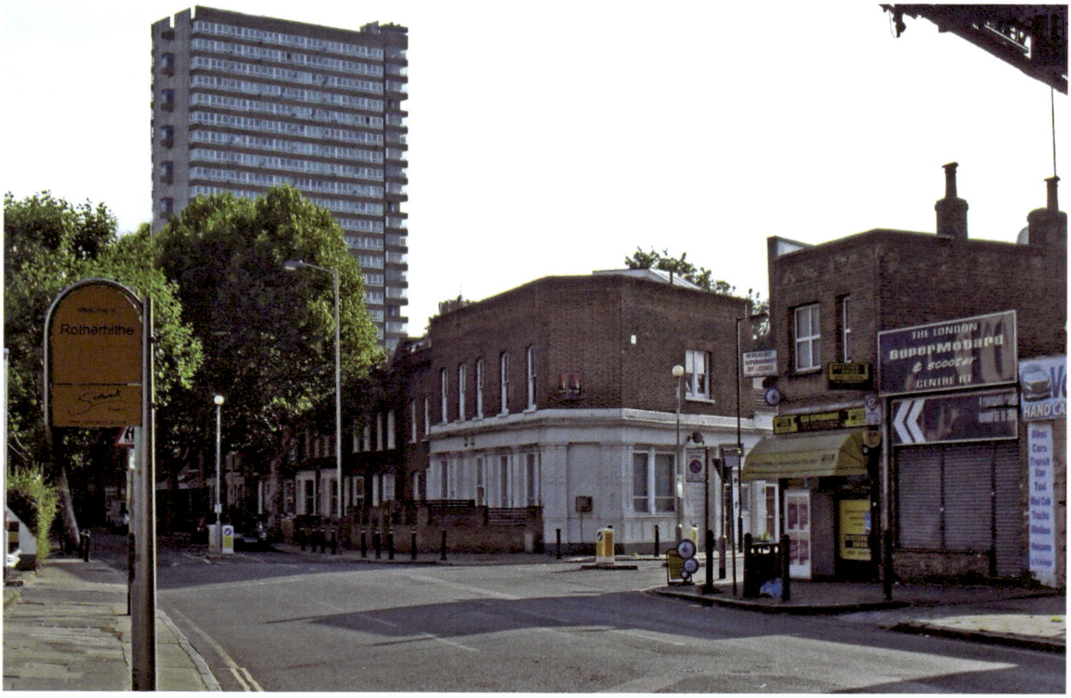

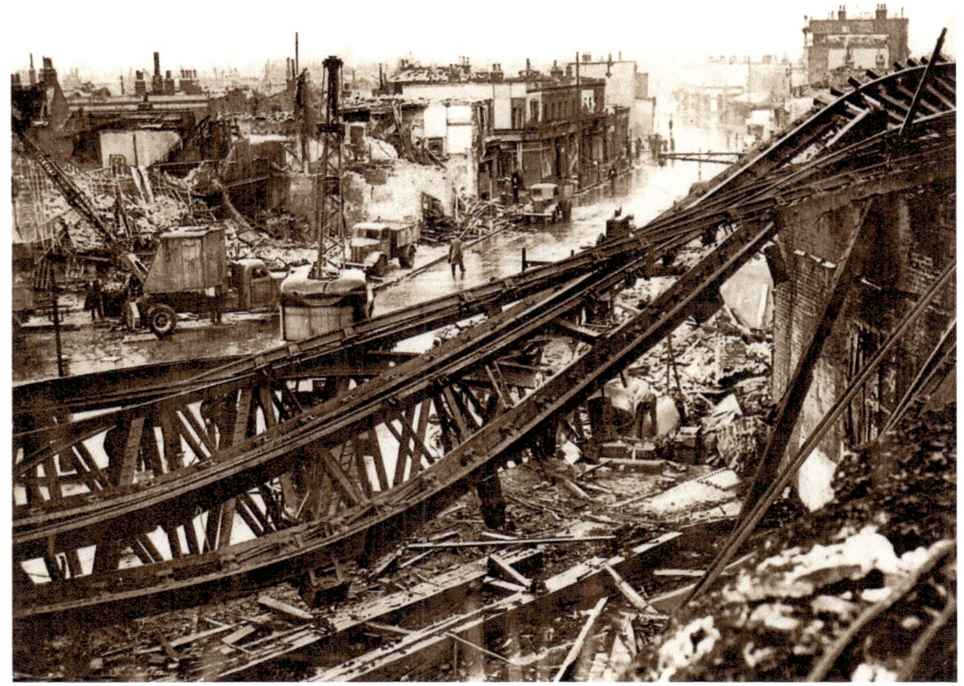

### John Bull Arch, Southwark Park Road, 1944

On 8 December 1940 a bomb fell near the railway, causing sixteen people sheltered beneath the arch to lose their lives. A V2 rocket exploded on 26 October 1944, killing eight and injuring over a hundred more. Damaged but largely intact, the arch was targeted again a month later. The bridge was shored up, but only two weeks later another V2 totally demolished it. The mass of twisted rails have gone, only to be echoed in these twisted tree branches.

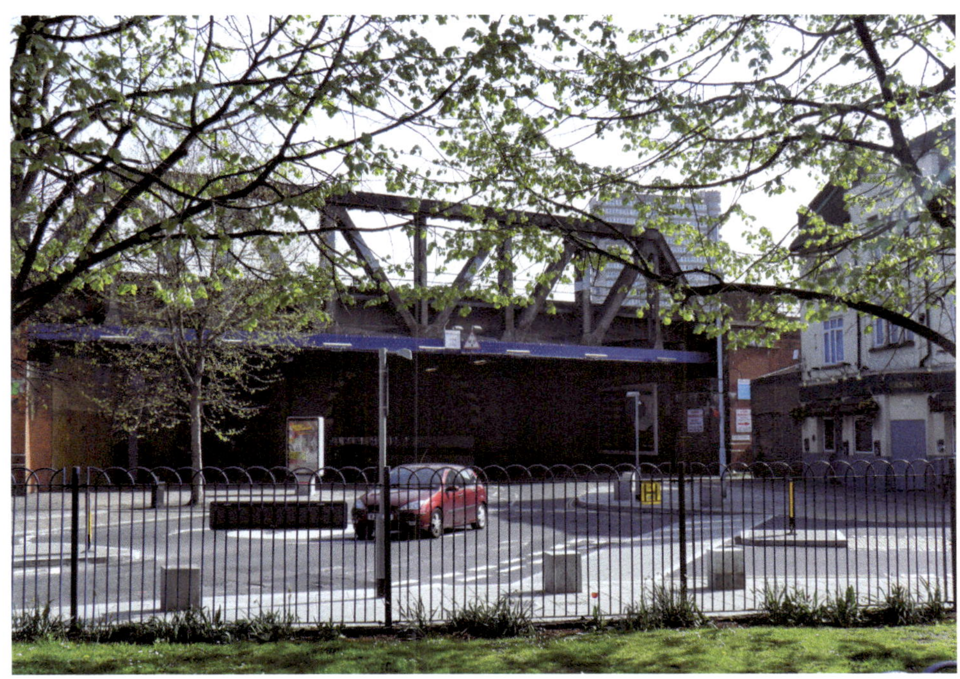

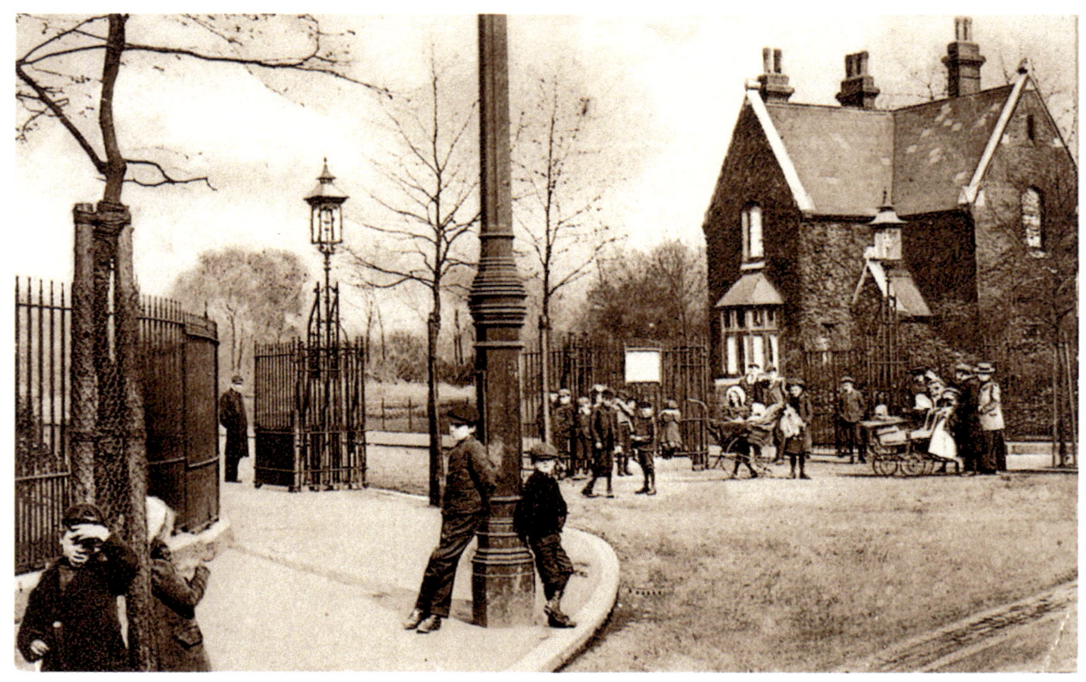

## Jamaica Gate, Southwark Park, 1908

Either side of the lamppost upon which the boys are leaning are two sapling trees, which have grown into a couple of marvellous specimens 100 years on. The lodge house featured was eventually demolished and reconstructed to the left of this picture. The soil there is so marshy that the house began to sink and the superintendent's wife's health suffered from the effects of damp and mould. Exactly where the tiger in the tree originated is a mystery!

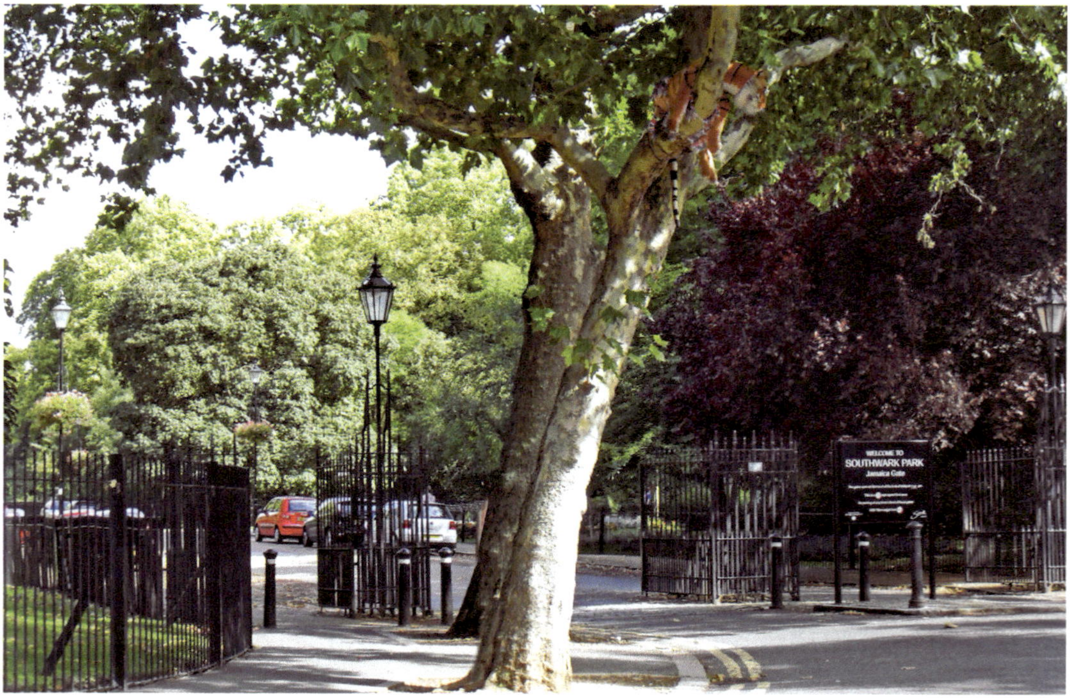

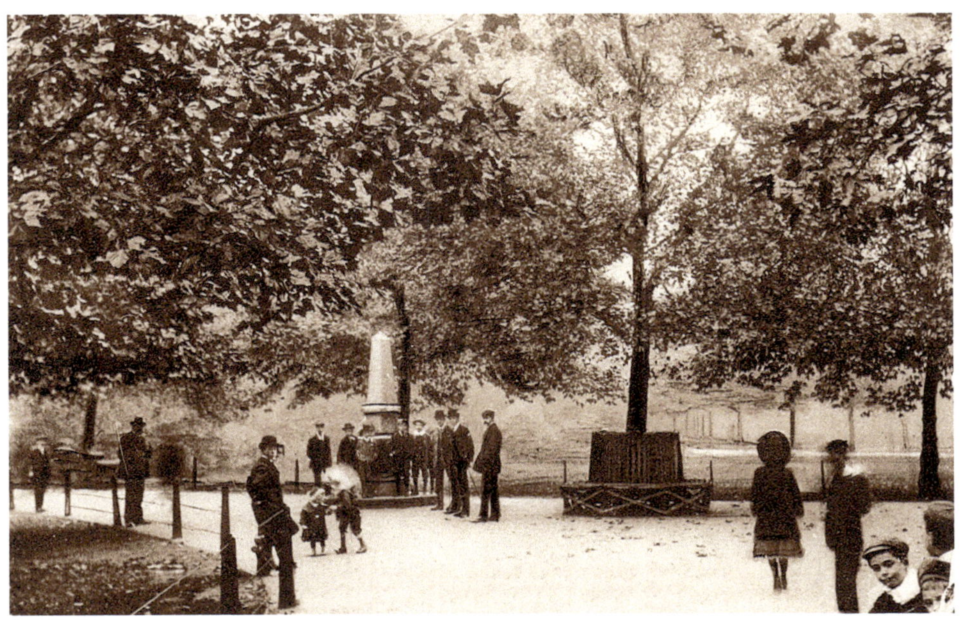

## Jabez West Memorial, Southwark Park, 1905

Jabez West, a local tanner, lived in Frean Street and flirted with politics, but his work with the Temperance Movement was more important. He was often seen bravely speaking against the demon drink outside pubs in the area. When he died in 1884 funding was obtained for an obelisk to his memory, which appeared in the park a year later. The drinking fountain was recently restored and is regularly used by the crows when they think nobody is looking!

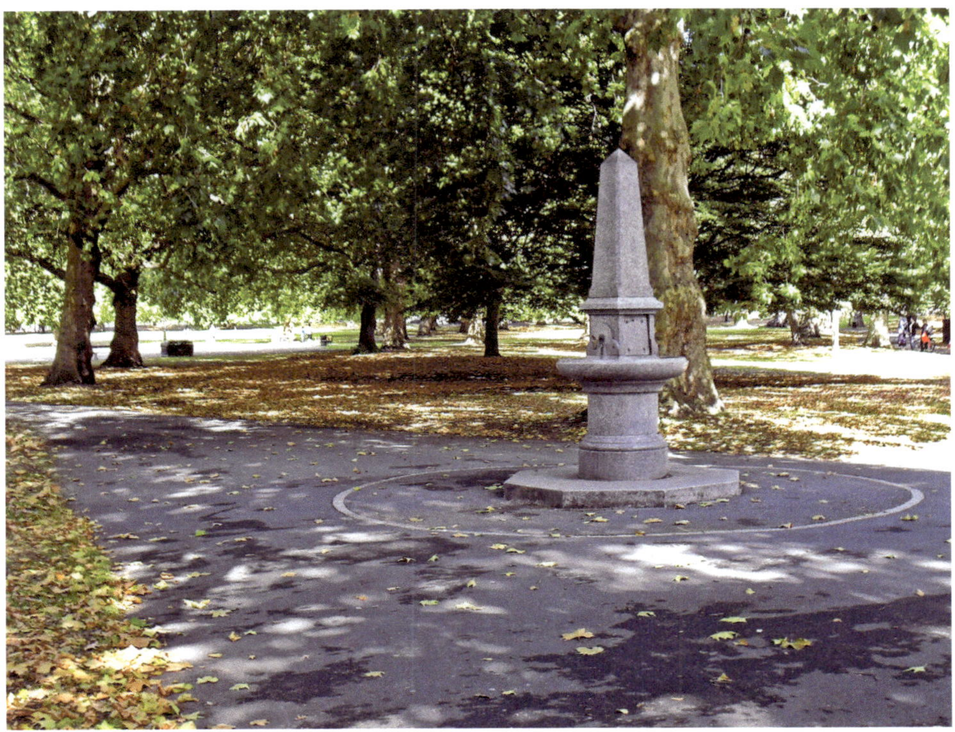

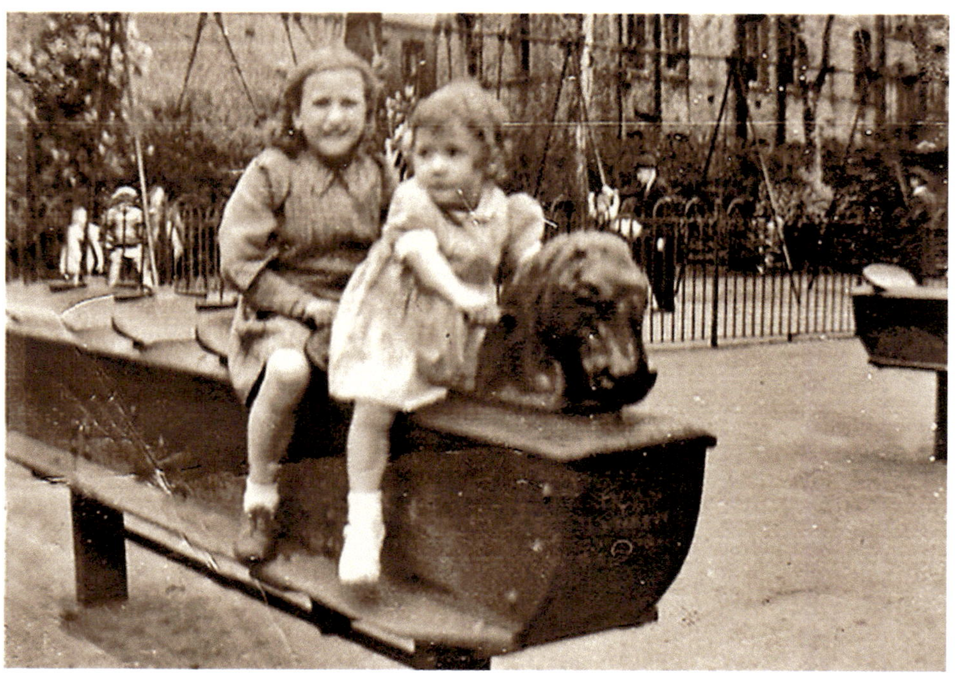

## Children's Playground, Southwark Park, 1950s

Janet and Brenda Donovan enjoyed the delights of this well-used playground, where children played, grew up and eventually brought their own children. In the background can be seen St Olave's Hospital, where local cricket hero Bobby Abel was treated after receiving a whack on the nose with a ball. Now that the children's park has moved, the old area is transformed into a very pleasant wildlife garden. (1950s photograph © Michael Holland)

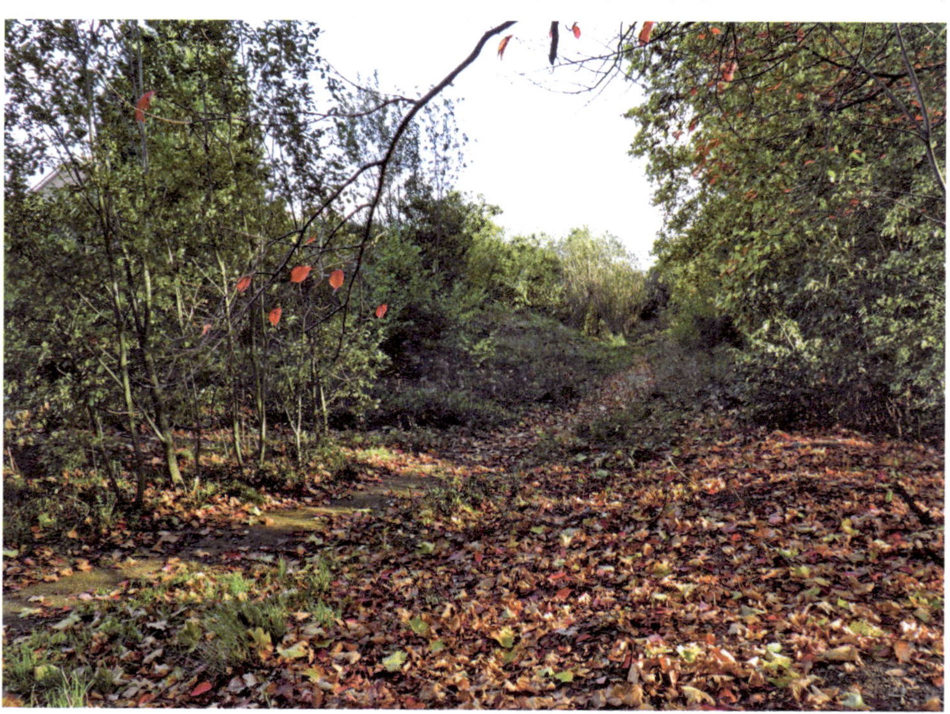

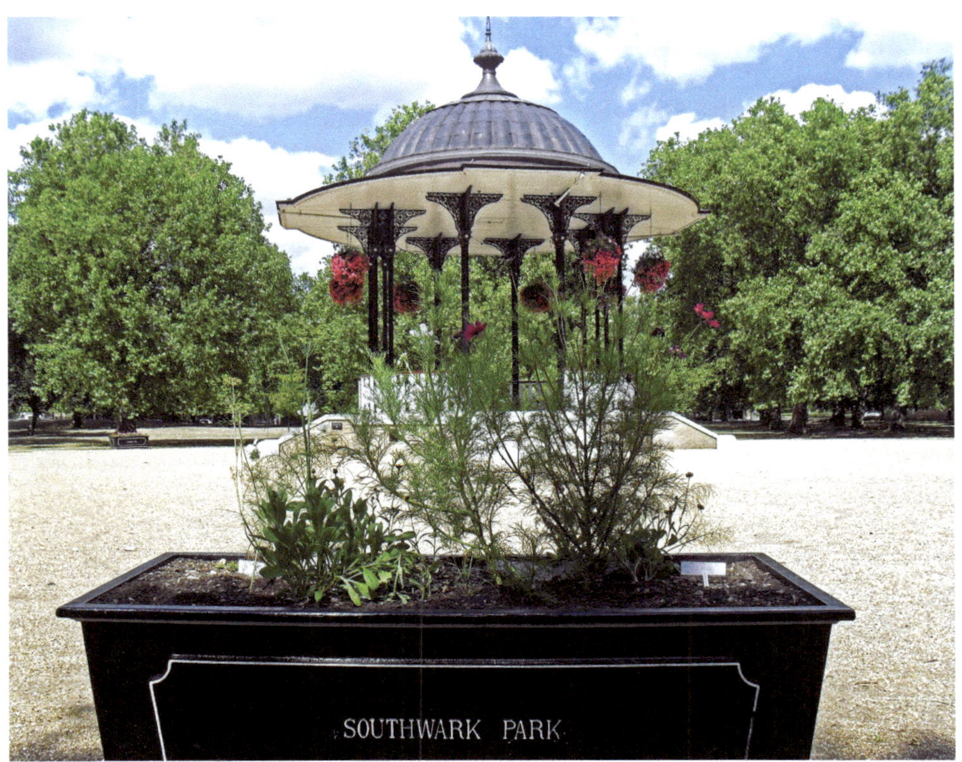



### The Bandstand, Southwark Park, 1910

Victorian Bermondsey was crowded, smoky, smelly and congested. There was nowhere for people to catch their breath and fill their lungs with clean air. Mortality rates were through the roof, with scarlet fever, TB and lung disease carrying off many people. These were grim times indeed. To the rescue came the Metropolitan Board of Works, which purchased land from the local gentry and laid out this park in 1869. Fifteen years later the bandstand appeared and filled the treetops with music, only for it to disappear mysteriously in the late 1950s. The one you see today is a replica which was constructed in 2002, financed by the Heritage Lottery Fund.

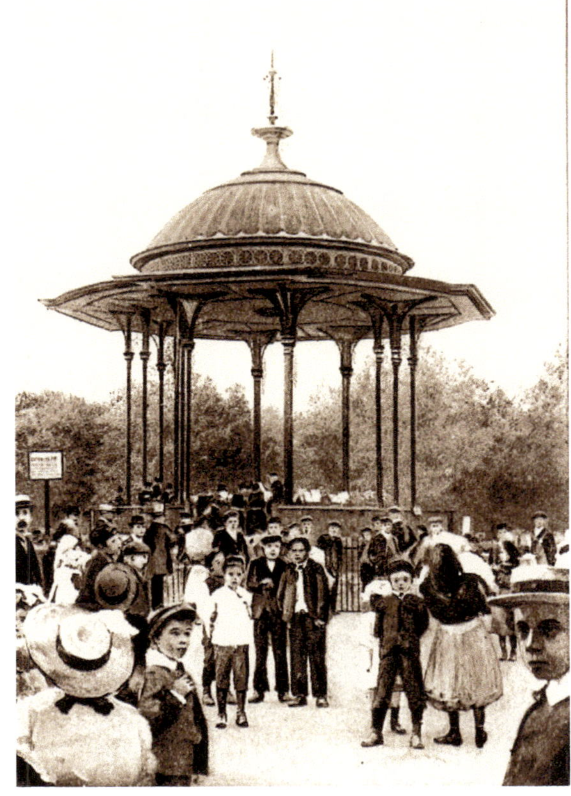

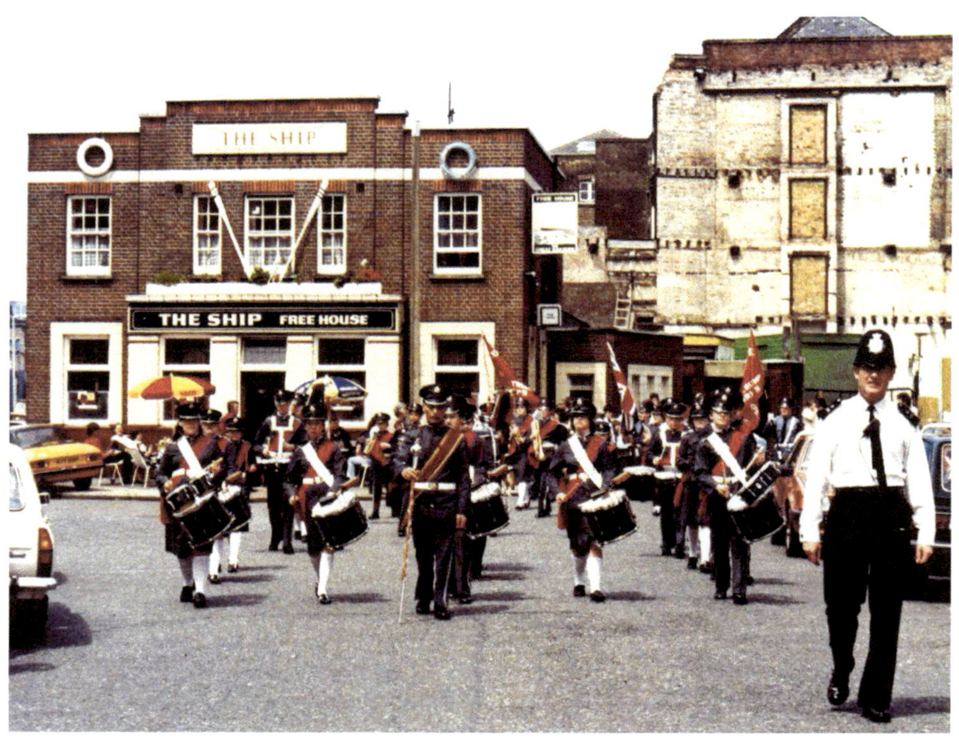



**The Ship Public House, Elephant Lane, 1982**

This band had just taken part in the Rotherhithe Festival, which at the time was held around this street. PC Christopher Lordan from Rotherhithe Police is escorting them back to base. Less than thirty years later the pub has been obscured, pleasantly, by these wonderful trees. (1982 photograph © Chris Lordan)

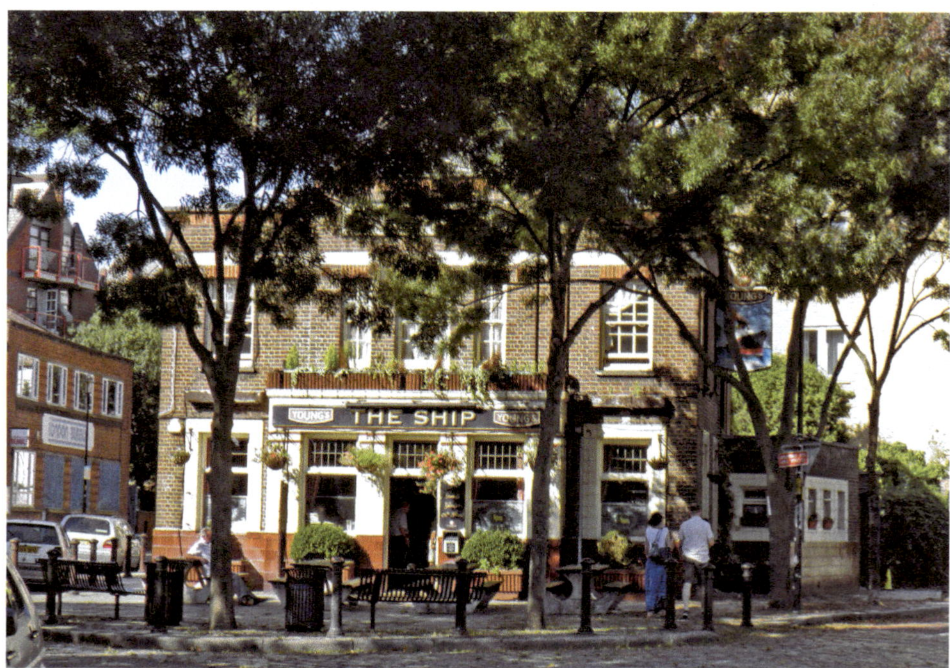

Built in 1814, a Dr William
Gaitskell lived here. He had
some very dubious habits.
From his house, local
legend claims, a tunnel led
down to the river where
youngsters were paid to
recover floating corpses
for the good doctor to
experiment on. It has
now been sealed up. In
1838 the building became
Rotherhithe Police Station,
where youngsters were
again paid for errands:
bringing in a fish and
chip supper for the local
plod! (1917 photograph ©
Metropolitan Police)

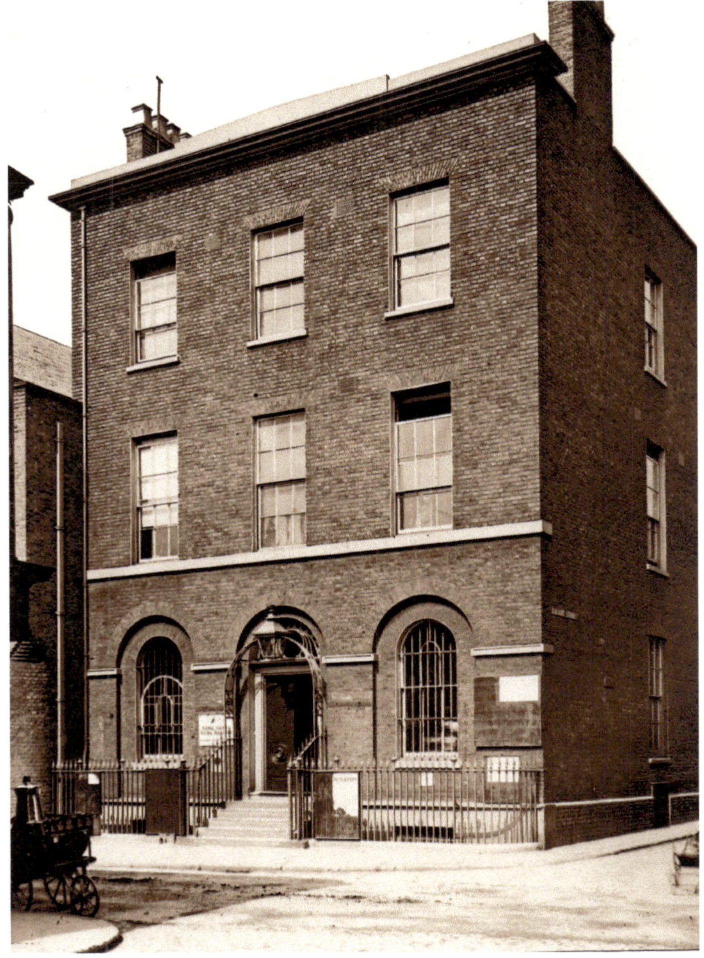

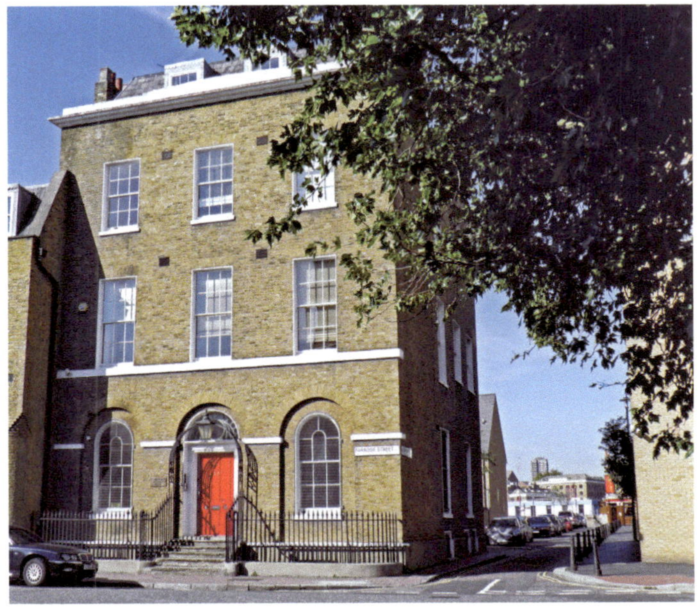

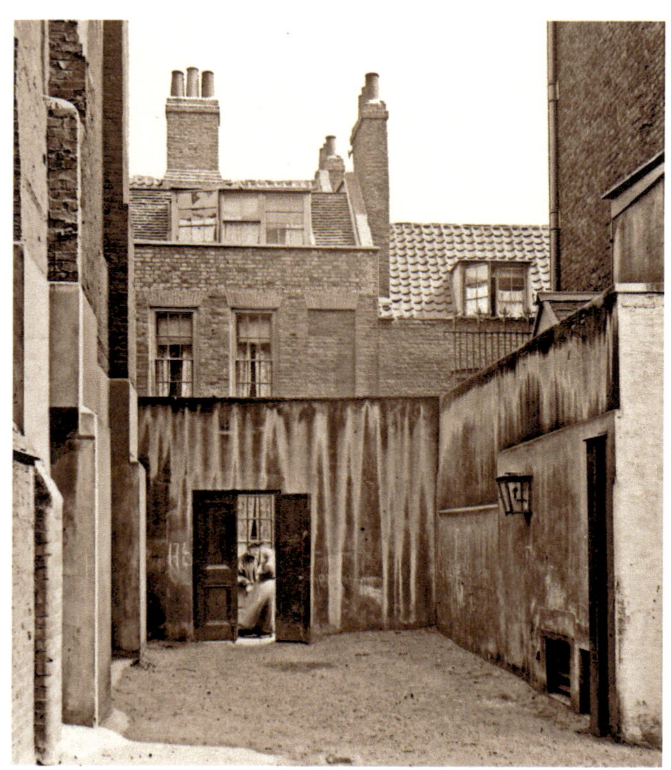



## Side Gate, Old Rotherhithe Police Station, 1900

The gate is in the same position but the backdrop has certainly changed. Many of the ancient houses that lined Paradise Street, in the background here, were demolished in the 1960s. Note the two women chatting, with their long skirts and shawls. The woman wearing the hat looks like she has been widowed for a number of years as she is not in full widow's weeds. (1900 photograph © Metropolitan Police)

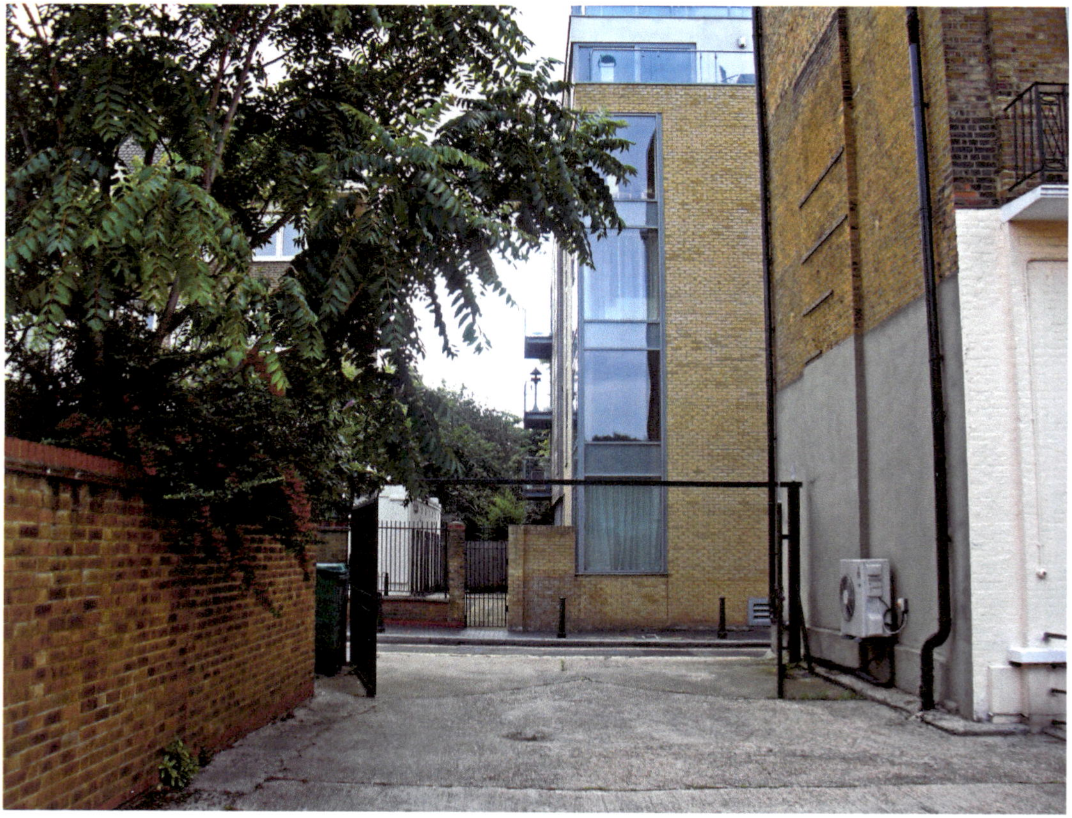

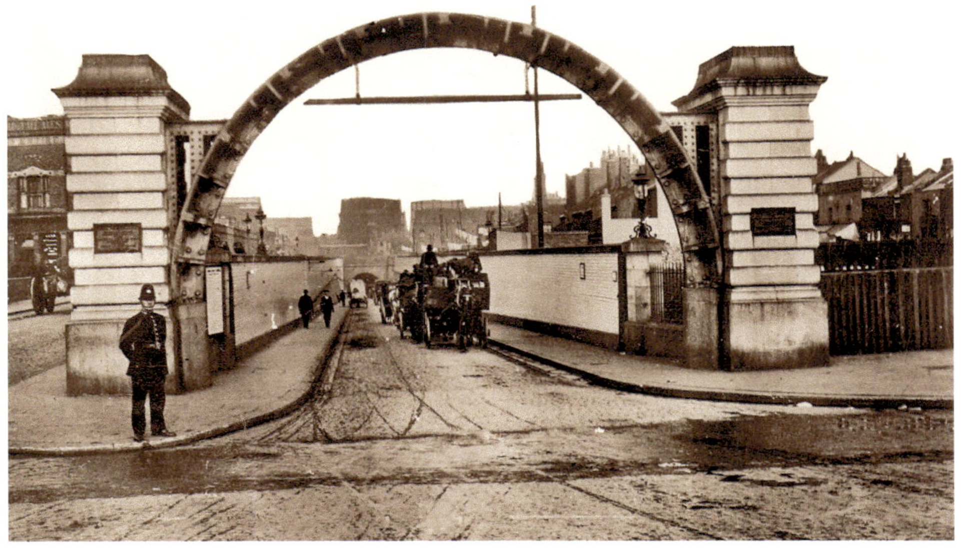

## Rotherhithe Tunnel, 1920

Designed by Maurice Fitzmaurice, the tunnel opened in 1908. The cutting shields, used to burrow beneath the Thames, were incorporated into the archway design and can still be seen. The old ironwork of the lamps remains above the pedestrian entrance. It would be possible to walk to Limehouse through the tunnel, but the fumes and treacherous drivers render this a dangerous, if not impossible, practice.

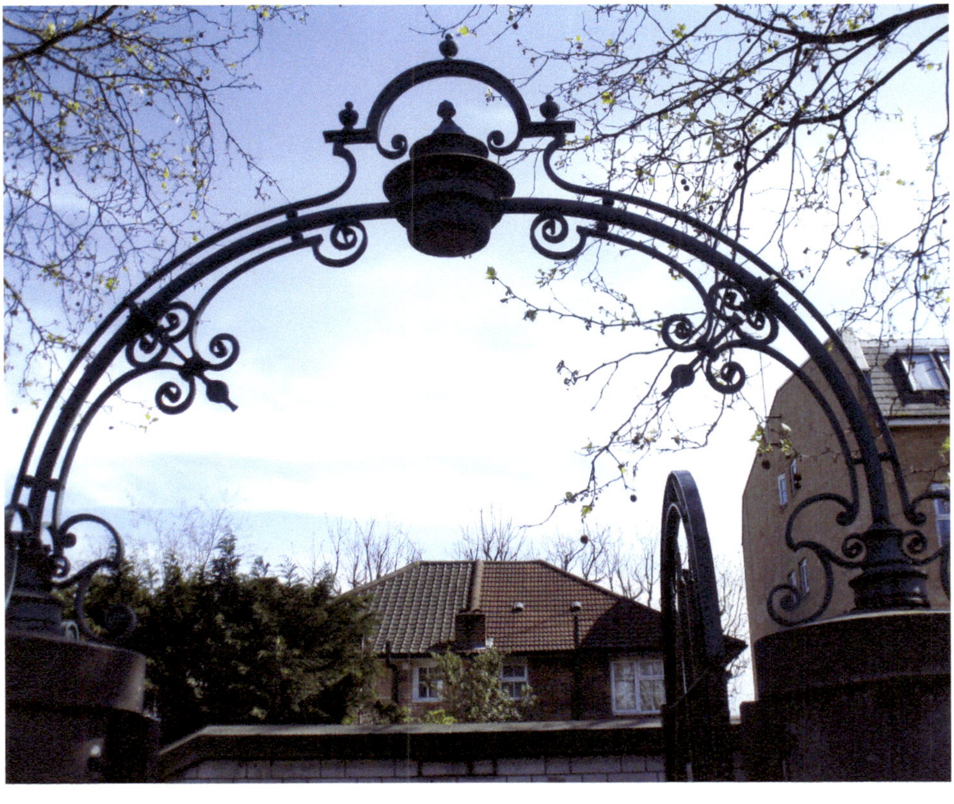

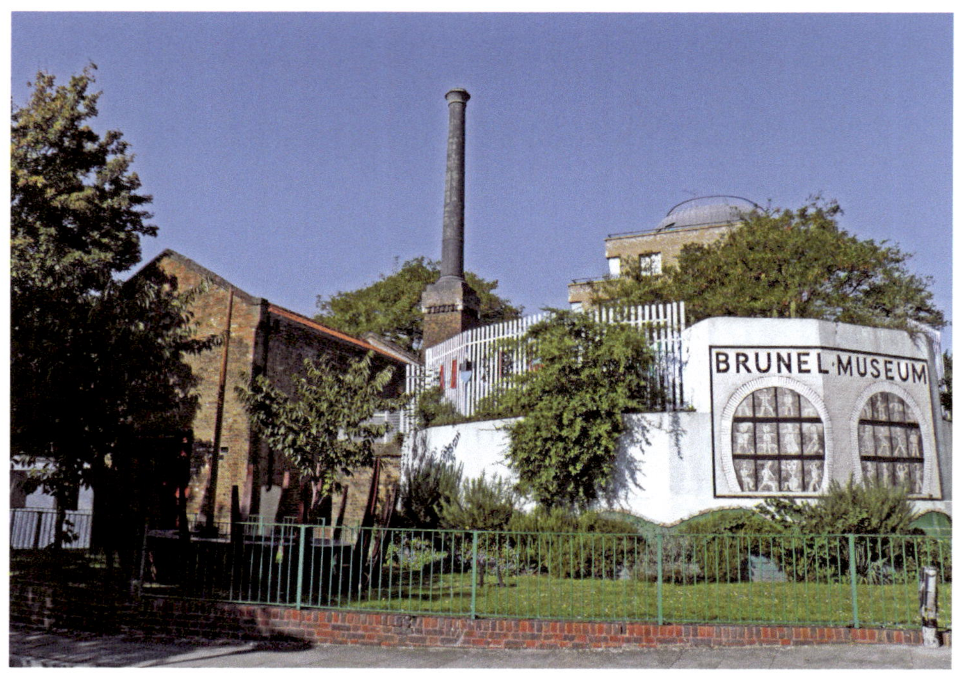

### Brunel Engine House, 1980s

The Brunels were responsible for this dilapidated shed, but what a story it told. An underwater tunnel, between Rotherhithe and Wapping; such a feat of engineering! The Rotherhithe shaft was topped by a powerful steam engine, which would whirr and chug as it pumped water out. In 1841 the two tunnels met, with much marvel and fanfare. The chimney has been carefully restored and in 1995 the building was awarded Grade II listing by English Heritage. (1980s photograph © Brunel Museum)

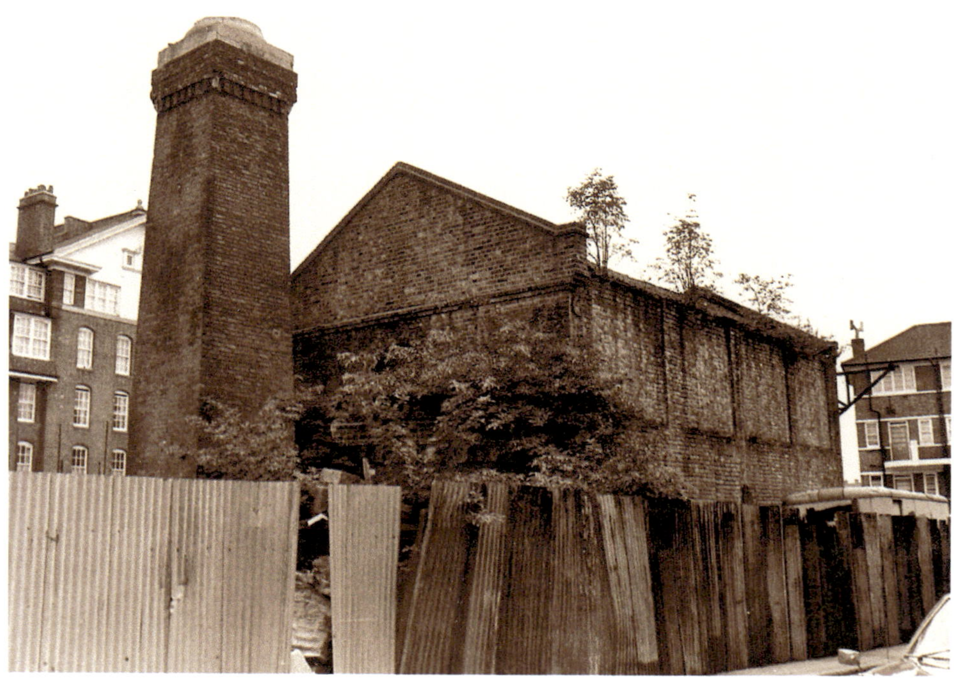

## Norwegian Church, 1929

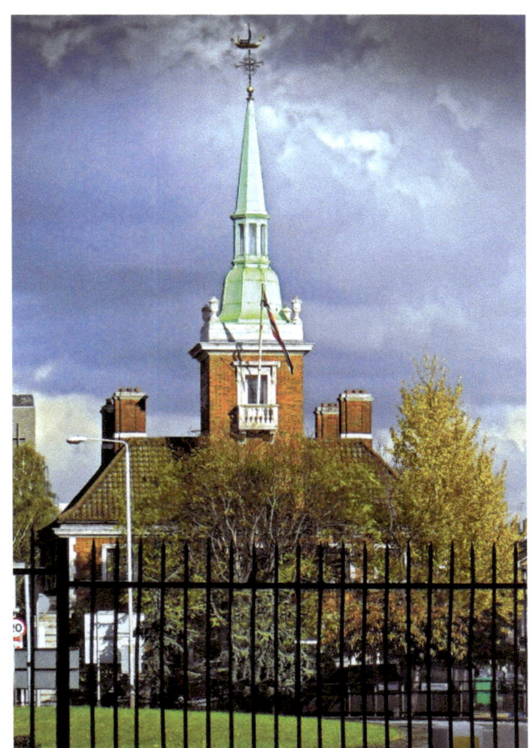

Sailing in with the pine wood were Baltic Jack Tars, some of whom settled in Rotherhithe. Even now there are Finnish, Swedish and Norwegian churches, which catered for sailors' spiritual needs while they were away from home. The Norwegian Church stands next to the Rotherhithe Tunnel and was consecrated in 1927. It is easily identified by its fabulous golden Viking ship, shining out from the steeple.

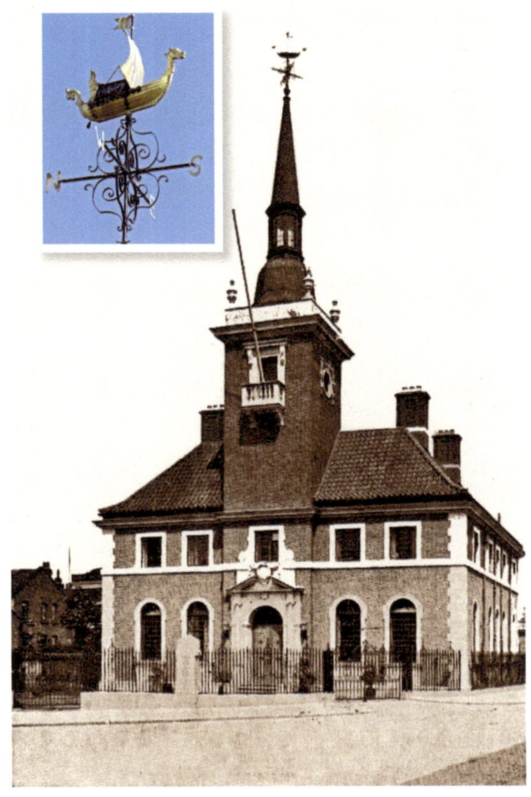

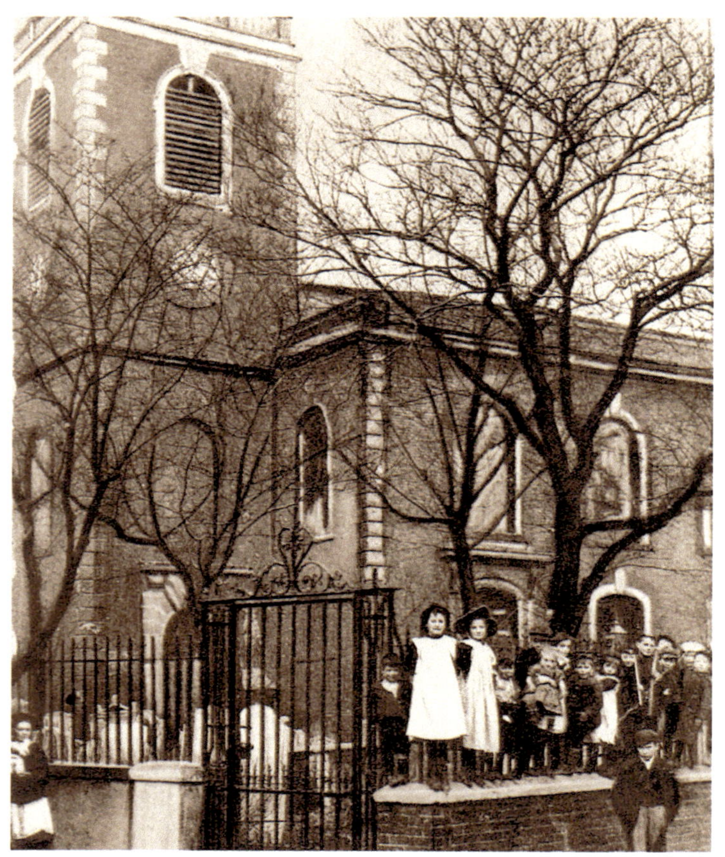



## St Mary, Rotherhithe, 1900

This is a church that inspires adventure stories. The present structure dates from 1714, but there has been a church here since at least the early twelfth century and it is just teeming with maritime history. A famous gravestone belongs to Prince Lee Boo of the Pelau Islands who sadly died from smallpox six months after being brought to England by a Rotherhithe resident, Captain Henry Wilson. Inside the church on a board is a list of benefactors to the parish school. One name of curiosity is Fortunatus Planta, who in 1774 donated £21 to the church. This seems a most unusual name for the times, so perhaps he too came from an exotic island. Further research may produce another adventure story just waiting to be told.

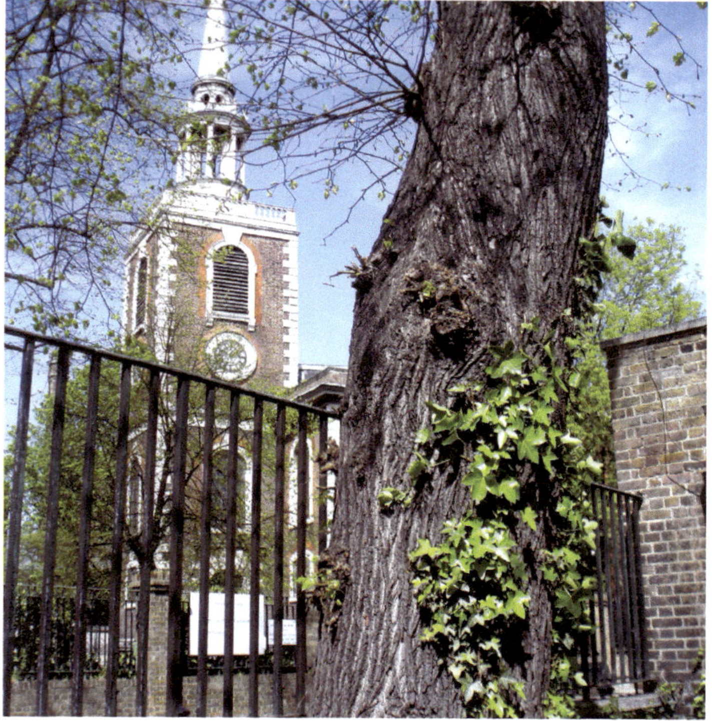

Taken from a painting in the church, this Gothic-looking building was destroyed on a summer's afternoon on 7 September 1940. Holy Trinity has the unhappy legacy of being the first church in Great Britain to be destroyed in the Blitz. It was during the first raids that day, when Surrey Docks was afire and chaos reigned. Very little of the church was left, with not a shred of its history to survive. The rebuilt church, designed by Thomas Ford and erected in 1957, is opposite Surrey Docks Farm, so between the birdsong can be heard the lowing of cows. It is truly a heavenly place. (1838 photograph © Holy Trinity, Rotherhithe)

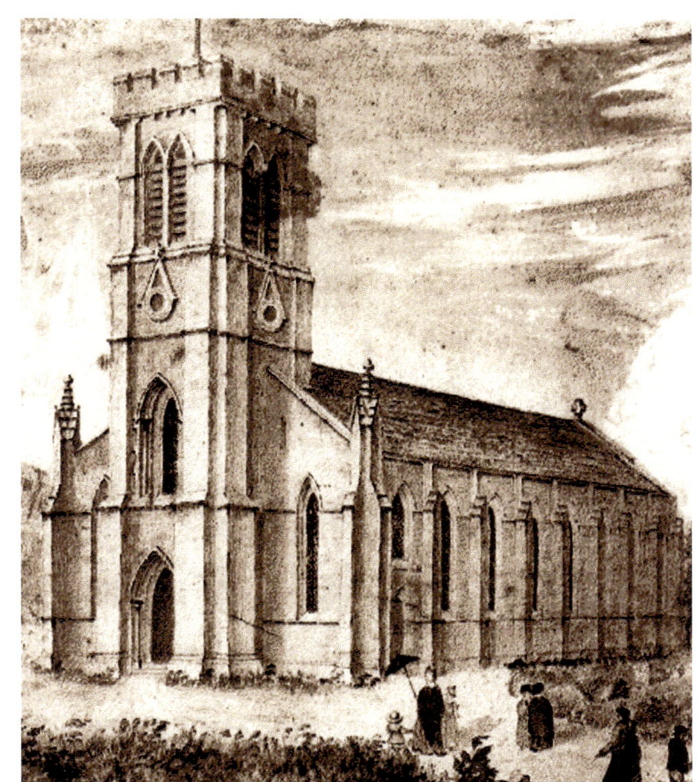

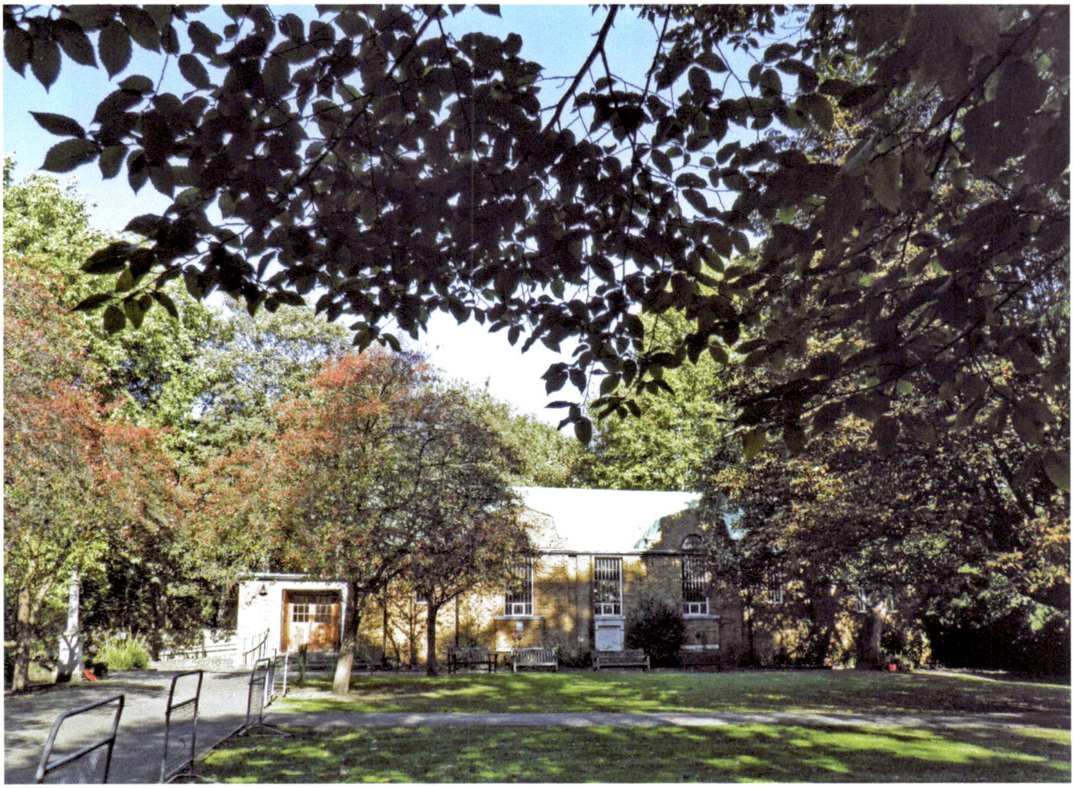

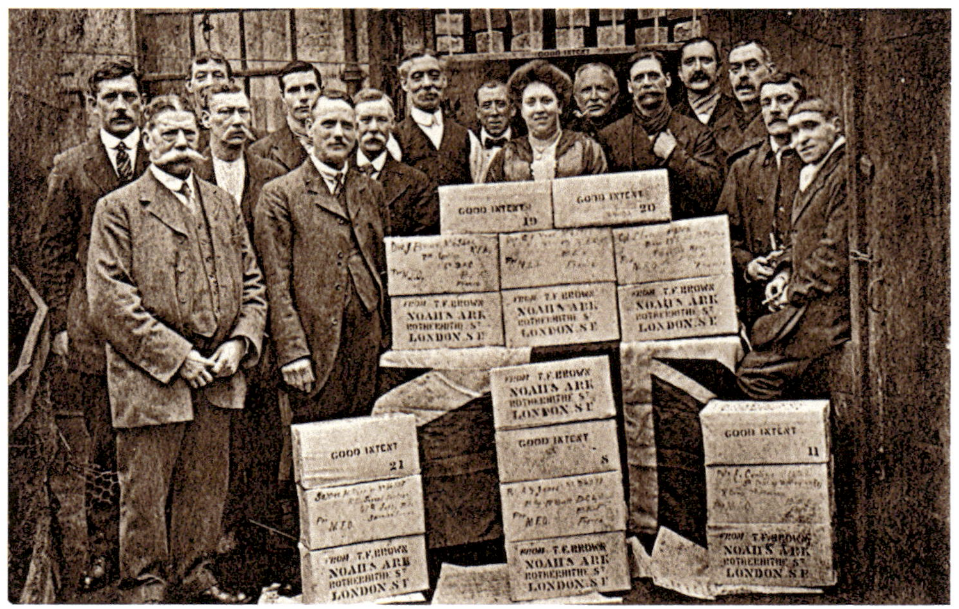



### The Noah's Ark Public House, Rotherhithe Street, 1916

This pub was first recorded in 1805 and situated in quaint-sounding Screw Post Lane. The licensee and regulars are seen here parcelling up supplies for the troops at the front in the First World War. Only one name on the boxes is legible, Sapper Risely, who thankfully is not recorded by the War Graves Commission. The pub, now demolished, closed in 1933 but perhaps some of those names on the boxes are shown on the memorial in Holy Trinity. (1916 photograph © D. Toogood)

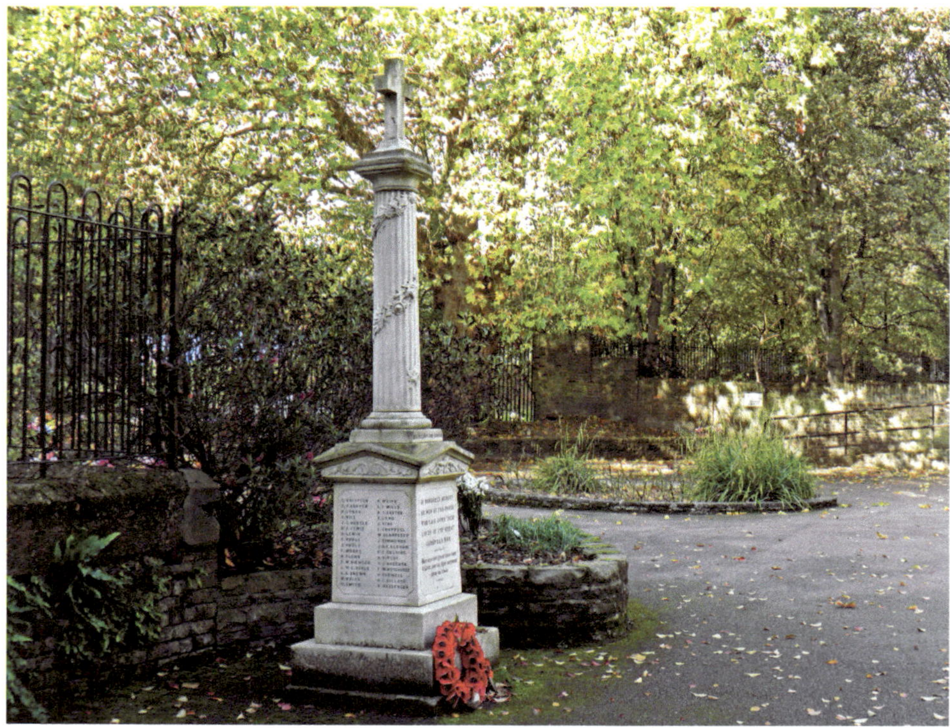

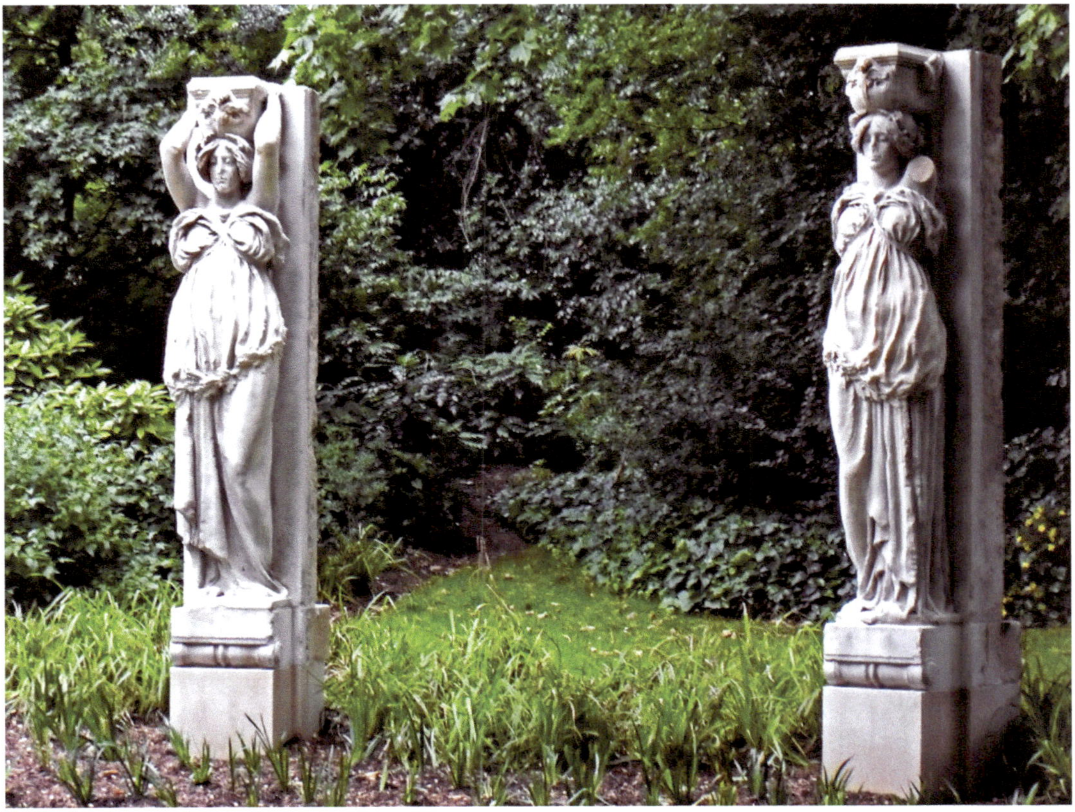

**Caryatids, Lower Road, 1908**
For many years these girls stood mouldering in the 1970s Heygate Estate in Walworth. They started life on Rotherhithe Town Hall but were removed after the war had ruined the building. The monstrous Heygate is now happily history and the restored ladies are to be seen in Southwark Park, a far more suitable place for such lovely statues.

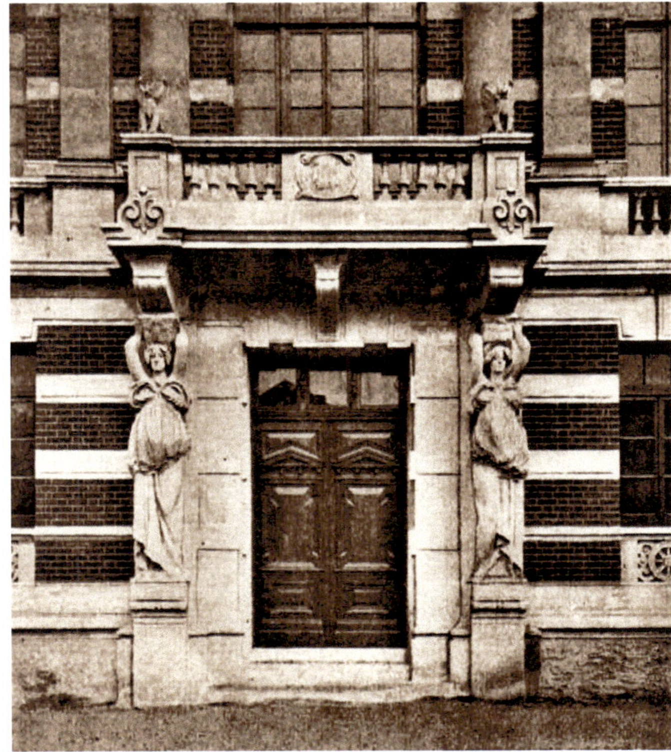

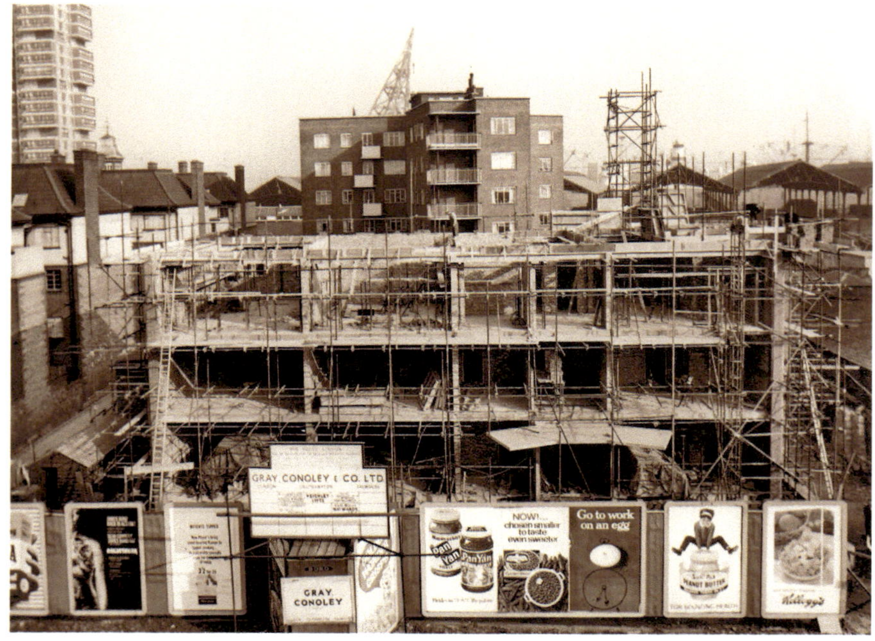



After the Second World War the effects of rationing, opportunity and possibly a sprinkling of anger changed things for the beat officer. It was goodbye, George Dixon! Lower Road was built for modern police use, and here 1960s consumerism can be glimpsed on the building site – it was a sad day when Pan Yan pickle disappeared from the shops! Now the station is looking very dated, but now that modern policing is again changing perhaps its days may be numbered. (1964 photograph © Metropolitan Police)

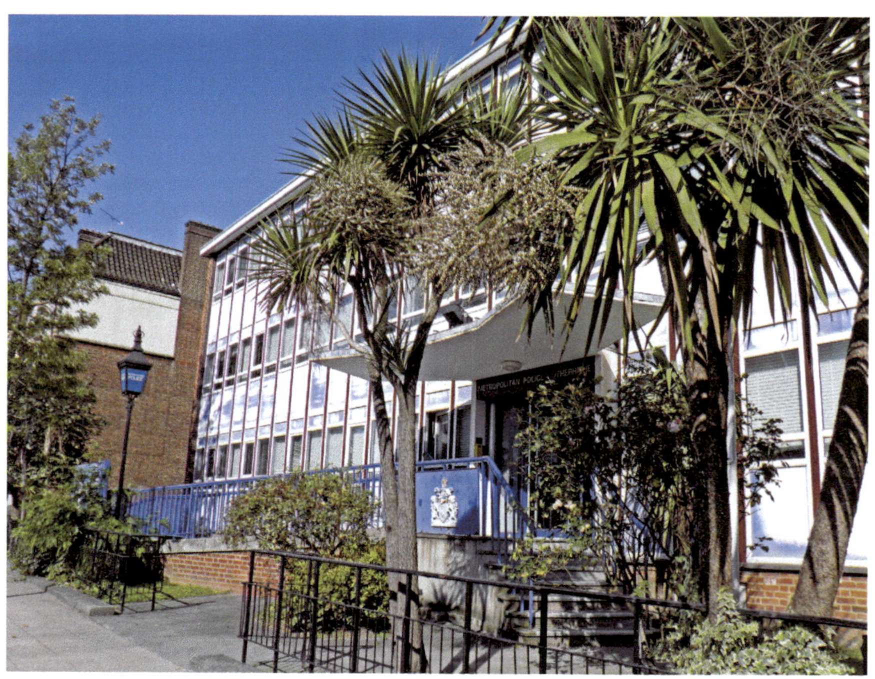

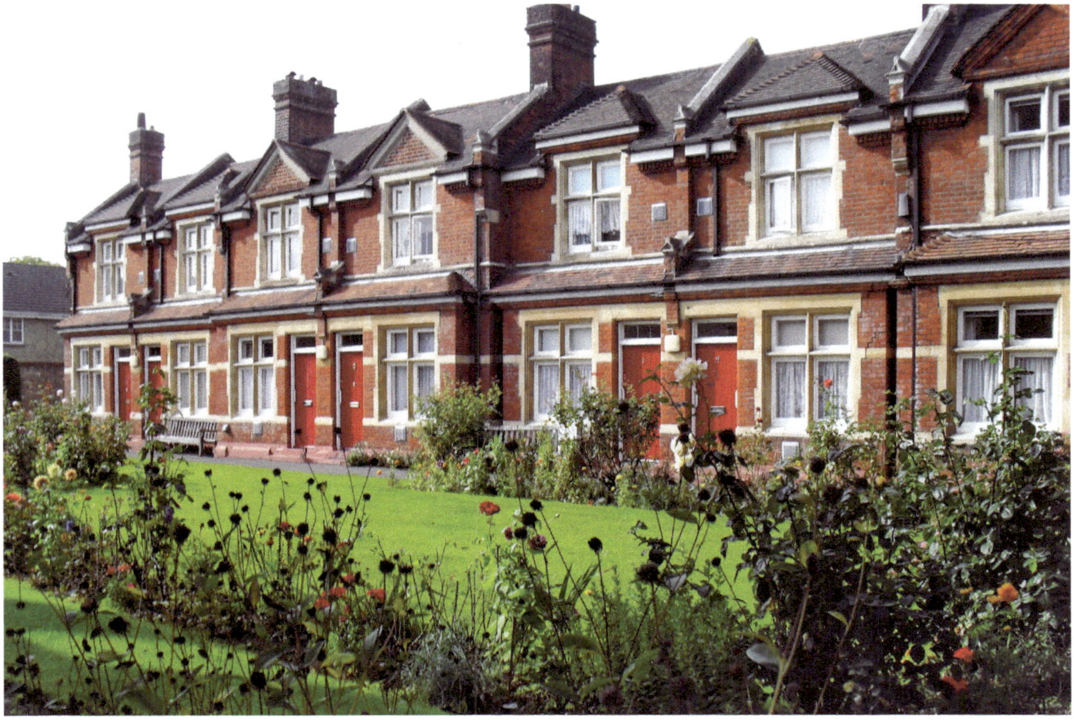

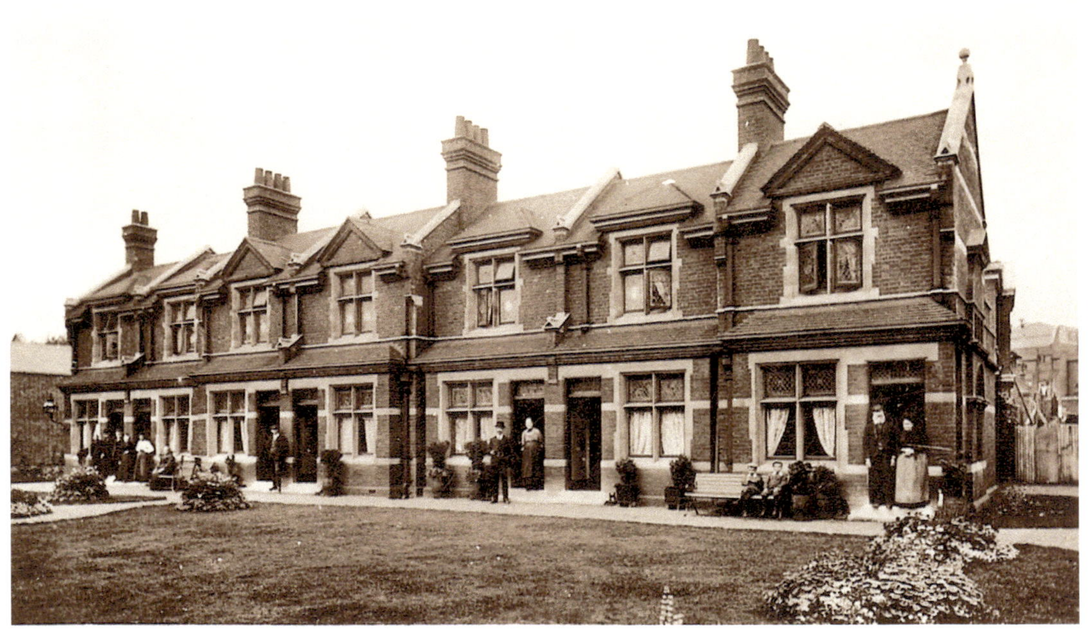

### Peele Almshouses, Lower Road, 1910

Charles Peele was a partner in the firm of Brandram Brothers, a chemical works situated near Canada Water. Peele bequeathed money to build almshouses for the elderly in memory of his mother, Helen, and they were opened in 1901. After such devastation to the rest of Lower Road during the war it is nothing short of a miracle that they survived; they look as good today as they did then.

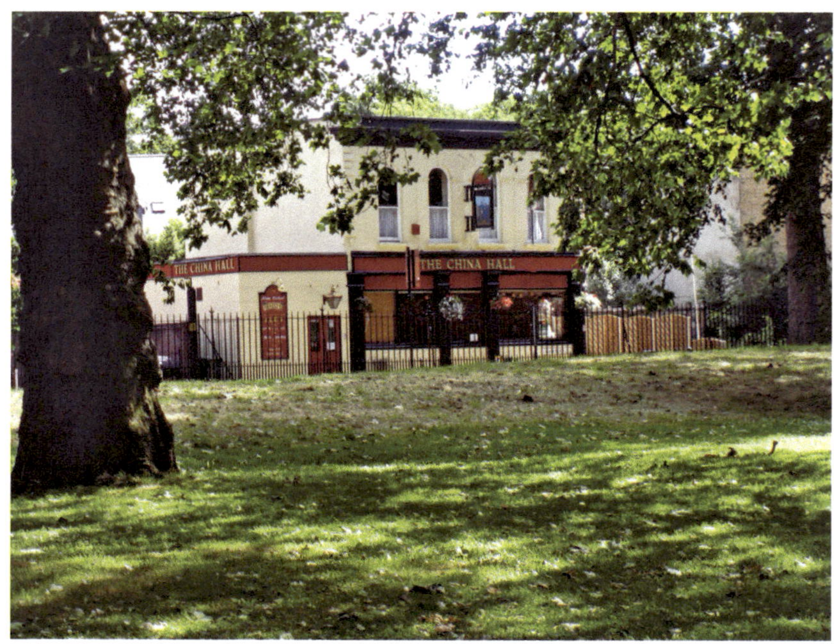

## The China Hall Public House, Lower Road, 1916

Jonathan Oldfield was an eighteenth-century china dealer, importing fine wares from the Orient. He converted an old inn, the Cock and Pie, (situated in a field of the same name) into a theatre. It caught fire and the site became a pub, the China Hall. A path, the Halfpenny Hatch, led across the market gardens (later Southwark Park) to the pub. Anyone who wished to use the path had to pay a halfpenny toll, but should they then drink in the China Hall the toll was refunded!

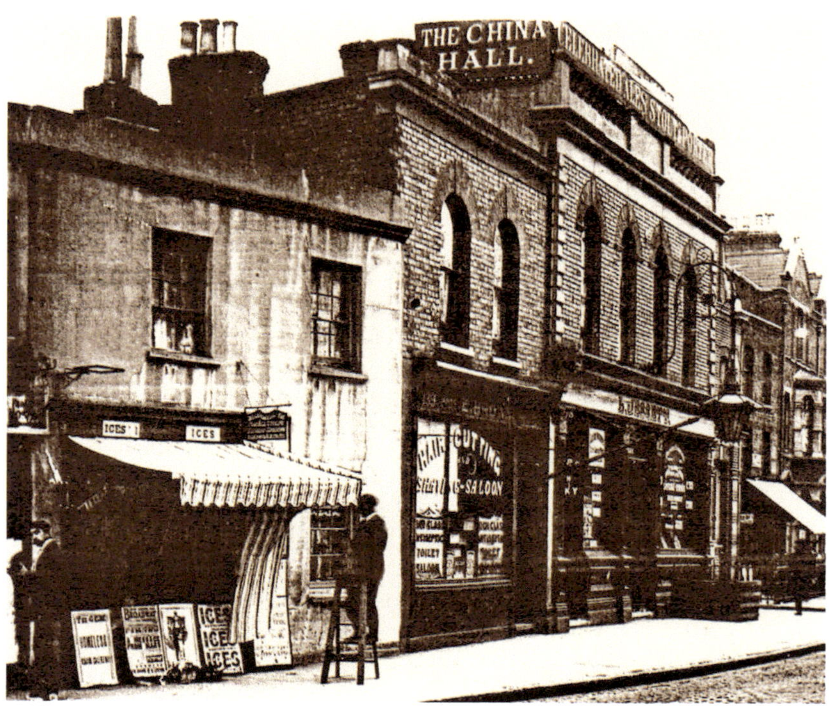

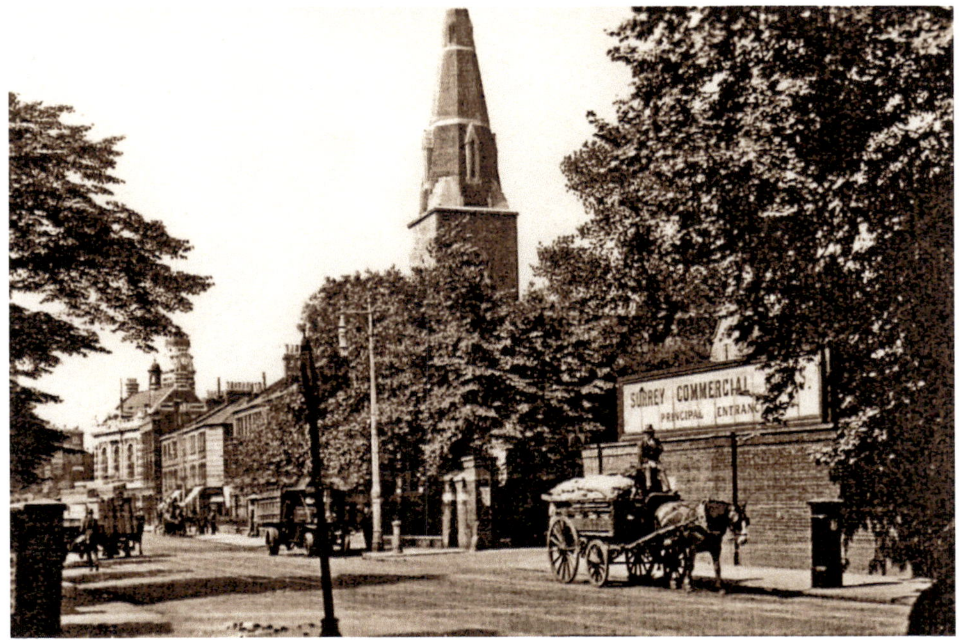


## All Saints Church, Lower Road, 1930

The horse and cart vies with a motorised goods lorry as the times begin to change in Lower Road. Much of this view, along with the church, was lost to the Blitz. The graveyard had already become a public open space before the war. Today it is a pleasant place to sit beneath the cherry blossom trees and escape from the constant stream of traffic outside.

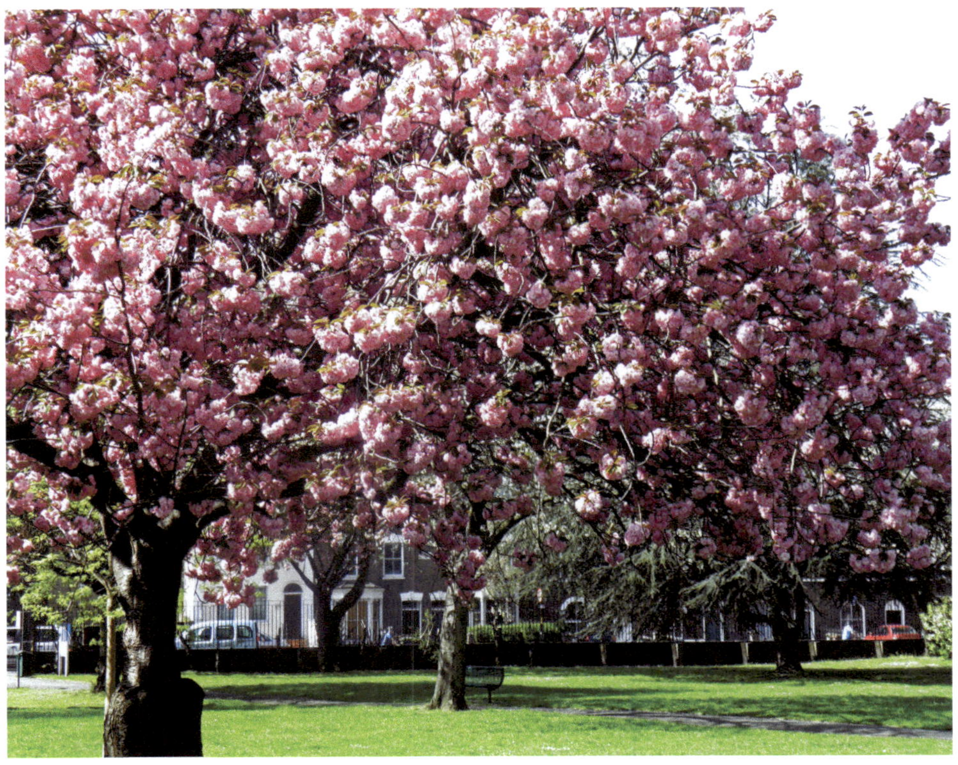

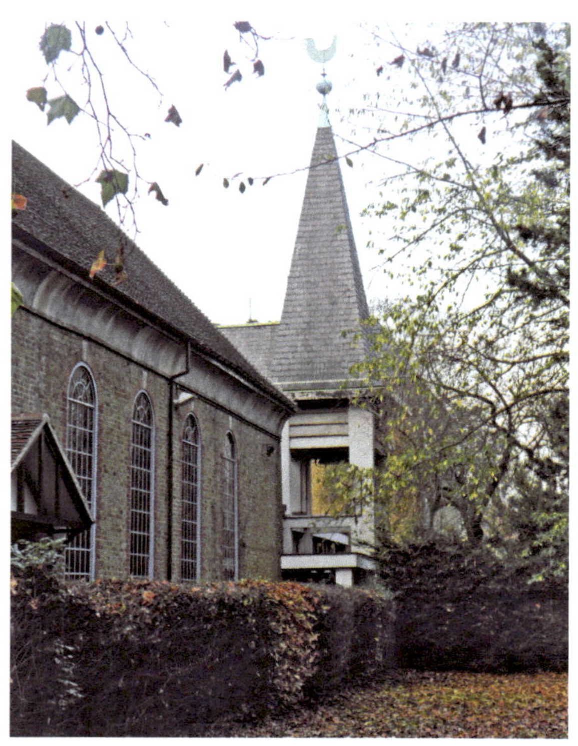

**Swedish Church, Lower Road, 1905**
The Swedish Seamen's Church, like its
Norwegian and Finnish equivalents,
accommodated mariners sailing
in from the Baltic. It was partially
rebuilt in 1966 after the extensive war
damage to Lower Road. The church
is also a hostel providing overnight
accommodation for Swedes visiting
London. (1905 photograph © Ingrid
Uhlén Gray)

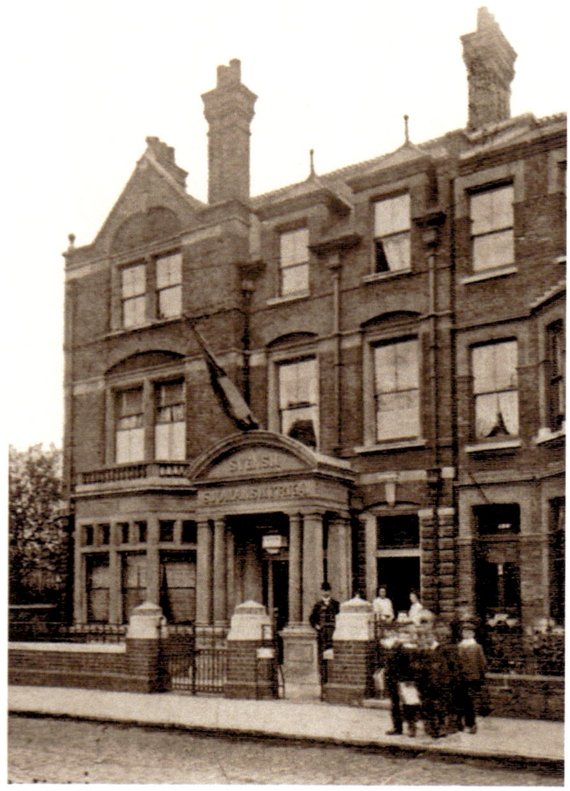

All the holes on a ship caused by wear and tear, along with any woodworm, were kept under control by the Caulker, who banged pieces of wood and tar into the vessel to keep it watertight. Issy Mendoza held down the licence of quite a few pubs and was probably a bit of a character in his day. He had travelled across the water after running a pub in the East End to manage the Jolly Gardeners. He then flitted over to the New Jolly Caulkers, but whether he was a jovial sort himself is unrecorded! Today the pub is an oriental restaurant.

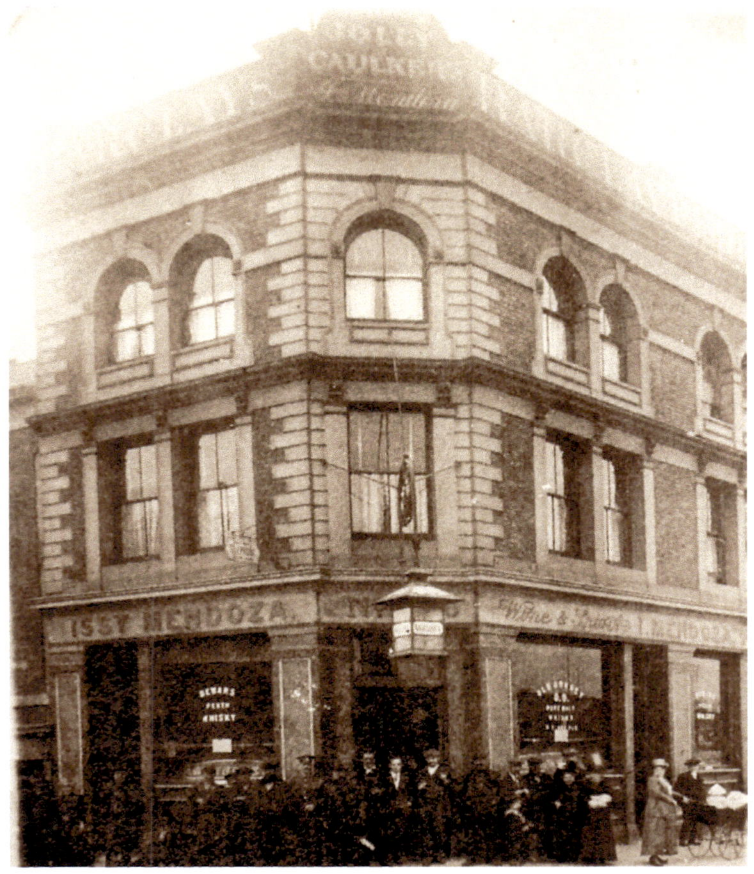

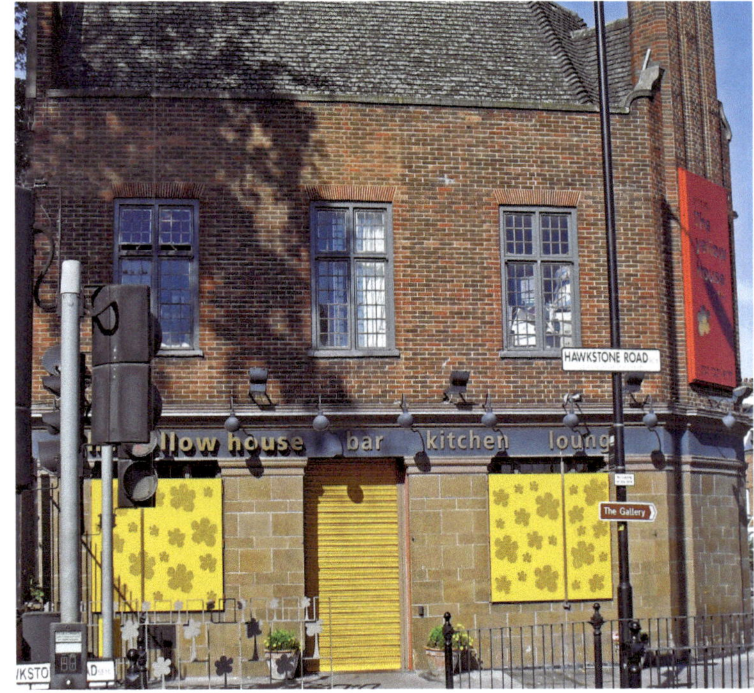

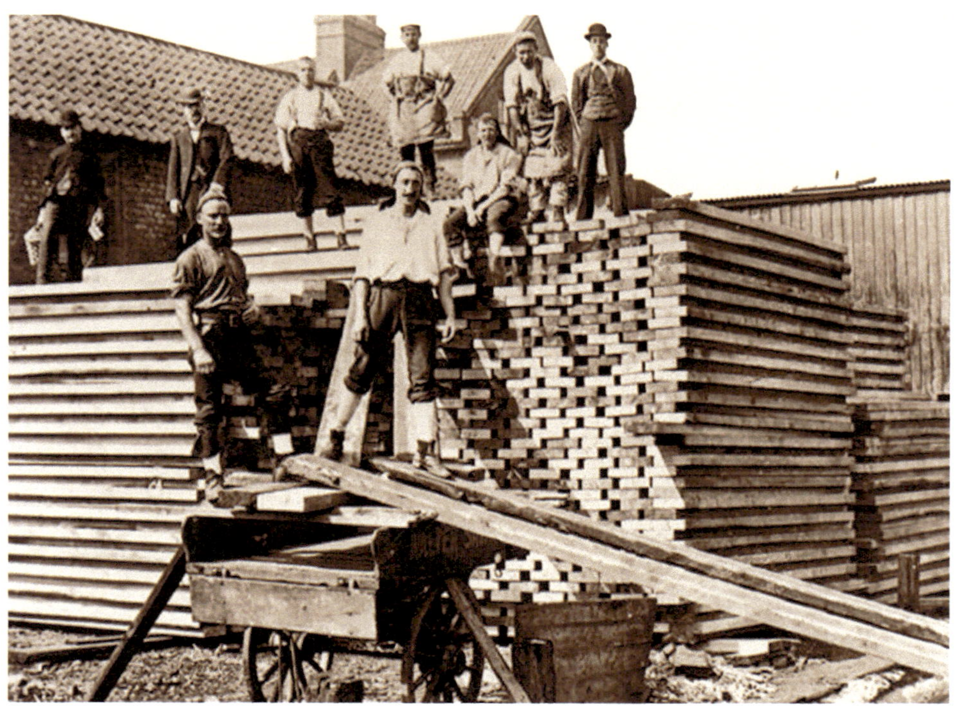



## Timber Pond, Surrey Docks, 1905

Surrey Docks stored timber and it had to be stacked, which was the job of the deal porters. Deal is a word describing softwood or pinewood. These men had to be highly skilled and very precise at their job. To load it high it had to be stacked straight; one lapse of concentration and the whole lot came crashing down. Now the docks are called quays and the timber has gone. This statue by Phillip Bews acknowledges the men that worked here.

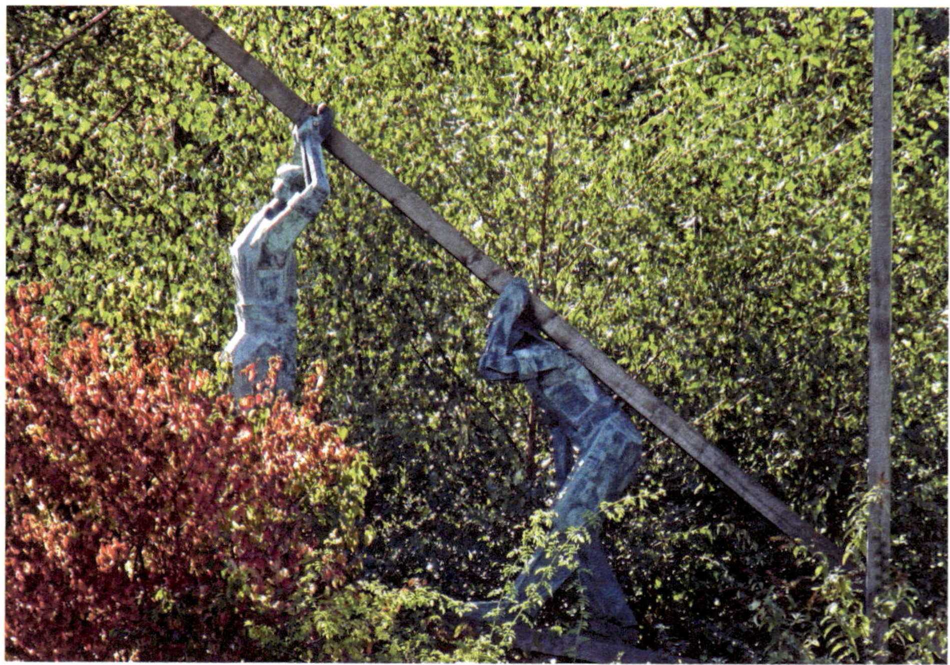

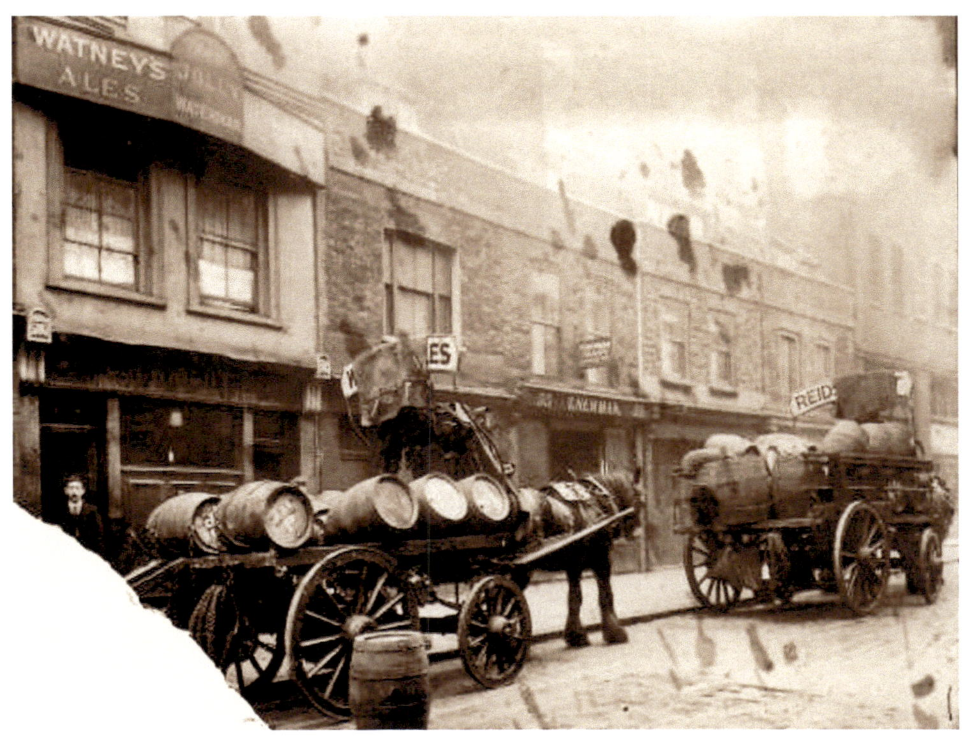

## The Jolly Waggoners Public House, Rotherhithe Old Road, 1918

Another jolly Rotherhithe watering hole! This little old pub now goes under the guise of Whelan's. It appears to have been at least partially rebuilt and enlarged, but the two original entrances remain in place. This well-loved photograph of the original pub, although badly damaged, still shows the dray horses and barrels used in every street before the advent of heavy traffic made it impossible. (1918 photograph © Boyd Sofield)

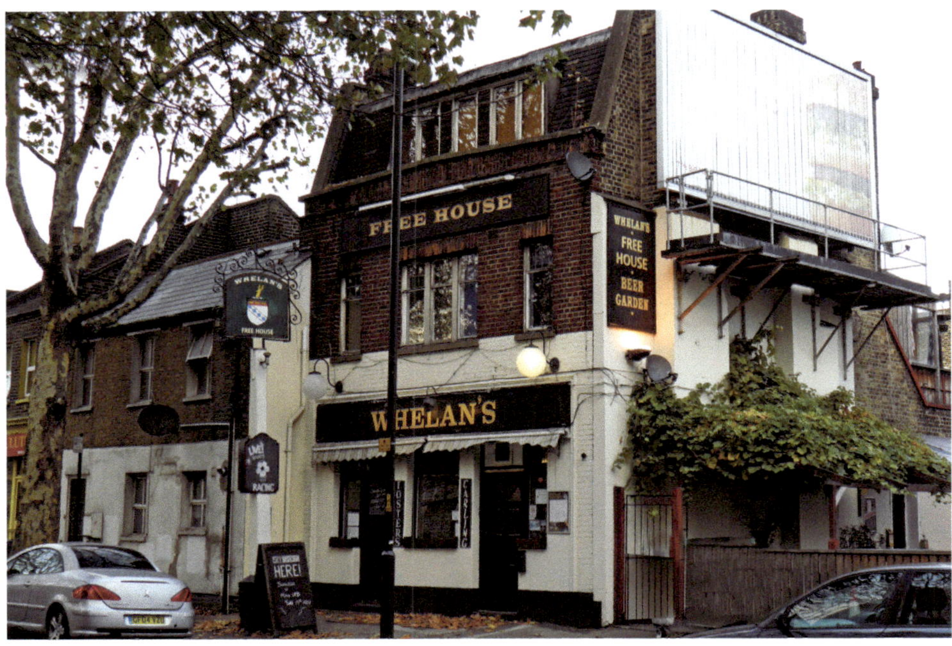

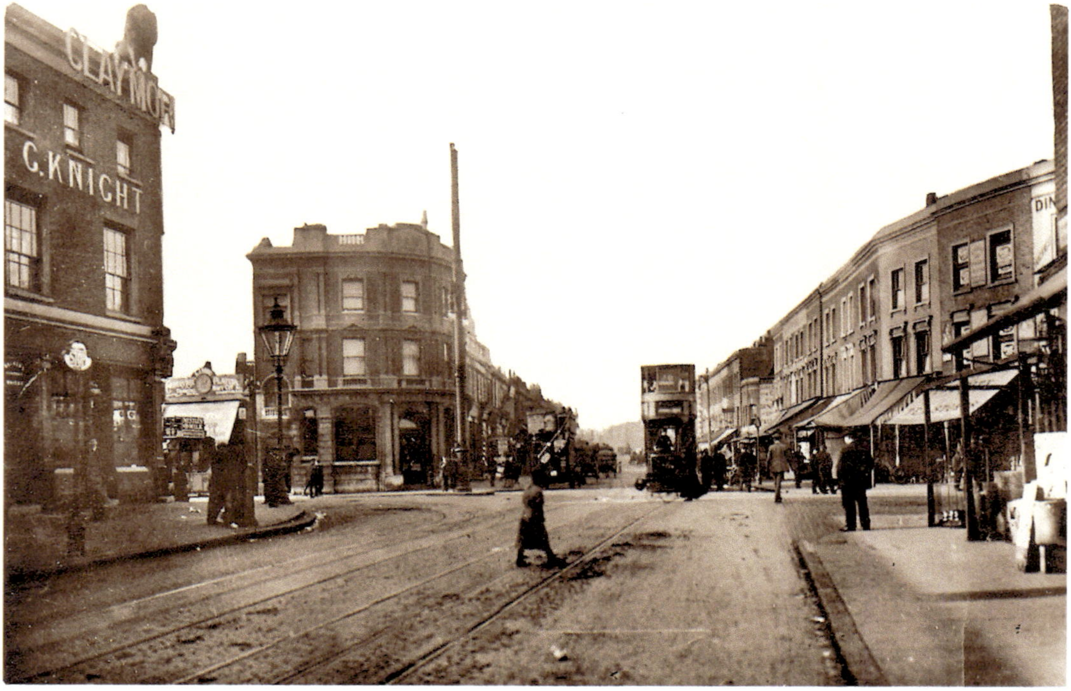

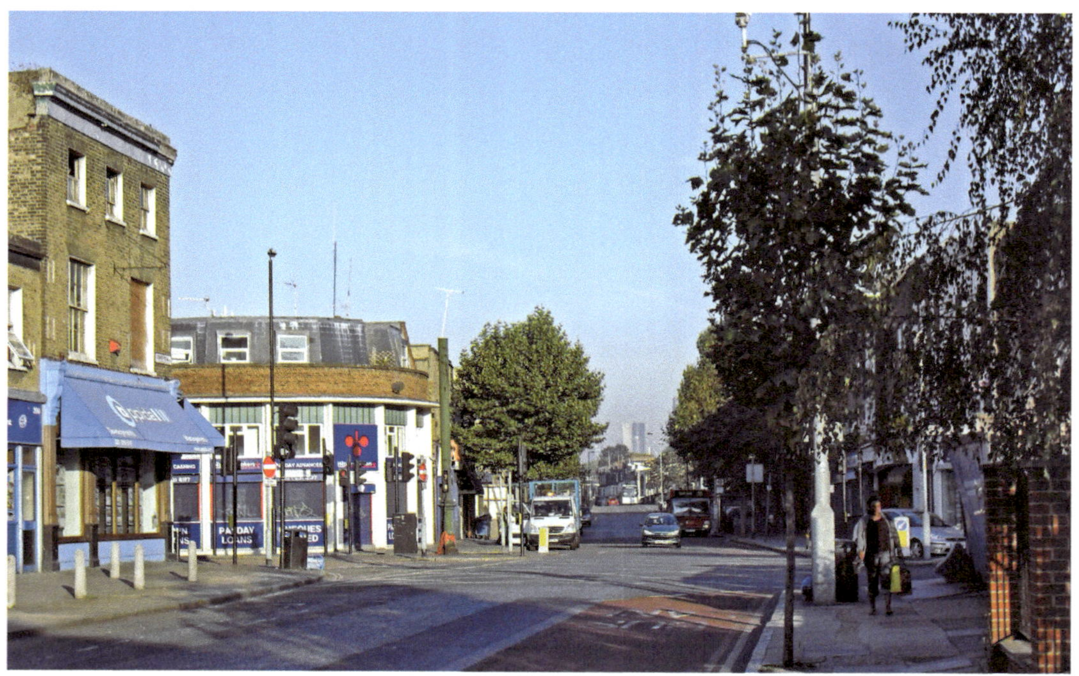

## The Red Lion Public House, Lower Road, 1920

This pub's rooftop statue gave the nickname for the shopping area that surrounded it. It was bombed on 20 January 1943, causing several people to lose their lives, including some of the staff of the bank opposite. The policeman who was on traffic duty at the time found himself thrown onto the tram line, surrounded by bags of silver! Despite several enquiries the Lion's fate remains unclear, but it seems likely it was badly damaged during that raid.

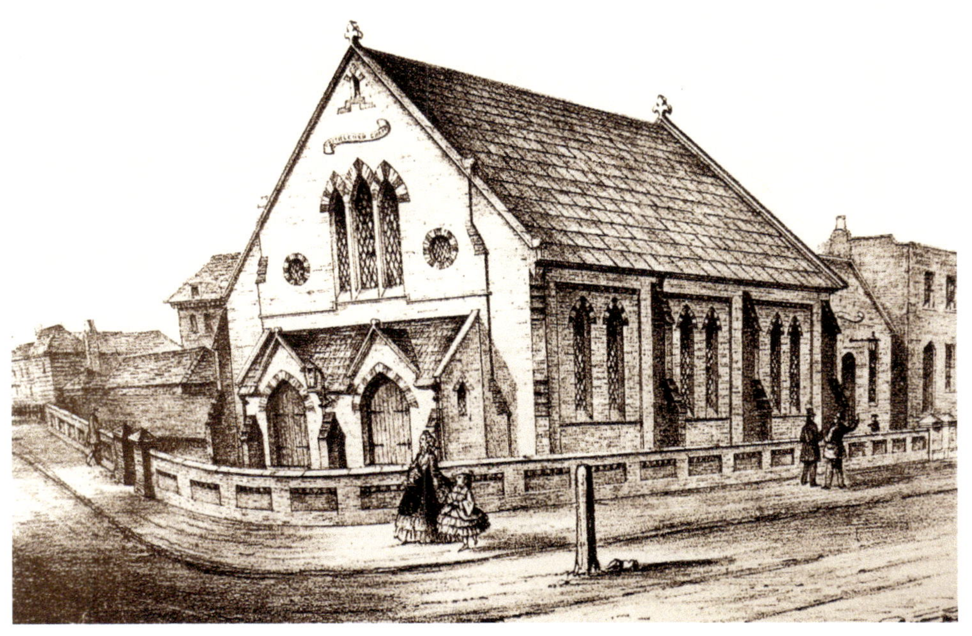

## Southwark Park Congregational Church, Hawkstone Road, 1886

This church was renamed the Bethlehem Methodist Chapel in 1886 and was again renamed St Winifred's in 1900. From the picture above the area appears to have a quiet country bridge leading to modest housing. The war is to blame for this now hectic junction, which leads to modern flats. The rebuilt church is now host to the Red Lion Boys' Club and various Sunday ministries.

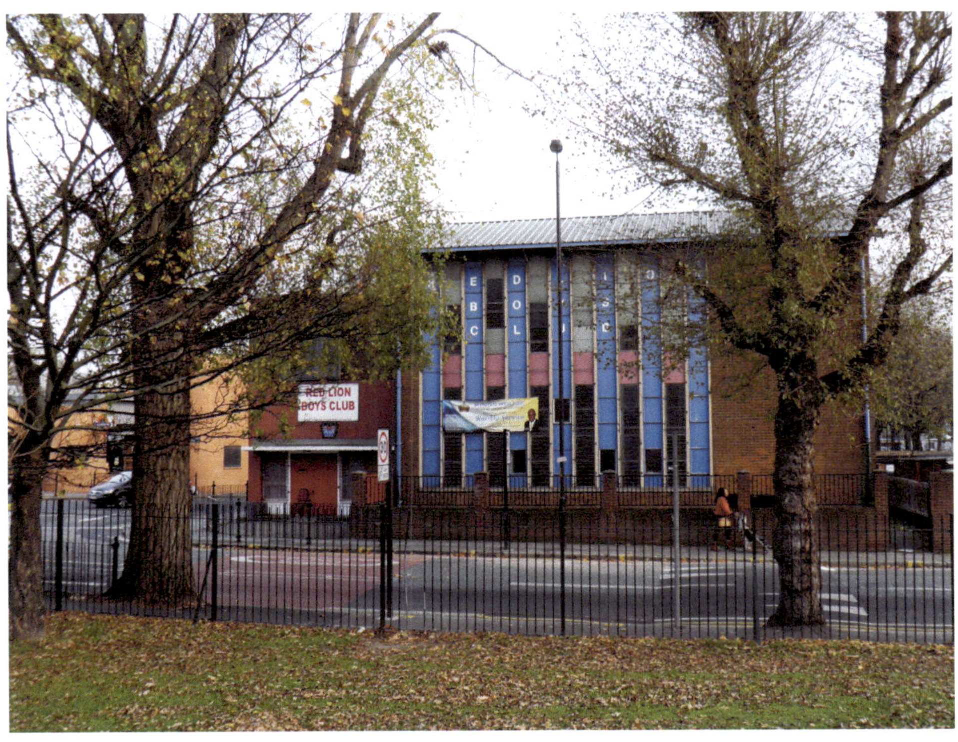

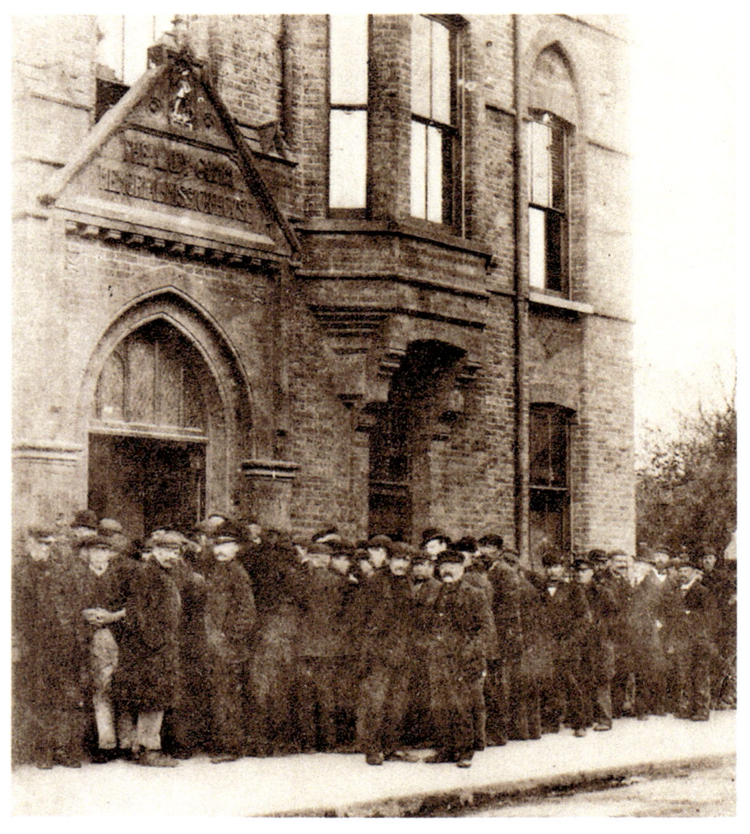

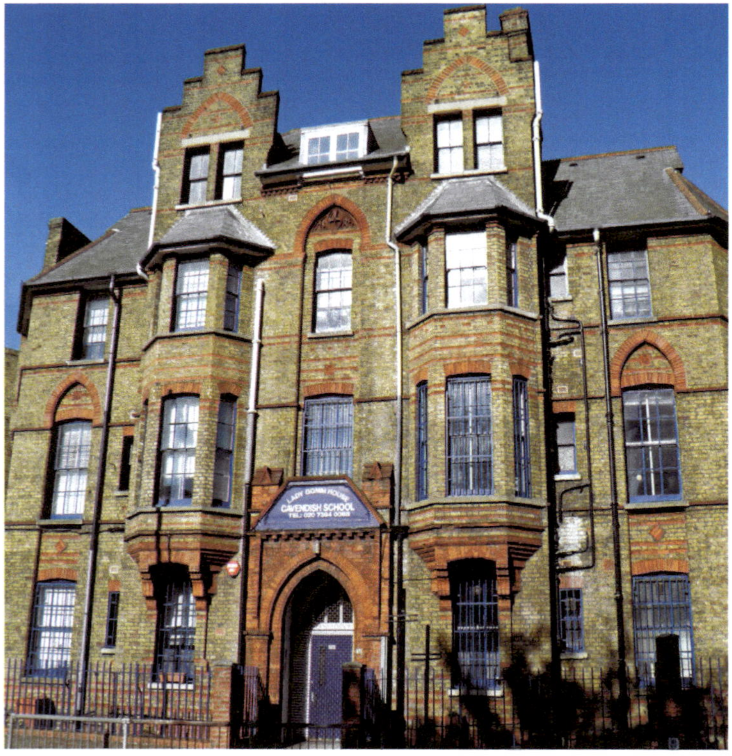



## Lady Gomm House, Hawkstone Road, 1900

These men might be unemployed dockers or foreign sailors. This mission house was built in memory of Lady Gomm, whose family were Lords of the Manor of Rotherhithe. Opening in 1884, it doubled as a mission house and accident hospital for injured dockers. Heavy bombing made it redundant, but in 1948 it became a youth club, before being used by social services and today it is the Cavendish School. (1900 photograph © Michael Holland)

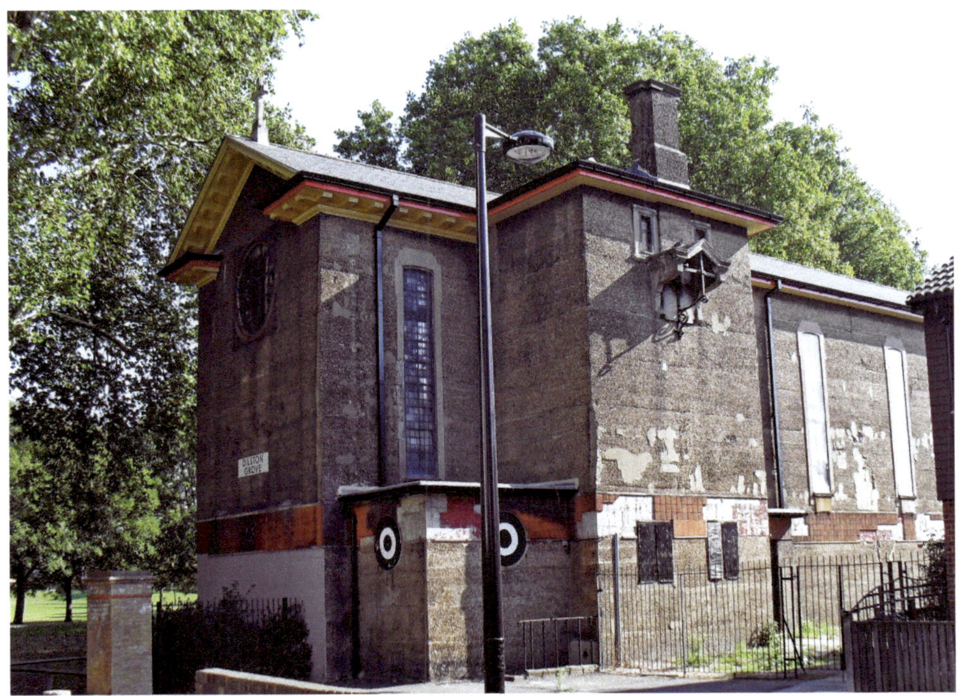

### Dilston Grove Church, 1911

Previously the Clare College Mission, this structure was rebuilt in 1911, being one of the first poured-concrete churches in the country. The architects were Sir John Simpson and Maxwell Ayrton. The ridges in the walls are where the concrete set before another layer was poured on top of a 'mould'. It is now an annexe of the Café Gallery in Southwark Park and is associated with the Bermondsey Artists' Group. Amazing pieces of performance art take place here.

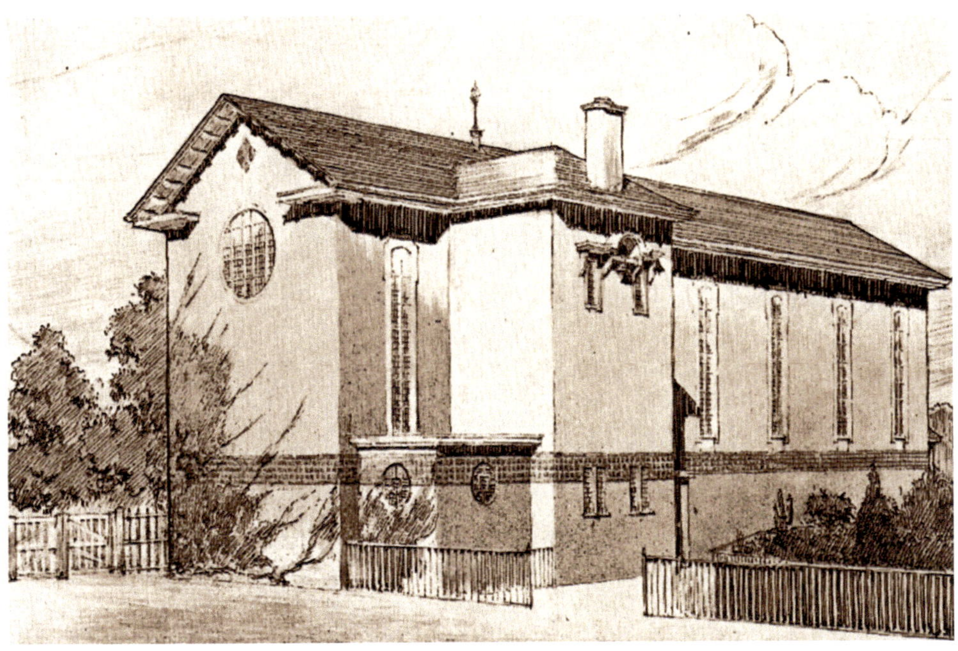

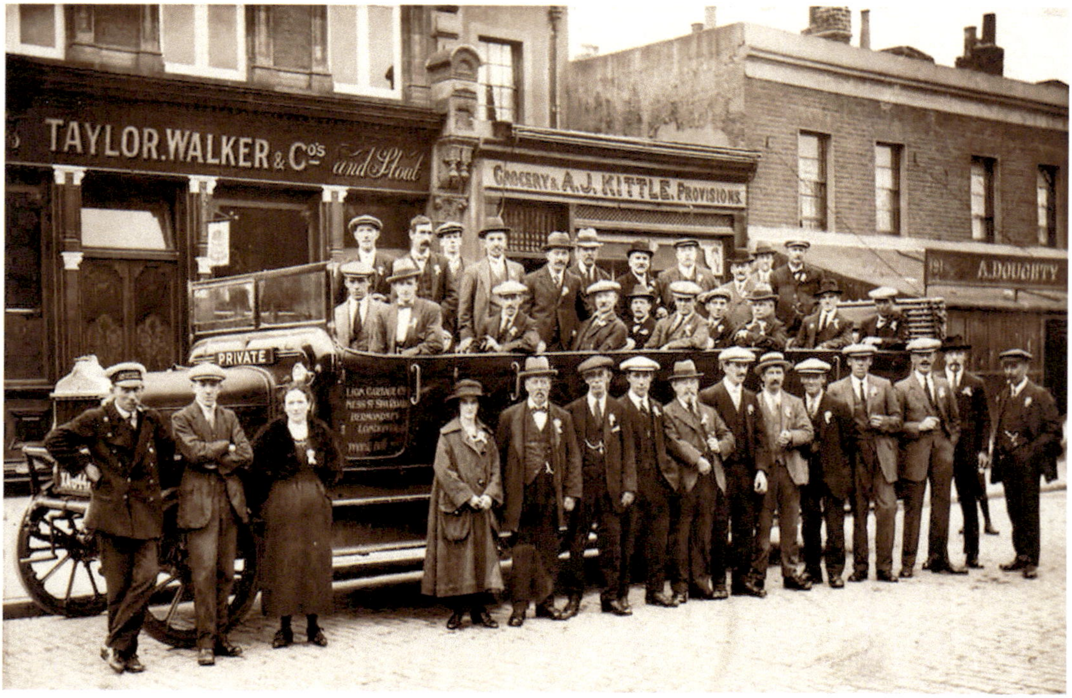

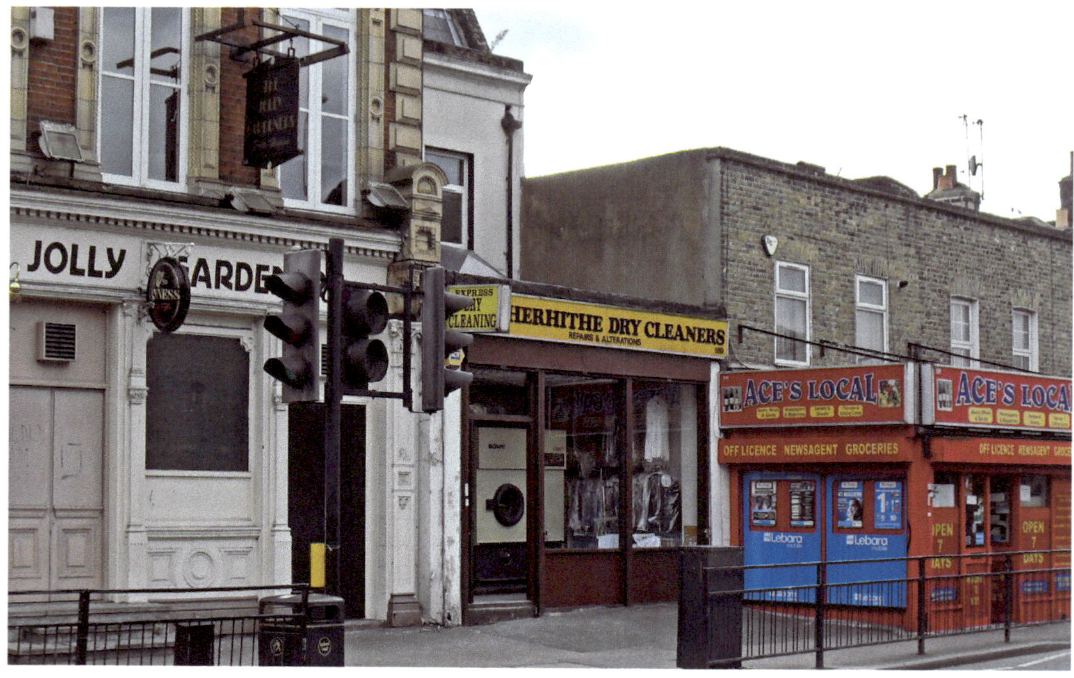

## Jolly Gardeners Beano, Rotherhithe New Road, 1925

Business was good for Lion Cartage of Spa Road, who provided all the beano coaches. This time the party are outside the Jolly Gardeners. Third from the right is Albert Tumner, looking pretty dapper in his Sunday best. The shops next door have (just) survived, complete with the 'braces' that are keeping up the shop extension of A. Doughty. The Gardeners pub was closed down by the police a few years ago. (1925 photograph © Boyd Sofield)

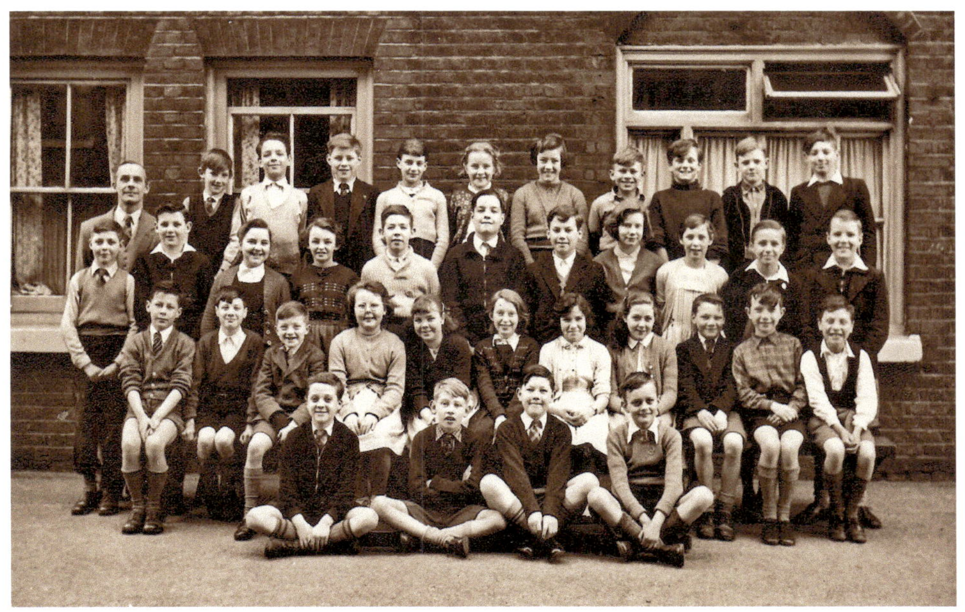

## Galleywall School, 1956

Galleywall Road is an ancient byway built between marshy fields and is the border between Bermondsey and Rotherhithe. Until the 1840s there was nothing of note along here, save for a glue works, but twenty years later terraced houses were covering the fields. This new population fuelled the need for education and, in 1877 the school was built. This class of eleven-year-olds are sitting outside the school caretaker's house, which still exists to the right of the modern picture. (1956 photograph © D. Toogood)

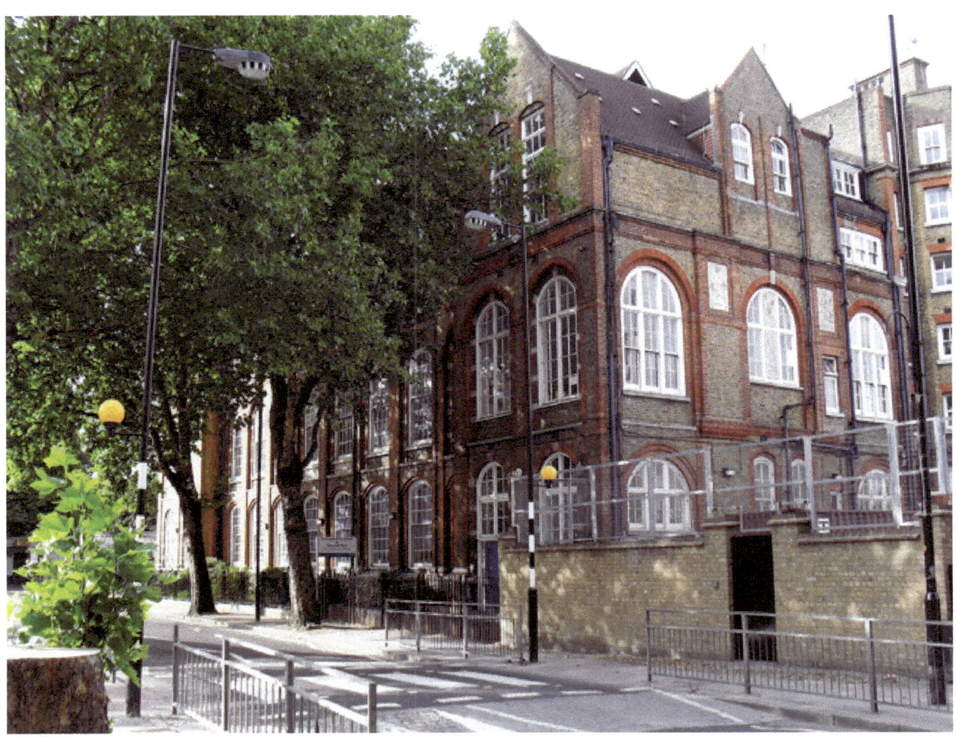

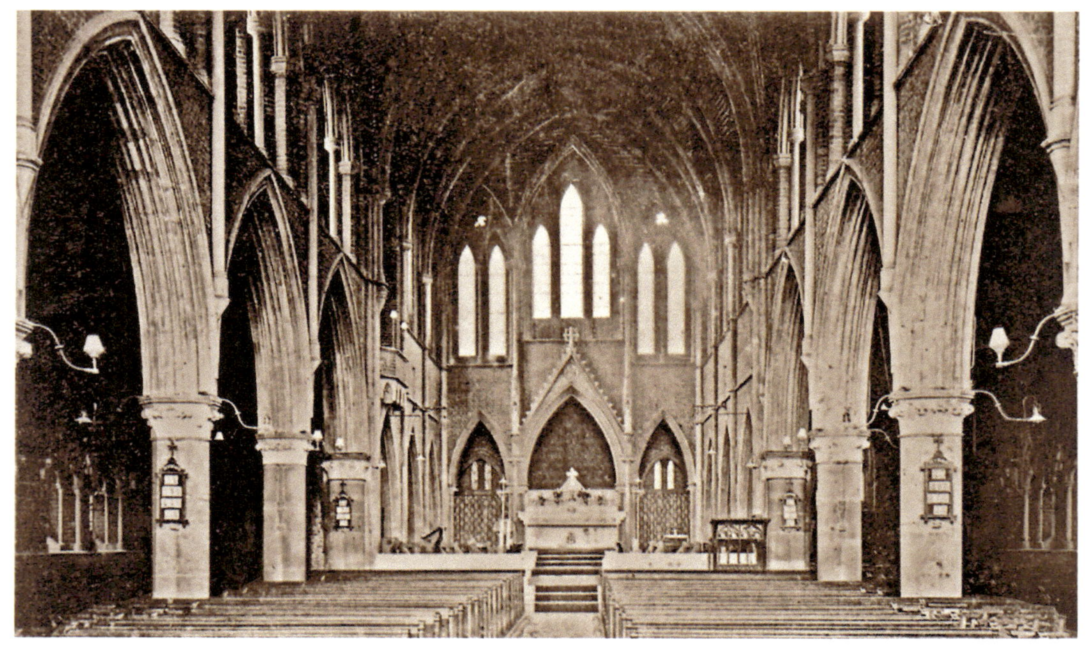

## St Augustine's Church, Lynton Road, 1920

Resembling a cathedral in this picture, the church was a very costly building project. Beforehand, Lynton Road had been gardens, bordered by streams and willow trees, so it was no surprise that deep foundations were needed. The roof over the nave was made of fir, probably delivered from the docks, and the chancel and two bays of the nave were built by Mr Shepherd of Bermondsey New Road. Still looking fabulous today, the building is residential and no longer consecrated.

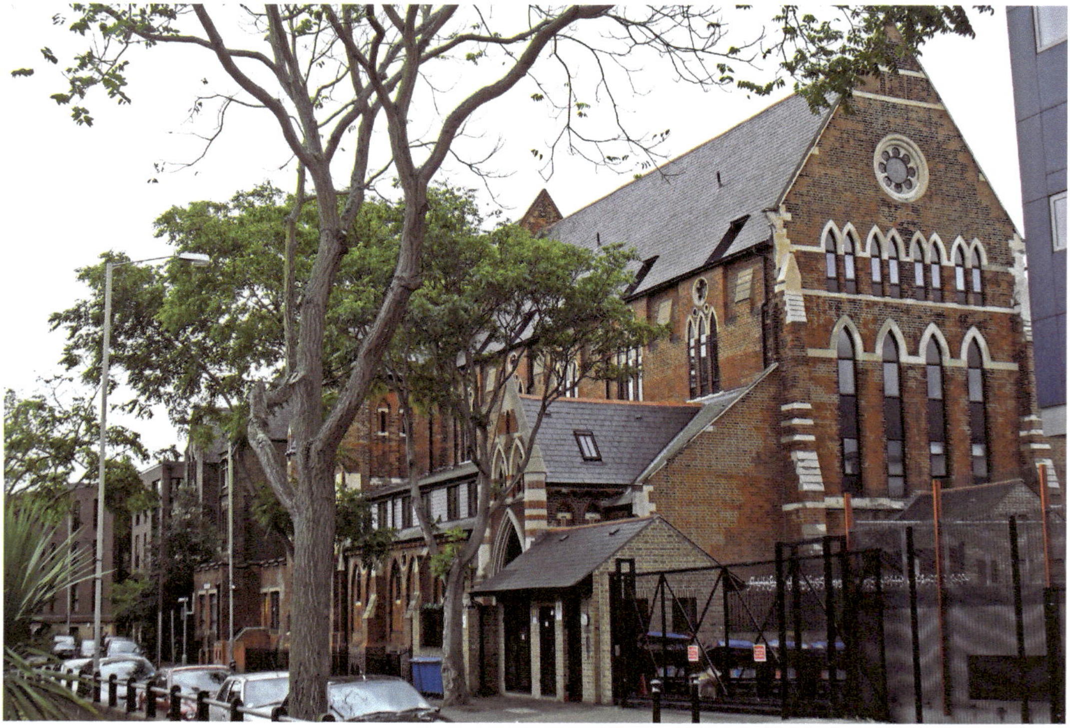

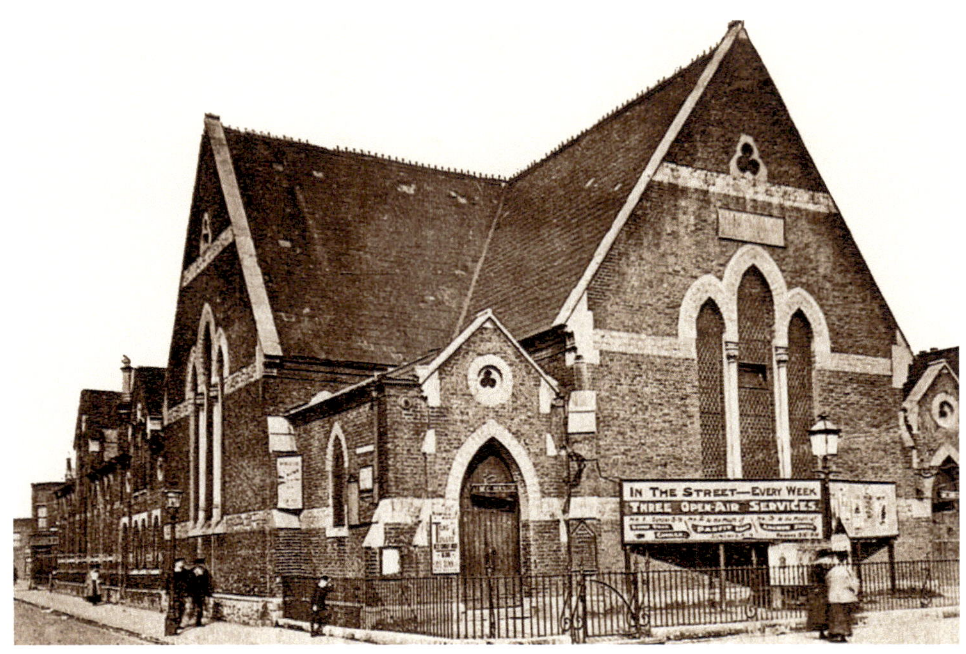


## Manor Church, Galleywall Road, 1910

In 1864 local landowner Abraham Batty, donated a huge sum of money to finance this church. Others contributed their time and skills to build it, and it celebrated its opening in 1865 with a huge bonfire and fireworks display. During the war it was used as a temporary mortuary and it was virtually destroyed by a V2 attack. Ten years after peace was declared, a new Manor Methodist Church sprang up in Galleywall Road but it has since seen two more incarnations.

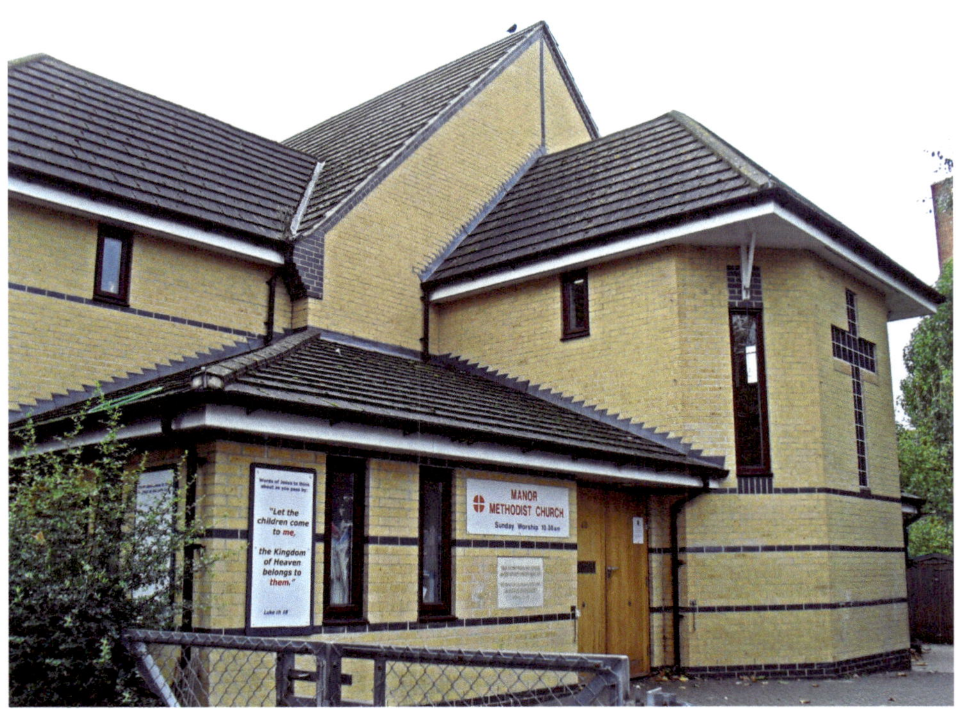

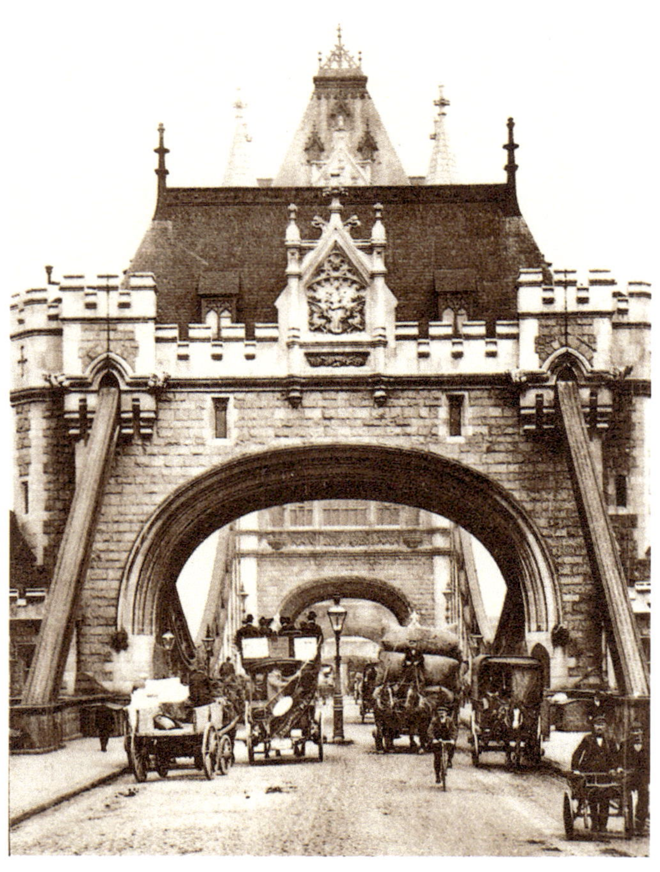

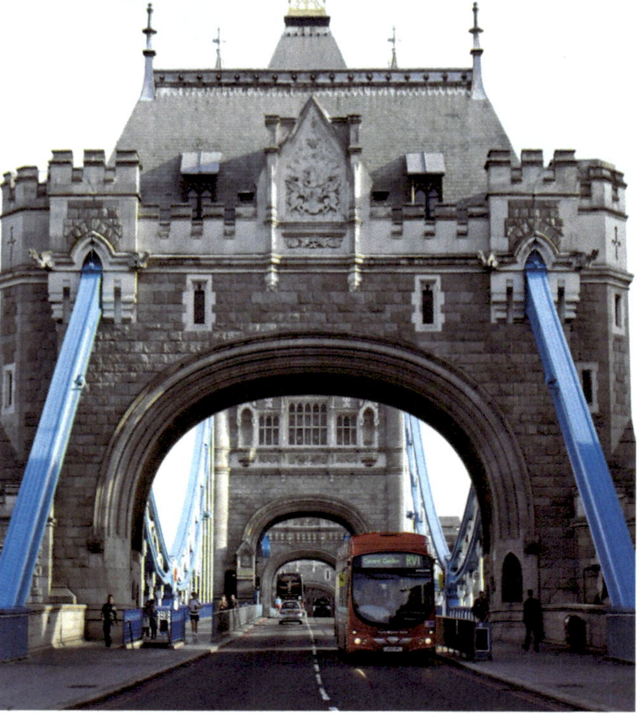

## Tower Bridge Approach, 1900

This scene has hardly changed; the horses have simply been replaced by buses. Although the bridge has changed over to electric power, it still has a bridgemaster on duty twenty four hours a day. The full length of the bridge is ½ mile and there is no charge to raise the bascules. Now, as always, river takes precedence over road and even US president Bill Clinton and his motorcade had to wait patiently until a boat had passed under!